AI IN PRACTICE

A Comprehensive Guide to Leveraging Artificial Intelligence in Business

Rick Spair

Introduction

"AI in Practice: A Comprehensive Guide to Leveraging Artificial Intelligence in Business" is a groundbreaking book that provides a comprehensive and practical exploration of the applications, strategies, and considerations involved in leveraging artificial intelligence (AI) in various business domains. Written for professionals, decision-makers, and enthusiasts alike, this book serves as a roadmap to help organizations harness the power of AI to drive innovation, improve efficiencies, and gain a competitive edge in the modern digital landscape.

The book covers a wide range of topics, starting with an introduction to AI and its impact on businesses. It explores the different types of AI, including machine learning, deep learning, natural language processing, and computer vision, providing readers with a solid understanding of the foundational concepts. The role of AI in digital transformation is also examined, highlighting how AI can revolutionize business operations, customer experiences, and overall organizational strategies.

One of the key focuses of the book is aligning AI strategies with business goals. It delves into the importance of understanding organizational objectives and developing AI initiatives that support and enhance those goals. The book provides insights into building the right team, including data scientists, engineers, and analysts, and emphasizes the need for collaboration between IT and business units to ensure the successful adoption and implementation of AI solutions.

Developing an AI strategy is another critical aspect covered in the book. It guides readers through the process of identifying use cases, prioritizing projects, and assessing the AI maturity of their organization. Furthermore, it offers practical guidance on creating an AI roadmap that aligns with the organization's long-term vision and goals.

Data management and infrastructure are explored in detail, emphasizing the importance of data quality, governance, and storage in AI projects. The book explores the considerations of cloud-based versus on-premises AI solutions, providing readers with insights to make informed decisions regarding their AI infrastructure.

Evaluating AI tools and platforms is another crucial aspect covered in the book. It offers readers a framework for assessing and selecting the right AI vendors and partners, considering factors such as functionality, scalability, and compatibility with existing systems. The book also discusses the pros and cons of open-source versus proprietary AI solutions, enabling readers to make informed choices based on their specific requirements.

The book emphasizes the agile methodologies for AI projects, promoting iterative development and continuous improvement. It explores how organizations can integrate AI solutions with existing systems and processes, ensuring seamless integration and minimizing disruption.

Ethical considerations in AI are given due attention in the book, discussing the importance of addressing bias, transparency, explainability, privacy, and data protection. It provides readers with a framework for ethical AI adoption and best practices for responsible AI implementation.

Measuring AI success and assessing the return on investment (ROI) are explored, with a focus on defining key performance indicators (KPIs) and evaluating the value created by AI projects. The book emphasizes the use of both quantitative and qualitative evaluation methods to gauge the impact and effectiveness of AI initiatives.

Upskilling and reskilling the workforce are discussed, highlighting the importance of continuous learning and development to adapt to the AI-driven landscape. It guides readers through identifying skill gaps and training needs within their organization and provides insights on creating a culture of innovation and learning.

The book explores emerging AI trends and technologies, offering readers a glimpse into the future of AI and its potential impact on businesses. It emphasizes the need to stay informed, adapt to regulatory changes, and continuously refine and evolve AI strategies to stay ahead in the competitive landscape.

Throughout the book, real-world case studies, examples, and best practices are provided to illustrate how organizations from various industries have successfully implemented AI solutions to achieve their business objectives.

In conclusion, "AI in Practice: A Comprehensive Guide to Leveraging Artificial Intelligence in Business" is a valuable resource for organizations looking to harness the power of AI. It equips readers with the knowledge, strategies, and considerations necessary to navigate the AI landscape and implement AI solutions that drive innovation, enhance customer experiences, and deliver tangible business value.

CONTENTS

Title Page

Introduction

Chapter 1: Overview of AI and Its Impact on Businesses

Chapter 2: Types of AI: Machine Learning, Deep Learning, Natural Language Processing, and Computer V

Chapter 3: The Role of AI in Digital Transformation

Chapter 4: Aligning AI Strategies with Business Goals

Chapter 5: Building the Right Team: Data Scientists, Engineers, and Analysts

Chapter 6: Collaboration between IT and business

Chapter 7: Identifying Use Cases and Prioritizing Projects

Chapter 8: Assessing the AI Maturity of Your Organization

Chapter 10: Creating an AI Roadmap

Chapter 11: Importance of Data Quality and Governance

Chapter 12: Data storage and processing requirements

Chapter 13: Cloud-based vs. On-Premises AI Solutions: A Comparison

Chapter 14: Evaluating AI Tools and Platforms

Chapter 15: Open Source vs. Proprietary AI Solutions: A Comparison

Chapter 16: Criteria for Selecting AI Vendors and Partners

Chapter 17: Agile Methodologies for AI Projects

Chapter 18: Iterative Development and Continuous Improvement in AI Projects

Chapter 19: Integration with Existing Systems and Processes in AI Projects
Chapter 20: Bias and Fairness in AI Algorithms
Chapter 21: Transparency and Explainability in AI Algorithms
Chapter 21: Privacy and Data Protection in the Age of AI
Chapter 22: Key Performance Indicators (KPIs) for AI Projects
Chapter 23: Assessing ROI and Value Creation in AI Projects
Chapter 24: Quantitative and Qualitative Evaluation Methods in AI Projects
Chapter 25: The Importance of Continuous Learning and Development
Chapter 26: Identifying Skill Gaps and Training Needs
Chapter 27: Creating a Culture of Innovation and Learning
Chapter 28: Emerging AI Technologies and Their Potential Impact on Businesses
Chapter 29: Preparing for AI-Driven Changes in the Workforce
Chapter 30: Staying Ahead of the Competition through AI Innovation
Chapter 31: Encouraging Experimentation and Risk-Taking
Chapter 33: Fostering Cross-Functional Collaboration
Chapter 34: Nurturing a Data-Driven Mindset Across the Organization
Chapter 35: Developing AI Governance Frameworks and Policies
Chapter 36: Ensuring Compliance with Data Protection and Privacy Regulations
Chapter 37: Auditing AI Systems and Processes
Chapter 38: Identifying and Mitigating AI-Related Security Threats
Chapter 39: Implementing Robust Access Controls and Monitoring
Chapter 40: Developing Incident Response Plans for AI-Related Breaches
Chapter 41: Designing AI Systems for Growth and Adaptability
Chapter 42: Optimizing AI Models and Algorithms for Performance
Chapter 43: Leveraging Cloud Computing and Edge Computing for AI Scalability
Chapter 44: Enhancing Customer Interactions with AI-Powered Chatbots and Virtual Assistants

Chapter 45: Personalizing Customer Experiences through AI-Driven Insights
Chapter 46: Leveraging AI for Predictive Analytics and Customer Segmentation
Chapter 47: Staying Informed on AI Trends and Emerging Technologies
Chapter 48: Adapting to Regulatory Changes and Industry Standards in the Era of AI
Chapter 49: Continuously Refining and Evolving Your AI Strategy for Long-Term Success
Chapter 50: Identifying and Addressing Common Roadblocks in AI Projects
Chapter 51: Ensuring Stakeholder Buy-In and Support in AI Projects
Chapter 52: Managing Organizational Change during AI Adoption
Chapter 53: Enhancing Data-Driven Decision-Making with AI Insights
Chapter 54: Leveraging AI for Competitive Intelligence and Market Analysis
Chapter 55: Implementing AI-Powered Dashboards and Visualization Tools
Chapter 56: Identifying Unique AI Opportunities within Your Industry
Chapter 58: Adapting AI Strategies to Industry-Specific Challenges and Opportunities
Chapter 59: Enhancing Network and Data Security with AI-Powered Tools
Chapter 60: Leveraging AI for Proactive Threat Detection and Response
Chapter 61: Implementing AI-Driven Cybersecurity Training and Awareness Programs
Chapter 62: Integrating AI and IoT for Enhanced Data Analysis and Insights
Chapter 63: Leveraging AI-Driven Analytics for Predictive Maintenance and Asset Management
Chapter 64: Optimizing IoT Device Performance and Energy Efficiency with AI
Chapter 65: Managing Intellectual Property (IP) Rights and Licensing in an AI-Driven World

Chapter 66: Utilizing AI Tools for Patent Analysis and Research
Chapter 67: Developing Strategies for Protecting AI-Generated Intellectual Property (IP)
Chapter 68: Navigating the International AI Ecosystem and Regulatory Environment
Chapter 69: Leveraging AI for Global Market Expansion and Business Growth
Chapter 70: Understanding the Impact of AI on International Trade and Competition
Chapter 71: Preparing IT Systems and Networks for AI-Driven Demands
Chapter 72: Evaluating Emerging Technologies for Potential AI Integration
Chapter 73: Future-proofing IT Infrastructure for Long-Term AI Success
Chapter 74: Cultivating a Strategic AI Vision for Your Organization
Chapter 75: Developing AI Leadership Skills and Competencies
Chapter 76: Building a Network of AI Champions and Advocates within Your Organization
Chapter 77: Aligning AI Strategy with Corporate Social Responsibility (CSR) and Ethical Values
Chapter 78: Implementing Ethical AI Principles in Your Organization's Culture
Chapter 79: Engaging Stakeholders in Discussions about AI Ethics and Responsible Technology Use
Chapter 80: Integrating AI as a Critical Component of Your Digital Transformation Strategy
Chapter 81: Leveraging AI to Enhance Digital Customer Experiences
Chapter 82: The Role of AI in Driving Digital Business Model Innovation
Chapter 83: Understanding the Interplay between AI, Blockchain, 5G, and Other Emerging Technologies
Chapter 84: Evaluating the Potential of AI-Driven Solutions in Various Technology Domains
Chapter 85: Preparing for the Convergence of AI and Other Disruptive Technologies

Chapter 86: Forming Strategic Alliances with AI Technology Providers and Partners
Chapter 87: Leveraging External AI Expertise and Resources for Business Growth
Chapter 88: Collaborating with academia, research institutions, and industry consortia on AI initiat
Chapter 89: Preparing for the Impact of AI on Workforce Composition and Skill Requirements
Chapter 90: Leveraging AI to Enhance Workforce Planning and Talent Management
Chapter 91: Encouraging a Culture of Lifelong Learning and Adaptability in the Age of AI
Chapter 92: Integrating AI into Board-Level Discussions and Decision-Making
Chapter 93: Ensuring Accountability and Transparency in AI Adoption and Use
Chapter 94: Managing the Impact of AI on Corporate Governance and Risk Management
Chapter 95: Reflecting on the Key Insights and Takeaways from the Guide
Chapter 96: Assessing Your Organization's Progress on the AI Journey
Chapter 97: Envisioning the Future of Your Organization in an AI-Driven World
Chapter 98: The Role of AI in Revolutionizing Healthcare Delivery
Chapter 99: Enhancing Education with AI-Powered Tools
Chapter 100: Optimizing Transportation Systems with AI-Driven Solutions
Chapter 101: Transforming the Energy Sector with AI-Driven Innovations
Chapter 102: Improving the Agriculture Industry Crop Yield and Resource Efficiency with AI Technolog
Chapter 103: Creating Intelligent Cities and Sustainable Urban Environments with AI
Chapter 104: Revolutionizing Banking and Finance with AI Technologies

Chapter 105: Enhancing User Experiences with AI in Entertainment Content
Chapter 106: Advancements in AI for Game Development and Gameplay
Chapter 107: Leveraging AI for Social Good and Humanitarian Initiatives
Chapter 108: A Comprehensive Overview of AI in Practice
Chapter 109: D&C

CHAPTER 1: OVERVIEW OF AI AND ITS IMPACT ON BUSINESSES

Artificial Intelligence (AI) is revolutionizing the way businesses operate, making significant impacts across various industries. AI refers to the simulation of human intelligence in machines, enabling them to perform tasks that typically require human intelligence, such as visual perception, speech recognition, decision-making, and problem-solving. With advancements in machine learning, deep learning, natural language processing, and computer vision, AI has become a powerful tool for businesses to drive innovation, enhance efficiency, and gain a competitive edge.

The impact of AI on businesses can be seen in several key areas:

Automation and Efficiency: AI enables businesses to automate repetitive and mundane tasks, freeing up human resources to focus on more complex and strategic activities. With AI-powered automation, businesses can streamline processes, improve operational efficiency, and reduce costs. For example, in manufacturing, AI-powered robots and intelligent systems can perform tasks such as assembly, quality control, and predictive maintenance with greater accuracy and speed.

Enhanced Customer Experience: AI technologies, such as chatbots and virtual assistants, have transformed customer interactions. Businesses can provide personalized and responsive customer support 24/7, improving customer satisfaction and loyalty. AI also enables businesses to analyze vast amounts of customer data to gain insights, deliver personalized recommendations, and tailor marketing campaigns, resulting in more targeted and effective customer engagement.

Data Analysis and Decision-Making: AI excels at analyzing large volumes of data quickly and extracting valuable insights. Businesses can leverage AI algorithms and machine learning models to uncover patterns, trends, and correlations in data that would be difficult for humans to identify. These insights empower businesses to make data-driven decisions, optimize processes, and identify new opportunities. AI-powered predictive analytics also enables businesses to anticipate customer behavior, market trends, and demand patterns, facilitating proactive decision-making.

Improved Productivity and Innovation: AI empowers employees by augmenting their capabilities and improving productivity. AI-powered tools, such as natural language processing and computer vision, enable employees to automate information retrieval, accelerate research, and perform complex analyses. This frees up time for employees to focus on higher-value tasks that require creativity and critical thinking. Additionally, AI can drive innovation by enabling businesses to develop new products and services, optimize existing offerings, and explore new business models.

Risk Management and Security: AI plays a crucial role in risk management and security. AI-powered algorithms can analyze vast amounts of data in real-time to identify anomalies, detect potential security threats, and predict risks. Businesses can leverage AI for fraud detection, cybersecurity, and compliance monitoring, safeguarding their operations and protecting sensitive data. AI can also enhance supply chain management by identifying potential disruptions and optimizing risk mitigation strategies.

However, the adoption of AI also raises important considerations and challenges for businesses:

Ethical and Social Impact: As AI becomes more pervasive, businesses must address ethical considerations. AI algorithms can be biased or discriminatory, leading to unfair outcomes. Ensuring fairness, transparency, and accountability in AI systems is crucial. Businesses must also address concerns regarding data privacy, security, and the responsible use of AI technologies.

Workforce Transformation: AI adoption may impact the workforce composition and require reskilling or upskilling employees to adapt to new roles and responsibilities. Businesses need to invest in training programs and create a culture of continuous learning to help employees embrace AI technologies and work effectively alongside them.

Integration and Implementation: Integrating AI technologies into existing systems and processes can be complex. Businesses must carefully plan and execute AI implementation strategies, ensuring seamless integration with legacy systems, data compatibility, and stakeholder buy-in. Additionally, scaling AI solutions across the organization requires robust infrastructure, data management practices, and efficient deployment strategies.

In conclusion, AI is transforming the business landscape, offering unprecedented opportunities for innovation, efficiency, and competitive advantage. Businesses that successfully harness the power of AI can unlock new growth potential, deliver enhanced customer experiences, optimize operations, and drive meaningful insights from data. However, businesses must also navigate ethical considerations, address workforce challenges, and carefully manage the integration and implementation of AI technologies to maximize its benefits. By embracing AI and adapting their strategies accordingly, businesses can position themselves for long-term success in an increasingly AI-driven world.

CHAPTER 2: TYPES OF AI: MACHINE LEARNING, DEEP LEARNING, NATURAL LANGUAGE PROCESSING, AND COMPUTER VISION

Artificial Intelligence (AI) encompasses a diverse range of technologies and methodologies that enable machines to perform tasks requiring human intelligence. Within the field of AI, several key subfields have emerged, each with its own unique focus and capabilities. Four prominent types of AI are machine learning, deep learning, natural language processing, and computer vision. These types of AI have revolutionized various industries and are driving advancements in automation, data analysis, language understanding, and visual perception.

Machine Learning:

Machine learning is a subset of AI that focuses on developing algorithms and statistical models that enable machines to learn from data and improve performance over time without being explicitly programmed. Machine learning algorithms analyze large datasets to identify patterns, correlations, and trends. They make predictions, classify data, and automate decision-making based on learned patterns. Machine learning is widely used in applications such as recommendation systems, fraud detection, predictive maintenance, and personalized marketing. Popular machine learning techniques include supervised learning, unsupervised learning, and reinforcement learning.

Deep Learning:

Deep learning is a specialized subset of machine learning that is inspired by the structure and function of the human brain. It involves the use of artificial neural networks, known as deep neural networks, to process and learn from complex patterns and data representations. Deep learning algorithms excel at automatically extracting features from raw data and learning hierarchical representations. This enables them to handle unstructured data like images, audio, and text. Deep learning has achieved remarkable success in areas such as computer vision, speech recognition, natural language processing, and autonomous systems. Convolutional Neural Networks (CNNs) and Recurrent Neural Networks (RNNs) are popular architectures used in deep learning.

Natural Language Processing (NLP):

Natural Language Processing is a branch of AI that focuses on the interaction between computers and human language. NLP enables machines to understand, interpret, and generate human language, both written and spoken. It involves tasks such as speech recognition, language translation, sentiment analysis, and text summarization. NLP algorithms process and analyze textual data, extracting meaning, semantic relationships, and context. They use techniques like machine translation, named entity recognition, sentiment analysis, and language generation to enable communication between humans and machines. NLP is employed in various applications, including chatbots, virtual assistants, customer support systems, and information retrieval.

Computer Vision:

Computer vision involves the extraction, analysis, and understanding of visual data by machines. It enables machines to perceive and interpret images and videos, replicating human visual capabilities. Computer vision algorithms process visual data, extract features, and recognize objects, faces, gestures, and scenes. They can perform tasks such as object detection, image classification, image segmentation, and image generation. Computer vision finds applications in fields like autonomous vehicles, medical imaging, surveillance systems, augmented reality, and robotics. Techniques such as convolutional neural networks and image processing algorithms are commonly used in computer vision.

The convergence of these AI types has led to powerful applications that combine their capabilities. For example, deep learning models are used in natural language processing tasks to analyze and generate human language. Machine learning algorithms are employed in computer vision to train models for image recognition and object detection. These intersections create opportunities for innovative solutions in various domains.

While these types of AI have transformed industries and unlocked unprecedented opportunities, they also present challenges. Large-scale data requirements, the need for computational power, and interpretability of AI models are areas that require attention. Ethical considerations, such as fairness, bias, and privacy, must be addressed to ensure responsible and accountable AI adoption.

In conclusion, machine learning, deep learning, natural language processing, and computer vision are key types of AI that have revolutionized industries and expanded the capabilities of machines. They enable automation, data analysis, language understanding, and visual perception, paving the way for groundbreaking applications in various fields. By leveraging these types of AI, businesses can drive innovation, improve decision-making, and enhance user experiences, opening new avenues for growth and transformation in the AI era.

CHAPTER 3: THE ROLE OF AI IN DIGITAL TRANSFORMATION

Digital transformation has become a critical priority for businesses across industries as they seek to leverage technology to drive innovation, enhance customer experiences, and remain competitive in the digital age. In this transformative journey, Artificial Intelligence (AI) plays a pivotal role. AI empowers organizations to harness the power of data, automate processes, gain insights, and make intelligent decisions at scale. It acts as a catalyst, enabling businesses to unlock new possibilities and reimagine their operations in the digital landscape.

Automation and Efficiency:

AI enables businesses to automate repetitive and manual tasks, significantly improving efficiency and productivity. By leveraging AI-powered tools and systems, organizations can streamline workflows, optimize resource allocation, and eliminate human errors. Robotic Process Automation (RPA) and intelligent automation solutions leverage AI algorithms to automate routine tasks, reducing operational costs and freeing up human resources to focus on more strategic activities. This automation-driven efficiency leads to increased productivity, faster response times, and improved customer satisfaction.

Data Analytics and Insights:

One of the most impactful contributions of AI to digital transformation is its ability to extract actionable insights from vast amounts of data. AI algorithms can analyze and process structured and unstructured data, uncovering patterns, correlations, and trends that would be difficult or impossible for humans to detect. Through techniques like machine learning and deep learning, AI models can make predictions, generate recommendations, and identify opportunities or risks in real-time. This data-driven decision-making enhances operational agility, enables proactive problem-solving, and drives business growth.

Enhanced Customer Experiences:

AI plays a crucial role in delivering personalized and seamless customer experiences, a key aspect of digital transformation. By analyzing customer data, AI algorithms can understand individual preferences, behavior patterns, and needs, allowing businesses to provide tailored products, services, and recommendations. AI-powered chatbots and virtual assistants enable businesses to offer round-the-clock customer support and personalized interactions. Natural Language Processing (NLP) and sentiment analysis help organizations gauge customer sentiment and sentiment, allowing them to address concerns, improve satisfaction, and build strong customer relationships.

Innovation and Product Development:

AI fosters innovation by enabling organizations to explore new frontiers and develop breakthrough products and services. Machine learning and deep learning algorithms can uncover market trends, identify emerging customer needs, and support the development of innovative solutions. AI-powered predictive analytics assists businesses in forecasting demand, optimizing pricing, and adapting to market changes. Moreover, AI enables rapid prototyping, simulation, and iterative design, accelerating the product development lifecycle and reducing time to market.

Intelligent Decision-Making:

AI empowers organizations to make intelligent decisions based on data-driven insights and predictions. By leveraging AI models, businesses can automate complex decision-making processes, optimize resource allocation, and minimize risks. AI algorithms can analyze market conditions, customer behavior, and internal data to provide recommendations for pricing, inventory management, and supply chain optimization. AI-powered systems can also identify anomalies, patterns, and outliers in real-time, enabling organizations to respond swiftly to changing conditions and mitigate risks effectively.

Continuous Learning and Adaptability:

AI promotes a culture of continuous learning and adaptability, which is vital for successful digital transformation. Machine learning algorithms can adapt and improve their performance over time by learning from new data and experiences. This adaptability allows businesses to stay ahead of the curve, anticipate customer needs, and adapt their strategies in real-time. By embracing AI, organizations foster a culture of innovation and agility, enabling them to navigate the evolving digital landscape with resilience.

However, incorporating AI into digital transformation initiatives requires careful consideration and planning:

Data Strategy and Infrastructure:

Effective AI implementation relies on a robust data strategy and infrastructure. Businesses need to ensure data quality, accessibility, and governance to feed AI algorithms with reliable and relevant data. They must invest in data management systems, data integration platforms, and cloud-based storage solutions to handle large volumes of data and facilitate seamless AI operations.

Skill Development and Talent Acquisition:

AI-driven digital transformation demands a skilled workforce capable of leveraging AI technologies effectively. Organizations must invest in upskilling and reskilling their employees to develop AI expertise. Additionally, acquiring AI talent through recruitment or partnerships with external experts can accelerate digital transformation initiatives and foster innovation.

Ethical Considerations:

AI adoption necessitates ethical considerations. Organizations must establish ethical guidelines and frameworks to ensure fairness, transparency, and accountability in AI systems. They should address biases, privacy concerns, and the responsible use of AI technologies to maintain trust and mitigate potential risks.

Change Management:

Implementing AI as part of digital transformation requires change management efforts. Organizations need to communicate the benefits of AI to employees, address concerns, and provide training and support throughout the transformation process. Building a culture that embraces AI and encourages innovation is vital for successful adoption.

In conclusion, AI is a fundamental enabler of digital transformation. Its capabilities in automation, data analytics, customer experience enhancement, innovation, intelligent decision-making, and continuous learning empower organizations to reimagine their operations, drive efficiency, and unlock new growth opportunities. However, successful integration of AI into digital transformation initiatives requires a strategic approach, addressing data, talent, ethical considerations, and change management. With AI as a driving force, businesses can thrive in the digital era and remain at the forefront of their industries.

CHAPTER 4: ALIGNING AI STRATEGIES WITH BUSINESS GOALS

Artificial Intelligence (AI) has become a transformative force across industries, offering businesses new opportunities to drive innovation, enhance operational efficiency, and deliver superior customer experiences. However, for organizations to fully leverage the potential of AI, it is crucial to align AI strategies with their overarching business goals. Alignment ensures that AI initiatives are purpose-driven, targeted, and contribute directly to the organization's success. Here are key considerations for aligning AI strategies with business goals:

Clearly Define Business Objectives:

The first step in aligning AI strategies with business goals is to clearly define the organization's objectives. This involves understanding the core mission, vision, and values of the business and identifying specific goals and outcomes that AI can help achieve. For example, business goals may include increasing revenue, improving customer satisfaction, optimizing operational processes, or gaining a competitive edge. By establishing clear business objectives, organizations can identify areas where AI can have the greatest impact.

Identify AI Opportunities:

Once business objectives are defined, the next step is to identify specific AI opportunities that align with those objectives. This involves conducting a thorough assessment of the organization's operations, processes, and challenges. By analyzing existing data assets, bottlenecks, and pain points, businesses can identify areas where AI can add value. For instance, AI may be applied to automate repetitive tasks, enhance decision-making processes, enable predictive analytics, or improve customer interactions. Prioritizing AI opportunities based on their potential impact and feasibility is essential.

Establish a Strategic Roadmap:

Developing a strategic roadmap is crucial to align AI initiatives with business goals. The roadmap outlines the steps, timelines, and resources required to implement AI solutions effectively. It should consider the organization's budget, technological capabilities, and the readiness of the workforce. The roadmap should prioritize AI projects based on their alignment with business goals, potential ROI, and strategic importance. It is also important to consider the scalability and sustainability of AI initiatives over the long term.

Collaborate Across Departments:

Aligning AI strategies with business goals requires close collaboration and coordination across different departments and stakeholders within the organization. The involvement of key stakeholders, including executives, business leaders, IT professionals, and subject matter experts, is crucial. Collaborative efforts ensure that AI initiatives address cross-functional needs and align with the organization's overall strategy. Regular communication and feedback loops enable continuous alignment and adjustment of AI strategies as business goals evolve.

Data-Driven Decision-Making:

AI strategies must be rooted in a strong data foundation. Data plays a critical role in fueling AI models and algorithms. Therefore, organizations need to prioritize data quality, integrity, and accessibility. This involves establishing data governance frameworks, implementing robust data management practices, and ensuring compliance with data privacy regulations. By leveraging data-driven insights, organizations can make informed decisions that align with their business goals.

Evaluate and Measure Impact:

To ensure ongoing alignment, it is essential to regularly evaluate and measure the impact of AI initiatives against business goals. Key performance indicators (KPIs) should be established to assess the effectiveness and ROI of AI projects. These KPIs may include metrics such as revenue growth, cost savings, customer satisfaction scores, or operational efficiency improvements. By tracking and analyzing these metrics, organizations can make data-driven decisions about the continuation, optimization, or adjustment of their AI strategies.

Agile Approach and Continuous Improvement:

Adopting an agile approach to AI implementation allows organizations to quickly iterate, learn, and adapt to changing circumstances. Agile methodologies enable incremental development, testing, and feedback, ensuring that AI initiatives remain aligned with business goals. Continuous improvement is essential to refine AI models, optimize processes, and address emerging business needs. By fostering a culture of innovation and learning, organizations can continuously align AI strategies with evolving business goals.

Stay Abreast of AI Developments:

AI is a rapidly evolving field, and staying informed about the latest developments and trends is essential for aligning AI strategies with business goals. Organizations should invest in ongoing research and learning to understand emerging AI technologies and their potential applications. Engaging with industry experts, attending conferences, and participating in AI-focused communities can provide valuable insights into how AI can support business objectives.

In conclusion, aligning AI strategies with business goals is a critical success factor in realizing the full potential of AI. By clearly defining business objectives, identifying AI opportunities, establishing a strategic roadmap, collaborating across departments, making data-driven decisions, evaluating impact, adopting an agile approach, and staying informed about AI developments, organizations can ensure that their AI initiatives contribute directly to their overall success. Through effective alignment, businesses can harness the power of AI to drive innovation, enhance efficiency, and achieve their strategic goals.

CHAPTER 5: BUILDING THE RIGHT TEAM: DATA SCIENTISTS, ENGINEERS, AND ANALYSTS

In the age of data-driven decision-making, businesses recognize the importance of building a capable and skilled team to leverage the power of data and extract valuable insights. To harness the potential of data, organizations need to assemble a multidisciplinary team that includes data scientists, engineers, and analysts. This team collaborates to ensure effective data collection, processing, analysis, and interpretation, ultimately driving informed decision-making and delivering actionable outcomes. Let us explore the roles and contributions of each team member in building a robust data-driven organization:

Data Scientists:

Data scientists are at the forefront of the data-driven revolution. They possess a unique blend of technical expertise, statistical knowledge, and business acumen. Data scientists are responsible for designing and implementing sophisticated algorithms and models to extract insights from data. They have expertise in machine learning, statistical analysis, data visualization, and programming languages like Python or R. Data scientists explore large and complex datasets to uncover patterns, trends, and correlations that provide valuable business insights. They also develop predictive models and algorithms to make accurate predictions and forecasts. Their role is pivotal in helping organizations make data-driven decisions, optimize processes, and drive innovation.

Key responsibilities of data scientists include:

Designing and implementing machine learning models and algorithms.

Analyzing large datasets and extracting insights.

Conducting statistical analysis and hypothesis testing.

Developing predictive models and forecasting techniques.

Collaborating with business stakeholders to understand their requirements.

Translating complex data insights into actionable recommendations.

Staying up-to-date with the latest advancements in data science techniques and tools.

Data Engineers:

Data engineers play a crucial role in building and maintaining the infrastructure required to handle large volumes of data efficiently. They are responsible for designing, implementing, and managing the data pipelines that enable the smooth flow of data from various sources to storage and analysis systems. Data engineers work closely with data scientists and analysts to ensure data availability, quality, and reliability. They develop data architectures, design database systems, and optimize data storage and retrieval processes. Additionally, they collaborate with IT teams to ensure data security, scalability, and compliance.

Key responsibilities of data engineers include:

Designing and implementing data pipelines for data ingestion, storage, and processing.

Integrating and transforming data from various sources.

Developing and maintaining databases and data warehouses.

Ensuring data quality and integrity.

Implementing data security and privacy measures.

Optimizing data storage, retrieval, and query performance.

Collaborating with data scientists and analysts to understand data requirements.

Data Analysts:

Data analysts are responsible for translating data into meaningful insights that drive decision-making across the organization. They focus on analyzing data, identifying trends, and producing reports and visualizations that communicate the findings effectively. Data analysts possess strong analytical and problem-solving skills, as well as proficiency in tools such as SQL, Excel, and data visualization platforms. They work closely with stakeholders from various departments to understand their data needs, develop analytical frameworks, and deliver actionable insights. Data analysts also play a vital role in monitoring key performance indicators (KPIs) and tracking the impact of business decisions.

Key responsibilities of data analysts include:

Collecting, cleaning, and organizing data for analysis.

Performing data exploration and descriptive analysis.

Developing and maintaining dashboards and reports.

Applying statistical techniques to uncover patterns and trends.

Collaborating with stakeholders to define data requirements.

Providing data-driven insights and recommendations.

Communicating findings effectively through visualizations and presentations.

Building a collaborative and effective data team requires a combination of technical skills, domain knowledge, and effective communication. Here are some key considerations for building the right team:

Define Roles and Responsibilities:

Clearly define the roles and responsibilities of data scientists, engineers, and analysts within the organization. This ensures clarity and avoids duplication of efforts. Each team member should have a clear understanding of their areas of expertise and how they contribute to the overall data strategy.

Foster Collaboration:

Encourage collaboration and cross-functional communication among team members. Foster an environment where data scientists, engineers, and analysts can work together, exchange ideas, and share insights. This collaboration facilitates a holistic approach to data-driven decision-making and promotes innovation.

Develop a Learning Culture:

Promote a culture of continuous learning and professional development within the data team. Encourage team members to stay updated with the latest advancements in their respective fields, attend conferences, participate in training programs, and share knowledge with colleagues. This enables the team to leverage emerging tools and techniques effectively.

Hire for Diversity:

Build a diverse team with a range of skill sets, experiences, and backgrounds. Diverse perspectives contribute to innovative problem-solving and bring fresh insights to the data analysis process. Encourage diversity in terms of technical skills, domain expertise, and educational backgrounds to foster a well-rounded team.

Supportive Infrastructure and Tools:

Provide the necessary infrastructure, tools, and technologies required for data scientists, engineers, and analysts to perform their tasks effectively. This includes access to relevant databases, data processing frameworks, programming languages, and data visualization platforms. Additionally, invest in training and support to ensure team members can leverage these resources efficiently.

Effective Leadership:

Strong leadership is vital for the success of a data team. Leaders should provide clear guidance, support professional development, and advocate for the team's needs within the organization. They should foster a culture of trust, collaboration, and innovation while aligning the team's efforts with the overall business goals.

In conclusion, building the right team comprising data scientists, engineers, and analysts is crucial for organizations seeking to embrace data-driven decision-making and maximize the value of their data assets. Each team member brings unique skills and perspectives, working together to extract insights, build robust data infrastructure, and provide actionable recommendations. By aligning their roles and responsibilities, fostering collaboration, promoting continuous learning, embracing diversity, providing the necessary resources, and providing effective leadership, organizations can build a high-performing data team that drives success in the data-driven era.

CHAPTER 6: COLLABORATION BETWEEN IT AND BUSINESS

Collaboration between IT and business units is essential in today's digital landscape, where technology plays a central role in driving innovation, efficiency, and business growth. The alignment and cooperation between these two critical components of an organization are crucial for successfully implementing technology solutions, leveraging data, and achieving strategic objectives. Let us explore the benefits and key considerations of collaboration between IT and business units:

Benefits of Collaboration:

Shared Understanding and Goals:

Collaboration fosters a shared understanding of business objectives, challenges, and opportunities. By working together, IT professionals gain insights into the specific needs of different business units, while business units develop a deeper understanding of technology capabilities. This shared understanding helps align efforts and ensures that technology solutions address the specific requirements of the business.

Innovation and Digital Transformation:

Collaboration between IT and business units drives innovation and digital transformation initiatives. IT professionals can provide valuable insights into emerging technologies, industry trends, and best practices. They can also identify opportunities for automation, process optimization, and data-driven decision-making. By collaborating with IT, business units can leverage technology to drive innovation, improve operational efficiency, and deliver enhanced customer experiences.

Efficient Technology Implementation:

When IT and business units collaborate closely, technology implementations become more efficient and effective. Business units provide insights into their operational processes, challenges, and requirements, enabling IT to design and deploy tailored technology solutions. The involvement of business units in the implementation process ensures that solutions are aligned with their needs and that potential roadblocks are addressed proactively.

Data-driven Decision-making:

Collaboration between IT and business units is essential for leveraging data and analytics effectively. IT professionals can help business units in collecting, storing, and managing data securely. They can also develop data analytics capabilities and provide insights to drive data-driven decision-making. Business units, on the other hand, contribute their domain expertise, identifying the relevant data points and defining the key business questions that need to be answered through analytics.

Change Management and User Adoption:

Technology implementations often require changes in processes, workflows, and user behavior. Collaboration between IT and business units ensures effective change management by involving stakeholders from the early stages of implementation. Business units can provide valuable input into user requirements, user interfaces, and training needs, ensuring that technology solutions are user-friendly and well-adopted across the organization.

Key Considerations for Collaboration:

Communication and Trust:

Open and effective communication is crucial for successful collaboration. Regular meetings, discussions, and knowledge-sharing sessions between IT and business units facilitate understanding, build trust, and ensure that everyone is on the same page. Transparent communication channels and a culture of trust enable productive collaboration, leading to better outcomes.

Joint Planning and Governance:

Collaboration should be formalized through joint planning and governance processes. IT and business units should work together to define technology strategies, prioritize initiatives, and allocate resources effectively. Establishing cross-functional committees or project teams with representation from both IT and business units helps ensure that decisions are made collectively, and the interests of all stakeholders are taken into account.

Cross-training and Skill Development:

Promoting cross-training and skill development initiatives between IT and business units is beneficial for both parties. IT professionals can benefit from understanding the specific business requirements, processes, and challenges, enabling them to develop tailored technology solutions. Business unit employees can benefit from gaining basic technology skills, allowing them to work more effectively with IT and understand the possibilities and limitations of technology implementations.

Change Agents and Champions:

Identifying change agents and champions within both IT and business units can drive collaboration and promote the adoption of technology solutions. These individuals can act as advocates, bridge the gap between the two groups, and drive cultural change within the organization. By promoting collaboration, they create a culture where IT and business units work together seamlessly.

Continuous Improvement and Feedback:

Collaboration between IT and business units should be an ongoing process of continuous improvement. Regular feedback sessions, retrospectives, and post-implementation reviews help identify areas for improvement and refine collaboration practices. This iterative approach ensures that collaboration evolves with changing business needs and technology advancements.

In conclusion, collaboration between IT and business units is crucial for organizations to leverage technology effectively, drive innovation, and achieve strategic objectives. By fostering shared understanding, promoting innovation, ensuring efficient technology implementations, enabling data-driven decision-making, and addressing change management, organizations can unlock the full potential of collaboration between IT and business units. By working together, IT and business units can drive organizational success in today's digital world.

CHAPTER 7: IDENTIFYING USE CASES AND PRIORITIZING PROJECTS

When implementing new technologies or embarking on digital transformation initiatives, organizations need to identify use cases and prioritize projects to maximize their return on investment and ensure successful outcomes. By carefully evaluating potential use cases and prioritizing projects based on strategic goals, feasibility, and impact, organizations can allocate their resources effectively and focus on initiatives that deliver the most significant value. Let us explore the process of identifying use cases and prioritizing projects:

Understand Business Objectives and Challenges:

To identify relevant use cases, it is essential to have a deep understanding of the organization's business objectives and challenges. This involves engaging with stakeholders across different departments, conducting interviews, and gathering insights into pain points, inefficiencies, and opportunities for improvement. By understanding the specific needs and goals of the organization, you can align technology initiatives with the strategic direction of the business.

Analyze Data and Processes:

Analyze available data and existing processes to identify areas where technology can have the most significant impact. Look for bottlenecks, manual tasks, and areas with a high potential for automation or optimization. Examine data sources, quality, and availability to determine how technology can enhance data-driven decision-making and enable more efficient processes. This analysis provides a foundation for identifying use cases that align with the organization's objectives.

Brainstorm and Ideation:

Conduct brainstorming sessions and workshops involving cross-functional teams to generate a wide range of ideas for potential use cases. Encourage participants to think creatively and explore different possibilities. These sessions can provide valuable insights into innovative ways technology can be applied to address business challenges and unlock new opportunities. The ideation process should be inclusive, involving representatives from IT, business units, and other relevant stakeholders.

Evaluate Feasibility and Impact:

Once a list of potential use cases is generated, evaluate their feasibility and impact. Feasibility assessment includes considerations such as technical complexity, data availability, resource requirements, and compatibility with existing systems. It is crucial to assess whether the organization has the necessary technological infrastructure, expertise, and resources to implement each use case effectively. Impact assessment involves analyzing the potential benefits and value each use case can bring to the organization, such as cost savings, revenue generation, customer satisfaction, or process optimization.

Align with Strategic Goals:

Evaluate each potential use case's alignment with the organization's strategic goals and priorities. Consider how each use case contributes to the overall vision and mission of the organization. Projects that align closely with strategic objectives should be given higher priority. This alignment ensures that technology initiatives support the organization's long-term growth and competitive advantage.

Perform Cost-Benefit Analysis:

Conduct a cost-benefit analysis for each potential use case to understand the potential return on investment. Assess the financial implications, including implementation costs, maintenance costs, and potential cost savings or revenue gains. Additionally, consider non-financial factors such as improved customer satisfaction, enhanced brand reputation, or increased operational efficiency. This analysis helps prioritize projects that offer the most significant value and align with the organization's financial objectives.

Consider Implementation Complexity and Dependencies:

Assess the implementation complexity and dependencies of each use case. Consider factors such as technical requirements, integration with existing systems, potential risks, and the availability of skilled resources. Projects that are easier to implement, have minimal dependencies, and can be executed within a reasonable timeframe should be prioritized initially. This approach ensures a smoother implementation process and reduces the risk of project delays or failures.

Seek Stakeholder Input:

Engage stakeholders from various departments and levels within the organization to gain their perspectives and input on potential use cases. Collaborate with business units, IT teams, senior management, and end-users to understand their requirements, pain points, and expectations. By involving stakeholders early in the process, you increase buy-in and ensure that the prioritized projects reflect the needs and priorities of the organization as a whole.

Develop a Prioritization Framework:

Develop a prioritization framework to objectively assess and compare potential use cases. The framework can include criteria such as strategic alignment, impact, feasibility, cost-benefit analysis, implementation complexity, and stakeholder input. Assign weights to each criterion based on their importance and score each use case accordingly. This framework helps in making informed decisions and justifying project prioritization.

Continuously Review and Adjust:

Project prioritization is an ongoing process. Continuously review and adjust the prioritization as business needs, market conditions, and technology advancements evolve. Regularly reassess the progress and impact of ongoing projects and incorporate new insights and feedback into the prioritization process. This iterative approach ensures that resources are allocated to the most relevant and valuable initiatives at any given time.

In conclusion, identifying use cases and prioritizing projects is a critical step in leveraging technology to drive organizational success. By understanding business objectives, analyzing data and processes, brainstorming ideas, evaluating feasibility and impact, aligning with strategic goals, performing cost-benefit analysis, considering implementation complexity, seeking stakeholder input, developing a prioritization framework, and continuously reviewing and adjusting, organizations can focus their efforts on initiatives that deliver the most significant value and contribute to long-term success. This systematic approach ensures effective resource allocation, reduces implementation risks, and maximizes the return on investment from technology initiatives.

CHAPTER 8: ASSESSING THE AI MATURITY OF YOUR ORGANIZATION

As organizations increasingly recognize the transformative potential of Artificial Intelligence (AI), assessing the AI maturity of your organization becomes crucial. AI maturity assessment helps organizations understand their current capabilities, identify areas for improvement, and develop a roadmap for AI adoption and advancement. By evaluating the organization's readiness, infrastructure, data, talent, and strategic alignment, businesses can gauge their AI maturity and take informed steps to enhance their AI capabilities. Let us explore key factors to consider when assessing the AI maturity of your organization:

Strategic Alignment:

Assessing strategic alignment involves evaluating how well AI initiatives align with the organization's overall goals and objectives. It involves understanding whether AI is considered a strategic priority by senior management and whether it is integrated into the organization's long-term plans. Evaluate how effectively AI initiatives support the organization's mission, vision, and business strategy. Strategic alignment ensures that AI is not implemented in isolation but rather contributes to the overall success of the organization.

Data Readiness:

An organization's data readiness is a critical factor in AI maturity assessment. Evaluate the quality, availability, and accessibility of your organization's data. Assess the organization's data infrastructure, data governance practices, and data management capabilities. Determine whether your organization has the necessary data infrastructure to support AI initiatives effectively. Consider factors such as data storage, data integration, data security, and data privacy. The availability of clean, relevant, and comprehensive data is essential for training AI models and generating accurate insights.

Technology Infrastructure:

Evaluate your organization's technology infrastructure to determine its readiness for AI implementation. Assess the availability and scalability of computing resources required for AI initiatives. Consider factors such as processing power, storage capacity, and network capabilities. Evaluate whether your organization has the necessary hardware, software, and tools to support AI development and deployment effectively. Additionally, assess the compatibility of existing systems and the ability to integrate AI technologies seamlessly.

Talent and Skills:

Evaluate the talent and skills within your organization related to AI. Assess the availability of skilled AI professionals such as data scientists, machine learning experts, and AI engineers. Consider the level of expertise in areas such as data analytics, statistical modeling, and programming languages. Evaluate the organization's ability to attract and retain top AI talent. Assess the availability of training and development programs to upskill existing employees in AI-related competencies. The presence of a skilled AI workforce is crucial for successful AI implementation and advancement.

Processes and Governance:

Assess the processes and governance frameworks related to AI within your organization. Evaluate how well AI initiatives are integrated into existing business processes and workflows. Consider whether there are dedicated teams or roles responsible for overseeing AI projects and governance. Assess the existence of guidelines and policies related to ethical AI practices, data privacy, and security. Evaluate the level of collaboration and communication between different teams involved in AI initiatives. Strong processes and governance structures ensure effective management, monitoring, and control of AI projects.

External Partnerships and Ecosystem:

Assess the organization's engagement with external partners, collaborations, and the AI ecosystem. Evaluate whether your organization actively seeks partnerships with AI technology providers, research institutions, startups, or industry consortia. Consider the extent to which your organization leverages external expertise and resources to advance its AI initiatives. Evaluate the organization's participation in AI-related events, conferences, and knowledge-sharing forums. Collaboration and engagement with the broader AI ecosystem can accelerate AI maturity by leveraging external knowledge, innovations, and emerging technologies.

ROI and Value Generation:

Assess the organization's ability to measure the return on investment (ROI) and value generation from AI initiatives. Evaluate whether the organization has mechanisms in place to track and measure the impact of AI projects on key performance indicators (KPIs) such as revenue growth, cost savings, customer satisfaction, or operational efficiency. Consider whether the organization has established frameworks to assess the value created by AI initiatives. Being able to demonstrate the tangible benefits of AI adoption is crucial for securing support and resources for future AI initiatives.

Continuous Learning and Improvement:

Assess the organization's commitment to continuous learning and improvement in the field of AI. Consider whether there is a culture of experimentation, innovation, and knowledge-sharing related to AI within the organization. Evaluate whether the organization actively monitors AI trends, research advancements, and emerging technologies. Consider whether the organization encourages employees to participate in AI training programs, attend conferences, or engage in professional development activities. A culture of continuous learning and improvement ensures that the organization stays updated with the latest AI developments and can adapt its AI strategies accordingly.

In conclusion, assessing the AI maturity of your organization is crucial for understanding its current capabilities, identifying areas for improvement, and charting a path for AI adoption and advancement. By evaluating strategic alignment, data readiness, technology infrastructure, talent and skills, processes and governance, external partnerships, ROI and value generation, and commitment to continuous learning, organizations can gauge their AI maturity and take strategic actions to enhance their AI capabilities. An effective AI maturity assessment provides insights that help organizations leverage AI as a transformative force and drive their success in the digital era.

Chapter 10: Creating an AI Roadmap

Creating an AI roadmap is a crucial step in harnessing the potential of Artificial Intelligence (AI) within an organization. An AI roadmap outlines the strategic plan for implementing AI initiatives, maximizing their value, and achieving the organization's business goals. It provides a clear vision, sets priorities, and guides the organization's AI journey. Let us explore key considerations for creating an effective AI roadmap:

Define Business Objectives:

The first step in creating an AI roadmap is to define the organization's business objectives. Identify the specific goals and outcomes that AI can help achieve. This may include increasing revenue, improving operational efficiency, enhancing customer experience, or driving innovation. By aligning AI initiatives with business objectives, the roadmap ensures that AI investments directly contribute to the organization's success.

Conduct Current State Assessment:

Assess the organization's current state in terms of AI readiness, capabilities, and infrastructure. Evaluate existing data assets, technology infrastructure, talent, and processes related to AI. Identify any gaps or areas for improvement. This assessment provides a foundation for designing the AI roadmap, as it helps prioritize initiatives and allocate resources effectively.

Identify Use Cases:

Identify specific use cases where AI can create value and impact. Consider the areas where AI can address business challenges, optimize processes, or generate insights. Engage with stakeholders across different departments to understand their needs and pain points. Prioritize use cases based on their strategic importance, feasibility, and potential impact on the organization's goals.

Set Key Milestones and Timelines:

Establish key milestones and timelines for the implementation of AI initiatives. Break down the roadmap into manageable phases or projects. This allows for a structured and incremental approach, ensuring that progress can be monitored, and adjustments can be made along the way. Each milestone should be clearly defined and aligned with the organization's strategic objectives.

Allocate Resources:

Determine the resources required to implement the AI roadmap effectively. This includes financial resources, technology infrastructure, talent acquisition or upskilling, and partnerships. Allocate the necessary budget and secure support from senior management. Consider the balance between in-house capabilities and external expertise, as well as the need for collaborations or partnerships to accelerate AI adoption.

Develop Technical Capabilities:

Assess and develop the technical capabilities required for successful AI implementation. This includes evaluating the organization's data infrastructure, such as data storage, data integration, and data governance. Consider the need for advanced analytics tools, cloud computing, or machine learning platforms. Ensure that the technology stack aligns with the organization's goals and supports the identified use cases.

Establish Data Governance:

Establish robust data governance practices to ensure data quality, privacy, and compliance. Develop data management frameworks, data access policies, and data security measures. This ensures that the organization's data assets are properly managed and protected. Data governance is essential for effective AI implementation, as high-quality and reliable data is crucial for training AI models and generating accurate insights.

Build a Skilled AI Workforce:

Invest in developing a skilled AI workforce. Identify the skills and competencies required for AI implementation and determine whether they exist within the organization or need to be acquired. Provide training and development opportunities to upskill existing employees in AI-related areas. Consider partnering with educational institutions or hiring external experts to bridge any skill gaps. A skilled workforce is essential for executing AI initiatives successfully.

Develop a Change Management Plan:

Implementing AI initiatives often involves changes in processes, workflows, and mindsets. Develop a change management plan to address potential resistance and facilitate smooth adoption. Communicate the benefits of AI to employees and stakeholders, provide training and support, and create a culture that embraces AI and encourages experimentation and innovation.

Monitor and Evaluate Progress:

Regularly monitor and evaluate the progress of AI initiatives against the roadmap's milestones. Establish key performance indicators (KPIs) and metrics to measure the impact of AI on business outcomes. Continuously assess the alignment of AI initiatives with evolving business needs and make adjustments to the roadmap, as necessary.

In conclusion, creating an AI roadmap is a strategic exercise that enables organizations to leverage the potential of AI effectively. By defining business objectives, conducting a current state assessment, identifying use cases, setting key milestones, allocating resources, developing technical capabilities, establishing data governance, building a skilled AI workforce, developing a change management plan, and monitoring progress, organizations can navigate their AI journey with clarity and purpose. An effective AI roadmap ensures that AI initiatives are aligned with business goals, maximizes the value of AI investments, and positions the organization for long-term success in the era of AI-driven innovation.

CHAPTER 11: IMPORTANCE OF DATA QUALITY AND GOVERNANCE

In today's data-driven world, organizations rely heavily on data to make informed decisions, drive innovation, and gain a competitive edge. However, the value and reliability of data depend on its quality and governance. Data quality refers to the accuracy, completeness, consistency, and timeliness of data, while data governance refers to the framework and processes for managing data throughout its lifecycle. Let us explore the importance of data quality and governance for organizations:

Informed Decision-Making:

High-quality data is essential for informed decision-making. When data is accurate, complete, and up-to-date, it provides a reliable basis for analysis and decision-making. Decision-makers can have confidence in the insights derived from data and make well-informed choices that drive positive business outcomes. Data quality ensures that decisions are based on trustworthy information, reducing the risk of errors, misinterpretation, and poor decision-making.

Enhanced Customer Experience:

Data quality and governance play a critical role in delivering an enhanced customer experience. By ensuring accurate customer data, organizations can personalize their interactions, deliver targeted marketing campaigns, and provide personalized products or services. Customers expect organizations to have a comprehensive and accurate understanding of their preferences and needs. Improving data quality and governance enables organizations to meet these expectations and deliver a seamless and personalized customer experience.

Efficient Operations:

Data is a vital asset for optimizing operational processes and improving efficiency. High-quality data allows organizations to identify bottlenecks, streamline workflows, and eliminate redundancies. Accurate and timely data supports effective inventory management, supply chain optimization, and resource allocation. By maintaining data quality and governance, organizations can optimize their operations, reduce costs, and improve overall productivity.

Regulatory Compliance:

Data governance is crucial for ensuring regulatory compliance. Organizations must adhere to various data protection and privacy regulations, such as the General Data Protection Regulation (GDPR) and the California Consumer Privacy Act (CCPA). Data governance frameworks enable organizations to establish processes and controls for data handling, security, and privacy. By implementing robust data governance practices, organizations can demonstrate compliance, mitigate risks, and protect the privacy of individuals.

Data Integration and Interoperability:

Data quality and governance are essential for data integration and interoperability. Organizations often operate with diverse data sources and systems, making it challenging to integrate and analyze data effectively. Poor data quality and inconsistent data formats can hinder integration efforts and lead to unreliable insights. Data governance practices, such as data standardization, data mapping, and data cleansing, ensure data compatibility and consistency across different systems, enabling seamless integration and interoperability.

Trust and Credibility:

Data quality and governance build trust and credibility both internally and externally. When organizations demonstrate a commitment to maintaining data quality, employees trust the data they work with and make data-driven decisions confidently. Externally, customers, partners, and stakeholders have confidence in an organization that can demonstrate accurate, reliable, and secure data practices. Trust and credibility enhance an organization's reputation and foster stronger relationships with customers and partners.

Data Analytics and AI:

Data quality is foundational to effective data analytics and Artificial Intelligence (AI) initiatives. High-quality data forms the basis for accurate predictive models, machine learning algorithms, and AI-driven insights. Poor data quality can lead to biased or inaccurate results, compromising the effectiveness of data analytics and AI applications. Data governance ensures that data is properly managed, validated, and cleansed, enabling organizations to leverage the full potential of data analytics and AI.

Risk Mitigation:

Data quality and governance help mitigate risks associated with data breaches, data loss, and unauthorized access. By implementing proper data governance practices, organizations can identify and assess data risks, implement security measures, and ensure data backup and recovery procedures are in place. Data quality controls and data governance frameworks help minimize the likelihood of data breaches and mitigate the impact in case of security incidents.

In conclusion, data quality and governance are crucial for organizations seeking to leverage data effectively and gain a competitive advantage. By ensuring data accuracy, completeness, and timeliness, organizations can make informed decisions, enhance the customer experience, optimize operations, and achieve regulatory compliance. Implementing data governance frameworks and practices ensures that data is properly managed, protected, and integrated, enabling organizations to unlock the full potential of their data assets. With reliable and high-quality data, organizations can drive innovation, gain insights, and thrive in today's data-centric business environment.

CHAPTER 12: DATA STORAGE AND PROCESSING REQUIREMENTS

Data storage and processing requirements play a vital role in today's data-driven landscape. As organizations collect, store, and analyze ever-increasing amounts of data, it is crucial to have the right infrastructure and processes in place to handle these demands efficiently and effectively. Let us explore the importance of data storage and processing requirements and key considerations for organizations:

Scalability and Flexibility:

Data storage and processing requirements should be scalable and flexible to accommodate the growing volume, variety, and velocity of data. Organizations need to anticipate future data growth and ensure that their storage and processing infrastructure can handle increased workloads without compromising performance. Scalable solutions, such as cloud-based storage and distributed computing frameworks, allow organizations to expand their capacity as needed and adapt to changing data demands.

Data Security and Privacy:

Data storage and processing requirements must prioritize data security and privacy. Organizations must implement robust security measures to protect sensitive data from unauthorized access, data breaches, and cyber threats. Encryption, access controls, data classification, and regular security audits are essential to ensure data confidentiality and integrity. Compliance with data protection and privacy regulations, such as GDPR and CCPA, is also crucial to maintain customer trust and meet legal requirements.

Accessibility and Availability:

Data storage and processing infrastructure should enable easy and reliable access to data for authorized users. Accessibility is particularly important for real-time analytics, decision-making, and customer service. Organizations need to ensure that data is available whenever it is required, minimizing downtime and disruptions. Implementing redundant storage systems, backup and recovery mechanisms, and disaster recovery plans ensure data availability and business continuity.

Performance and Speed:

Efficient data storage and processing are essential for maintaining high performance and speed. As organizations analyze and extract insights from large datasets, they require fast and responsive systems to deliver results in a timely manner. Optimized storage technologies, high-speed networks, and parallel processing frameworks, such as distributed computing or in-memory computing, can significantly enhance data processing speed and overall system performance.

Data Integration and Interoperability:

Data storage and processing infrastructure should support seamless integration and interoperability across different data sources and systems. Organizations often operate with diverse data types and formats, and integrating data from various sources is crucial for comprehensive analysis and decision-making. Compatibility with different database systems, data integration tools, and APIs enables efficient data exchange and integration, enabling organizations to gain a holistic view of their data assets.

Cost Optimization:

Organizations need to consider cost optimization when designing data storage and processing solutions. Traditional on-premises infrastructure requires significant upfront investments in hardware, software, and maintenance. Cloud-based storage and processing solutions offer cost advantages by providing pay-as-you-go models, scalability, and reduced maintenance overhead. Careful evaluation of cost structures, considering factors such as data storage volumes, processing requirements, and the organization's budget, helps optimize costs and ensure a cost-effective data infrastructure.

Data Governance and Compliance:

Effective data storage and processing requirements should align with data governance and compliance frameworks. Organizations must establish policies, processes, and controls to manage data throughout its lifecycle, ensuring data quality, privacy, and security. Data governance practices include data classification, data retention policies, metadata management, and data lineage tracking. Compliance with industry regulations and standards, such as HIPAA or PCI-DSS, is critical to avoid legal and reputational risks.

Analytics and Machine Learning:

Data storage and processing requirements need to support advanced analytics and machine learning initiatives. Organizations increasingly rely on analytics to gain insights, make data-driven decisions, and develop predictive models. Storage and processing infrastructure should be designed to handle the complex computational requirements of advanced analytics and machine learning algorithms. Implementing specialized data processing frameworks, such as distributed computing frameworks (e.g., Hadoop, Spark), facilitates the efficient processing of large datasets for analytics purposes.

Data Lifecycle Management:

Effective data storage and processing requirements should consider the entire data lifecycle, including data ingestion, storage, processing, analysis, archiving, and disposal. Organizations should have strategies and mechanisms in place to manage data throughout its lifecycle, optimizing storage utilization, ensuring data retention compliance, and minimizing storage costs. Data lifecycle management also includes strategies for data cleansing, data transformation, and data deduplication to maintain data quality and optimize processing efficiency.

Future-Proofing:

When designing data storage and processing requirements, organizations should consider future needs and technological advancements. The landscape of data storage and processing technologies is rapidly evolving, with new innovations and solutions emerging regularly. Organizations need to consider technologies like cloud computing, edge computing, and advanced storage architectures to future-proof their infrastructure and stay ahead of the curve.

In conclusion, data storage and processing requirements are critical for organizations to effectively manage and leverage their data assets. Scalability, security, accessibility, performance, integration, cost optimization, governance, analytics support, data lifecycle management, and future-proofing are key considerations for designing a robust data storage and processing infrastructure. By addressing these requirements, organizations can efficiently handle growing data volumes, gain valuable insights, and unlock the full potential of their data for informed decision-making and competitive advantage.

CHAPTER 13: CLOUD-BASED VS. ON-PREMISES AI SOLUTIONS: A COMPARISON

As organizations embrace Artificial Intelligence (AI) technologies, they face a crucial decision: whether to adopt cloud-based or on-premises AI solutions. Both options offer unique advantages and considerations that organizations must evaluate based on their specific needs, resources, and priorities. Let us explore the key factors to consider when comparing cloud-based and on-premises AI solutions:

Infrastructure and Scalability:

Cloud-based AI solutions leverage the infrastructure provided by cloud service providers (CSPs), offering virtually unlimited scalability. Organizations can access computational resources, storage, and AI-specific services on-demand, scaling up or down based on their requirements. This flexibility eliminates the need for organizations to invest in and manage their own hardware infrastructure. On the other hand, on-premises AI solutions require organizations to set up and maintain their infrastructure, which may involve higher upfront costs and ongoing maintenance efforts. Scalability is limited to the capacity of the on-premises hardware.

Cost Considerations:

Cost is a significant factor when comparing cloud-based and on-premises AI solutions. Cloud-based solutions typically operate on a pay-as-you-go model, allowing organizations to pay only for the resources they consume.

This can be cost-effective, particularly for organizations with fluctuating AI workloads or limited budgets. Cloud-based solutions also eliminate the need for upfront infrastructure investments and ongoing maintenance costs. On the other hand, on-premises solutions involve upfront capital expenses for hardware and software, as well as ongoing operational costs for maintenance, upgrades, and energy consumption. The total cost of ownership for on-premises solutions may be higher in the long run.

Security and Privacy:

Data security and privacy considerations are paramount when evaluating AI solutions. Cloud service providers invest heavily in robust security measures, including physical security, network security, data encryption, and access controls. They comply with industry standards and regulations, offering comprehensive security frameworks. Cloud providers often have dedicated teams of security experts and the resources to address emerging threats effectively. However, concerns about data privacy and control may arise when sensitive data is stored and processed in the cloud. On-premises solutions provide organizations with greater control over their data, enabling them to implement security measures according to their specific requirements and compliance standards. This can be particularly important for organizations operating in highly regulated industries or those with strict data governance policies.

Maintenance and Upgrades:

Cloud-based AI solutions alleviate the burden of infrastructure maintenance and software upgrades. The responsibility for maintaining and updating the infrastructure lies with the cloud service provider, allowing organizations to focus on AI implementation and application development. CSPs regularly update their services with the latest features, security patches, and performance improvements, ensuring organizations have access to state-of-the-art AI technologies. In contrast, on-premises solutions require organizations to manage hardware maintenance, software updates, and compatibility issues. This demands dedicated IT resources and may involve downtime during upgrades.

Time to Deployment and Agility:

Cloud-based AI solutions offer rapid deployment and agility. Organizations can quickly provision resources and start using AI services, reducing the time to market for AI applications. Cloud providers offer pre-built AI models, frameworks, and APIs that expedite AI development and reduce the need for building AI infrastructure from scratch. This agility allows organizations to experiment, innovate, and scale AI initiatives faster. In contrast, on-premises solutions require time for hardware acquisition, installation, configuration, and software setup. The deployment process may involve more extensive planning and implementation timelines, potentially delaying time-sensitive AI projects.

Customization and Control:

On-premises AI solutions provide organizations with greater customization and control over their AI infrastructure. Organizations can tailor their AI environment to specific requirements, integrate with existing systems seamlessly, and customize algorithms and models to suit their unique needs. This level of customization is particularly important for organizations with specialized AI requirements or those working with sensitive or proprietary data that cannot be stored externally. Cloud-based solutions, while offering a wide range of services and configurations, may have limitations in terms of customization and control, as they operate within the framework provided by the CSP.

Connectivity and Latency:

Connectivity and latency considerations are essential for AI applications that require real-time or low-latency processing. On-premises solutions provide direct access to local data, minimizing the dependency on external networks and reducing latency. This can be critical for applications such as autonomous vehicles, industrial automation, or real-time monitoring. In contrast, cloud-based solutions rely on network connectivity to transfer data to and from the cloud, which can introduce additional latency. However, CSPs often have data centers distributed globally, allowing organizations to select data centers in proximity to their operations to mitigate latency issues.

Compliance and Regulatory Requirements:

Organizations operating in highly regulated industries may have specific compliance and regulatory requirements regarding data storage and processing. Some regulations restrict data residency and require data to be stored within specific geographic boundaries. In such cases, on-premises solutions provide organizations with greater control and visibility over data storage locations, ensuring compliance with local regulations. Cloud providers offer compliance certifications and data residency options, but organizations must ensure that their chosen CSP meets the specific requirements of their industry and jurisdiction.

In conclusion, the choice between cloud-based and on-premises AI solutions depends on various factors, including scalability needs, cost considerations, security requirements, customization preferences, and compliance obligations. Cloud-based solutions offer scalability, cost-effectiveness, rapid deployment, and maintenance-free infrastructure. On the other hand, on-premises solutions provide greater control, customization, and potentially better latency for applications requiring real-time processing or data residency compliance. Organizations should carefully evaluate their specific requirements and weigh the benefits and trade-offs of each approach to make an informed decision that aligns with their business objectives and resources.

CHAPTER 14: EVALUATING AI TOOLS AND PLATFORMS

As organizations embrace Artificial Intelligence (AI) technologies, the need to evaluate and select the right AI tools and platforms becomes crucial. The market is filled with a wide range of AI solutions, making it challenging to determine which ones best meet the organization's specific needs and requirements. Effective evaluation of AI tools and platforms ensures that organizations invest in solutions that align with their goals and enable successful AI implementation. Let us explore key considerations for evaluating AI tools and platforms:

Functionality and Suitability:

The first consideration when evaluating AI tools and platforms is their functionality and suitability for the organization's specific use cases. Assess whether the tools and platforms have the necessary features and capabilities to address the organization's AI requirements. Consider factors such as data processing capabilities, algorithm availability, integration options, model deployment methods, and scalability. The tools and platforms should align with the organization's objectives and support the specific AI tasks and applications it aims to develop.

Performance and Efficiency:

Evaluate the performance and efficiency of the AI tools and platforms. Consider factors such as processing speed, accuracy, and resource utilization. Assess the scalability of the solutions to handle large datasets or high workloads effectively. Look for benchmarks, case studies, or customer testimonials that provide insights into the performance of the tools and platforms. Additionally, consider the compatibility of the tools and platforms with the organization's existing infrastructure to ensure optimal performance and integration.

Ease of Use and User Experience:

User experience and ease of use are critical factors to consider when evaluating AI tools and platforms. The solutions should have an intuitive user interface and provide a smooth workflow for data ingestion, model development, and deployment. Consider the accessibility of documentation, tutorials, and support resources that can assist users in effectively utilizing the tools and platforms. A user-friendly interface and comprehensive support contribute to better adoption and productivity among users.

Integration Capabilities:

Evaluate the integration capabilities of the AI tools and platforms with the organization's existing systems and workflows. Consider whether the solutions can seamlessly integrate with data sources, databases, analytics tools, or other AI frameworks. Integration capabilities are essential for data ingestion, data preprocessing, model training, and integrating AI insights into existing business processes. The ability to integrate with other tools and platforms enhances the overall AI ecosystem within the organization.

Scalability and Flexibility:

Assess the scalability and flexibility of the AI tools and platforms. AI initiatives often require processing large volumes of data or handling fluctuating workloads. Evaluate whether the solutions can scale up or down to meet the organization's evolving needs. Consider whether the tools and platforms can leverage cloud computing resources or distributed computing frameworks to ensure scalability. Flexibility is also important, as organizations may need to customize or extend the functionalities of the tools and platforms to suit their specific requirements.

Vendor Credibility and Support:

Evaluate the credibility and reputation of the vendors providing the AI tools and platforms. Consider factors such as their track record, industry experience, customer base, and financial stability. Assess the level of support offered by the vendors, including the availability of technical support, updates, and ongoing maintenance. Evaluate customer reviews, case studies, and references to gain insights into the vendor's commitment to customer success and satisfaction.

Data Privacy and Security:

Data privacy and security are critical considerations when evaluating AI tools and platforms. Assess the vendors' data privacy policies, data protection measures, and compliance with relevant regulations, such as GDPR or CCPA. Evaluate the security features offered by the tools and platforms, including encryption, access controls, and data governance capabilities. The solutions should provide robust security mechanisms to protect sensitive data and ensure the privacy of both customer and organizational information.

Total Cost of Ownership (TCO):

Evaluate the total cost of ownership (TCO) of the AI tools and platforms. Consider not only the upfront costs but also the ongoing expenses, such as licensing fees, maintenance costs, and potential additional costs for scaling or customization. Assess the pricing models of the solutions, such as subscription-based, usage-based, or one-time licensing fees. Additionally, consider the potential return on investment (ROI) the tools and platforms can deliver in terms of improved efficiency, productivity, and business outcomes.

Future-Proofing and Roadmap:

Consider the future development roadmap of the AI tools and platforms. Assess the vendors' commitment to innovation, their plans for incorporating new AI technologies, and their ability to adapt to evolving market trends. Evaluate whether the tools and platforms align with the organization's long-term AI strategy and can support future growth and requirements. Future-proofing ensures that the organization can leverage advancements in AI technologies and stay competitive in the rapidly evolving AI landscape.

In conclusion, evaluating AI tools and platforms requires a comprehensive assessment of their functionality, performance, user experience, integration capabilities, scalability, vendor credibility, data privacy and security, TCO, and future-proofing. A thorough evaluation process helps organizations select the right AI solutions that align with their objectives, enable effective AI implementation, and drive success in their AI initiatives. By carefully considering these factors and conducting proper due diligence, organizations can make informed decisions and maximize the value of their AI investments.

CHAPTER 15: OPEN SOURCE VS. PROPRIETARY AI SOLUTIONS: A COMPARISON

When considering the adoption of Artificial Intelligence (AI) solutions, organizations face a fundamental choice between open source and proprietary options. Open-source AI solutions provide freely available source code and allow users to modify and distribute it, while proprietary solutions are developed and owned by specific companies, offering closed-source software. Both options have their advantages and considerations, which organizations must evaluate based on their specific needs, resources, and objectives. Let us explore the key factors to consider when comparing open source and proprietary AI solutions:

Flexibility and Customization:

Open-source AI solutions provide organizations with maximum flexibility and customization options. As the source code is freely available, organizations can modify, extend, and adapt the software to meet their specific requirements. This level of flexibility allows organizations to tailor the AI solution to their unique needs and integrate it seamlessly with their existing infrastructure. Proprietary solutions, on the other hand, offer limited customization options, as the source code is not accessible. Organizations must rely on the features and functionalities provided by the vendor, which may not align perfectly with their requirements.

Community Support and Collaboration:

Open-source AI solutions benefit from a vibrant community of developers and users who contribute to the improvement and evolution of the software. These communities provide valuable resources, documentation, forums, and collaborative environments where users can seek assistance, share knowledge, and exchange ideas. The collective efforts of the community lead to faster bug fixes, feature enhancements, and continuous improvement of the software. In contrast, proprietary solutions depend on the support and development resources provided by the vendor. While the vendor's expertise can be valuable, it may not match the collaborative nature and collective knowledge of an open-source community.

Cost Considerations:

Cost is a significant factor when evaluating AI solutions. Open-source solutions are generally free to use, allowing organizations to avoid licensing fees and reduce upfront costs. Additionally, organizations have the flexibility to deploy open-source solutions on their own infrastructure, avoiding cloud service costs. However, it is important to consider that implementing and maintaining open-source solutions may require dedicated resources with the necessary technical skills. Proprietary solutions, on the other hand, often involve licensing fees and ongoing costs for support, updates, and maintenance. The total cost of ownership should be carefully evaluated, considering not only the upfront expenses but also the long-term costs associated with each option.

Security and Reliability:

Security and reliability are critical considerations for AI solutions. Open-source solutions benefit from the scrutiny of a large community of developers, which often leads to quicker identification and resolution of security vulnerabilities. The transparency of open-source code allows for independent security audits and the ability to address issues promptly. However, organizations must still ensure that they implement proper security measures and keep their open-source software up to date. Proprietary solutions, developed and maintained by specific companies, may provide dedicated security teams and undergo rigorous testing and validation. Organizations must evaluate the vendor's reputation, track record, and security practices to assess the reliability and security of the proprietary solution.

Support and Documentation:

Proprietary solutions often come with dedicated support services provided by the vendor. This includes technical assistance, troubleshooting, and access to experts who can help organizations navigate any issues or challenges. Proprietary solutions also tend to have comprehensive documentation and training materials tailored to the specific software. In contrast, open-source solutions rely on community-driven support, where organizations may have to depend on forums, online communities, and user-driven documentation. While open-source communities can be robust and supportive, the level of support may vary, and organizations may need to invest additional resources in finding the right assistance.

Feature Availability and Innovation:

Proprietary solutions may have a competitive advantage in terms of advanced features and innovation. Companies invest heavily in research and development to create cutting-edge AI technologies and functionalities that differentiate their offerings in the market. Proprietary solutions often provide a comprehensive suite of tools and features tailored to specific use cases. Open-source solutions may lag behind in terms of feature availability or require additional development efforts to match the capabilities of proprietary solutions. However, open-source communities can quickly adopt and integrate new AI advancements, and they often serve as a breeding ground for innovation and experimentation.

Vendor Lock-In and Long-Term Viability:

Consider the implications of vendor lock-in when evaluating proprietary solutions. Organizations become reliant on the vendor's software and ecosystem, making it difficult to switch to alternative solutions in the future. In contrast, open-source solutions provide the freedom to transition between different software options or build upon existing solutions without dependency on a single vendor. It is also essential to evaluate the long-term viability of open-source projects, ensuring they have an active community and ongoing development support. Proprietary solutions, backed by dedicated companies, often provide a sense of stability and continuity.

In conclusion, the choice between open source and proprietary AI solutions depends on several factors, including flexibility, customization, community support, cost considerations, security, support, feature availability, vendor lock-in, and long-term viability. Open-source solutions offer flexibility, customization, community collaboration, and cost advantages, but require technical expertise and may have limited support. Proprietary solutions often provide dedicated support, advanced features, and a sense of reliability, but come with licensing costs, potential vendor lock-in, and limited customization. Organizations must carefully evaluate their specific needs and priorities to make an informed decision that aligns with their AI strategy and resources.

CHAPTER 16: CRITERIA FOR SELECTING AI VENDORS AND PARTNERS

Selecting the right AI vendors and partners is crucial for the successful implementation of Artificial Intelligence (AI) initiatives within an organization. The choice of vendors and partners significantly impacts the quality, effectiveness, and long-term viability of AI projects. To ensure a successful partnership, organizations need to consider several key criteria when evaluating potential AI vendors and partners. Let us explore these criteria in detail:

Expertise and Experience:

Evaluate the expertise and experience of AI vendors and partners. Consider their track record in delivering AI solutions, their industry knowledge, and the depth of their technical expertise. Assess their experience in working with organizations of similar size, industry, or AI requirements. Vendors and partners with a proven track record and domain expertise are better positioned to understand the unique challenges and requirements of the organization, ensuring the successful implementation of AI projects.

Technology and Solution Fit:

Assess whether the AI vendor's technology and solutions align with the organization's specific needs and requirements. Consider the breadth and depth of their AI offerings, including the availability of AI models, algorithms, frameworks, and tools that address the organization's use cases.

Evaluate the compatibility and integration capabilities of the vendor's solutions with the organization's existing infrastructure and systems. The vendor's technology and solutions should provide a good fit for the organization's AI strategy, goals, and long-term vision.

Scalability and Performance:

Scalability and performance are crucial considerations when selecting AI vendors and partners. Organizations should assess the vendor's ability to handle large volumes of data, scale AI solutions to meet growing demands, and deliver real-time or near-real-time performance for time-sensitive applications. Evaluate the vendor's infrastructure, computational resources, and the ability to leverage distributed computing or cloud computing technologies to ensure scalability and performance as data volumes and workloads increase.

Data Privacy and Security:

Data privacy and security are paramount in AI implementations. Evaluate the vendor's data privacy and security practices, including their policies, compliance with industry regulations, and data protection measures. Assess their ability to safeguard sensitive data and ensure confidentiality, integrity, and availability throughout the AI lifecycle. Consider whether the vendor's solutions offer encryption, access controls, secure data transfer mechanisms, and auditing capabilities to address security concerns. It is essential to ensure that the vendor follows best practices and standards for data privacy and security.

Support and Collaboration:

Consider the level of support and collaboration offered by the AI vendor or partner. Evaluate the vendor's responsiveness, availability of technical support, and the quality of their customer service. Assess their ability to provide timely assistance, troubleshoot issues, and resolve technical challenges. Additionally, consider the vendor's approach to collaboration and their willingness to work closely with the organization's team, offering guidance, training, and knowledge transfer. A strong support system and collaborative approach contribute to a successful and productive partnership.

References and Case Studies:

Request references and case studies from the AI vendor or partner. This allows the organization to gain insights into their previous projects, the outcomes achieved, and the satisfaction levels of their customers. References and case studies provide valuable information on the vendor's ability to deliver on their promises, their level of expertise, and the quality of their solutions. Contacting references and studying case studies help validate the vendor's claims and provides a realistic perspective on their capabilities and compatibility with the organization's requirements.

Vendor Stability and Roadmap:

Assess the stability and long-term viability of the AI vendor or partner. Evaluate their financial stability, company size, and market presence. Consider the vendor's commitment to research and development, their vision for future advancements in AI, and their ability to adapt to evolving technology trends. A vendor with a solid financial footing, a clear roadmap, and a commitment to innovation is more likely to provide ongoing support, updates, and continuous improvement to their AI solutions.

Pricing and Value for Money:

Evaluate the pricing models and value for money offered by the AI vendor or partner. Consider the total cost of ownership, including licensing fees, implementation costs, support fees, and any additional expenses. Assess the pricing structure, whether it aligns with the organization's budget and scalability requirements. It is essential to strike a balance between cost and the value delivered by the vendor's AI solutions. Consider the ROI potential and the long-term value that the vendor's solutions can bring to the organization.

In conclusion, selecting the right AI vendors and partners requires careful consideration of their expertise, technology fit, scalability, data privacy and security measures, support and collaboration, references and case studies, vendor stability, roadmap, and pricing. A thorough evaluation process ensures that organizations choose vendors and partners who not only meet their current AI requirements but also align with their long-term strategic goals. By selecting the right AI vendors and partners, organizations can leverage their expertise, technology, and support to drive successful AI implementations and achieve desired business outcomes.

CHAPTER 17: AGILE METHODOLOGIES FOR AI PROJECTS

As organizations undertake Artificial Intelligence (AI) projects, they face the challenge of effectively managing the complexity and uncertainty inherent in AI development. Traditional project management approaches may struggle to accommodate the iterative and evolving nature of AI projects. Agile methodologies provide a flexible and adaptive framework that is well-suited for AI projects, enabling organizations to embrace uncertainty, iterate quickly, and deliver value in a dynamic AI landscape. Let us explore how Agile methodologies can be applied to AI projects:

Iterative and Incremental Development:

Agile methodologies emphasize iterative and incremental development, where AI projects are divided into small, manageable increments called sprints. Each sprint focuses on delivering a specific set of AI features or functionality. This approach allows organizations to gather feedback early and frequently, enabling them to adapt and refine their AI models and algorithms based on real-world insights. Through iterative development, organizations can continually improve their AI solutions, address emerging challenges, and respond to evolving requirements.

Cross-Functional Collaboration:

Agile methodologies promote cross-functional collaboration among AI project teams. This typically includes data scientists, engineers, domain experts, and stakeholders from various business units. By bringing together individuals with different skill sets and perspectives, organizations can leverage their collective expertise to solve complex AI problems. Collaboration fosters effective communication, knowledge sharing, and a shared understanding of project goals, leading to better AI outcomes. Regular meetings, such as daily stand-ups, promote collaboration and ensure that everyone is aligned and working towards a common vision.

Prioritization and Value-driven Approach:

Agile methodologies prioritize delivering value to the organization and its stakeholders. Through techniques such as user stories, organizations identify the most valuable AI features or use cases and prioritize them accordingly. This enables organizations to focus on delivering AI functionality that provides the highest business impact. By continuously reevaluating priorities, organizations can adapt to changing needs, emerging opportunities, or unexpected challenges, ensuring that AI projects remain aligned with strategic objectives and deliver meaningful outcomes.

Rapid Feedback and Adaptation:

Agile methodologies emphasize obtaining rapid and frequent feedback to inform decision-making and course correction. In AI projects, this feedback is crucial for evaluating model performance, data quality, and the effectiveness of AI algorithms. By gathering feedback from end-users, stakeholders, and domain experts early and continuously, organizations can identify areas for improvement, refine AI models, and make informed decisions about further iterations. This feedback loop facilitates the adaptation and refinement of AI solutions, enabling organizations to deliver higher-quality and more effective AI applications.

Continuous Integration and Testing:

Agile methodologies promote continuous integration and testing to ensure the quality and stability of AI solutions. By integrating code and data regularly, organizations can identify and address integration issues or bottlenecks early in the development cycle. Automated testing helps validate the functionality, accuracy, and performance of AI models, reducing the risk of errors or discrepancies. Continuous integration and testing practices support the reliability and robustness of AI solutions, enabling organizations to deliver more reliable and consistent results.

Transparency and Visibility:

Agile methodologies foster transparency and visibility throughout AI projects. By using visual management tools like Kanban boards or project dashboards, teams can track progress, monitor tasks, and visualize the status of AI development. This transparency promotes accountability, facilitates communication, and enables stakeholders to have a clear understanding of project status and progress. Regular project demonstrations or showcases provide stakeholders with opportunities to provide feedback, validate project direction, and ensure alignment with business objectives.

Empirical Process Control:

Agile methodologies follow an empirical process control approach, where decisions are based on empirical evidence rather than assumptions. This approach aligns well with AI projects, as they involve experimentation, data analysis, and evidence-based decision-making. By collecting and analyzing data on AI performance, user feedback, and project metrics, organizations can make informed decisions about optimizing AI models, prioritizing future iterations, or adapting project direction. The empirical process control approach enables organizations to embrace uncertainty, learn from feedback, and continuously improve their AI solutions.

Flexibility to Embrace Change:

One of the core principles of Agile methodologies is embracing change. This is particularly relevant in AI projects, where requirements, data, and business needs can evolve rapidly. Agile methodologies enable organizations to adapt to changes, accommodate new insights, and incorporate emerging technologies or techniques into their AI development process. By embracing change, organizations can harness the potential of AI innovation and remain responsive to evolving business demands and market dynamics.

In conclusion, Agile methodologies provide a well-suited framework for managing the complexity and uncertainty inherent in AI projects. By embracing iterative and incremental development, fostering cross-functional collaboration, prioritizing value, gathering rapid feedback, emphasizing continuous integration and testing, promoting transparency and visibility, following an empirical process control approach, and embracing change, organizations can effectively manage AI projects and deliver high-quality AI solutions that align with business goals. Applying Agile methodologies to AI projects allows organizations to navigate the dynamic AI landscape, adapt to emerging requirements, and achieve successful AI outcomes.

CHAPTER 18: ITERATIVE DEVELOPMENT AND CONTINUOUS IMPROVEMENT IN AI PROJECTS

In the realm of Artificial Intelligence (AI) projects, iterative development and continuous improvement are essential methodologies that enable organizations to create robust and effective AI solutions. Rather than following a linear and fixed approach, iterative development emphasizes the creation of prototypes, gathering feedback, and making incremental improvements. Continuous improvement, on the other hand, focuses on the ongoing enhancement of AI models, algorithms, and processes to optimize performance and deliver better results over time. Let us delve into the significance of iterative development and continuous improvement in AI projects:

Iterative Development:

Prototype Creation:

Iterative development encourages the creation of prototypes or minimum viable products (MVPs) early in the development process. These prototypes serve as working models that capture the core functionality or features of the AI solution. By quickly building and testing prototypes, organizations can gather valuable feedback from stakeholders, users, and domain experts. This feedback loop allows for early validation of the AI concept, identification of potential challenges, and adjustments to the solution's direction.

Agile and Adaptive Approach:

Iterative development aligns well with agile methodologies, emphasizing flexibility and adaptability. Rather than attempting to define all requirements upfront, organizations iterate through multiple development cycles, known as sprints or iterations. Each iteration focuses on refining the AI solution based on feedback and new insights. This iterative approach allows organizations to adapt to changing requirements, emerging trends, and evolving business needs, ensuring that the AI solution remains relevant and aligned with stakeholder expectations.

User-Centric Design:

Iterative development places a strong emphasis on user-centric design. By involving end-users early in the development process, organizations can gather insights into user preferences, needs, and pain points. These user insights drive iterative improvements, ensuring that the AI solution aligns with user expectations and provides a seamless user experience. User feedback guides the refinement of features, interface design, and overall usability, ultimately enhancing user satisfaction and adoption.

Risk Mitigation and Early Issue Identification:

Iterative development helps organizations mitigate risks and identify issues early in the AI development lifecycle. By breaking the development process into smaller iterations, organizations can address potential risks incrementally, reducing the impact of unforeseen challenges. The iterative nature of development allows for ongoing testing, validation, and course correction. Early issue identification enables organizations to rectify problems before they escalate, enhancing the overall quality and reliability of the AI solution.

Continuous Improvement:

Data Analysis and Model Evaluation:

Continuous improvement in AI projects involves a systematic approach to analyzing data, evaluating model performance, and identifying areas for enhancement. Organizations continuously collect and analyze data to assess the effectiveness and accuracy of AI models. By leveraging metrics, key performance indicators (KPIs), and feedback from stakeholders, organizations can gain insights into model performance, identify areas of improvement, and make data-driven decisions to optimize the AI solution.

Model Refinement and Optimization:

Continuous improvement focuses on refining and optimizing AI models and algorithms. Organizations employ techniques such as hyperparameter tuning, feature engineering, and model selection to enhance the performance and accuracy of AI models. By iteratively fine-tuning models based on data analysis and feedback, organizations can reduce errors, increase prediction accuracy, and optimize resource utilization. Continuous improvement enables organizations to deliver AI solutions that provide better results and meet evolving business needs.

Incorporating New Data and Techniques:

To achieve continuous improvement, organizations must leverage new data and incorporate cutting-edge techniques and technologies. As more data becomes available over time, organizations can enhance their AI models by retraining and updating them with the latest information. Additionally, advancements in AI research and techniques present opportunities to incorporate state-of-the-art algorithms and methodologies. By staying updated with emerging trends and adopting new techniques, organizations can ensure their AI solutions remain at the forefront of innovation.

Feedback Integration and Learning Loops:

Continuous improvement thrives on feedback integration and learning loops. Organizations gather feedback from various sources, such as end-users, stakeholders, and domain experts, and incorporate it into the AI solution's improvement process. This feedback-driven approach enables organizations to address user requirements, align the AI solution with business goals, and stay responsive to changing needs. By creating learning loops that facilitate feedback integration, organizations establish a culture of continuous learning, improvement, and innovation.

Benchmarking and Comparison:

Continuous improvement involves benchmarking AI solutions against industry standards, best practices, and competitor offerings. Organizations evaluate the performance of their AI models, algorithms, and processes against established benchmarks or key industry metrics. By analyzing comparative data and identifying gaps, organizations can set improvement targets, prioritize enhancement initiatives, and strive to achieve superior performance and competitiveness.

In conclusion, iterative development and continuous improvement are crucial for the success of AI projects. Iterative development allows organizations to build prototypes, gather feedback, and make incremental improvements, ensuring alignment with user expectations and evolving requirements. Continuous improvement focuses on refining AI models, optimizing performance, and incorporating new data and techniques to deliver better results over time. By embracing these methodologies, organizations can develop robust and effective AI solutions that provide meaningful business value, remain adaptable to changing needs, and drive continuous innovation in the AI landscape.

CHAPTER 19: INTEGRATION WITH EXISTING SYSTEMS AND PROCESSES IN AI PROJECTS

Integrating new Artificial Intelligence (AI) systems and processes with existing systems is a critical aspect of AI projects. Successful integration ensures seamless collaboration between AI solutions and the organization's established infrastructure, workflows, and processes. It allows organizations to leverage the power of AI while maximizing the value of their existing investments. Let us explore the key considerations and best practices for integrating AI with existing systems and processes:

Understand Existing Systems and Processes:

Before integrating AI systems, it is crucial to thoroughly understand the organization's existing systems and processes. This includes identifying the various data sources, applications, databases, and workflows that are currently in place. It is important to assess how data flows within the organization, what data is available for AI purposes, and how different systems interact with each other. Understanding the existing landscape provides insights into the potential integration points and helps in identifying any constraints or challenges.

Identify Integration Points:

Identify the specific integration points where AI systems can seamlessly connect with existing systems and processes. This involves determining how AI-generated insights, predictions, or recommendations can be integrated into decision-making processes or existing applications. Consider areas where AI can enhance existing workflows, automate manual tasks, or provide real-time data for better decision-making. It is essential to identify the touchpoints where AI can add value without disrupting existing operations.

Data Integration and Data Flows:

Data integration is a critical aspect of AI system integration. Determine how AI systems will access and consume data from existing systems and processes. This may involve extracting data from databases, APIs, or other data sources, transforming it into a suitable format, and loading it into AI systems. Establish robust data pipelines and ensure the integrity, security, and quality of data as it flows between systems. Consider the frequency of data updates and establish processes for synchronizing and refreshing data to keep AI systems up to date.

Application and Process Integration:

Integration of AI systems with existing applications and processes is key to enabling smooth collaboration. Evaluate the compatibility of AI solutions with existing applications and systems, such as customer relationship management (CRM), enterprise resource planning (ERP), or supply chain management (SCM) systems. Identify the best approach to integrate AI outputs, such as predictions or recommendations, into existing applications and processes, ensuring they are easily accessible and actionable for end-users. This may involve developing APIs, building connectors, or utilizing middleware solutions to facilitate seamless data and information exchange.

Scalability and Performance Considerations:

Consider the scalability and performance requirements when integrating AI systems with existing infrastructure. AI systems may have varying resource requirements, such as computational power, memory, or storage. Ensure that the existing infrastructure can accommodate the increased demands of

AI workloads. Evaluate the need for additional hardware, cloud resources, or optimization techniques to ensure smooth integration and efficient processing. Pay attention to system response times, throughput, and overall performance to ensure that AI integration does not degrade the overall system performance.

Security and Privacy:

Integrating AI systems with existing systems necessitates careful attention to security and privacy considerations. Assess the potential impact of AI integration on data security and privacy, ensuring that sensitive information is protected throughout the integration process. Implement appropriate access controls, data encryption, and monitoring mechanisms to safeguard data integrity and prevent unauthorized access. Ensure compliance with relevant regulations, such as data protection or industry-specific security standards, during AI integration.

Change Management and User Adoption:

Integrating AI systems with existing systems and processes requires effective change management and user adoption strategies. Communicate the purpose and benefits of AI integration to stakeholders and end-users, addressing any concerns or resistance to change. Provide training and support to users to ensure they understand how to interact with AI outputs and incorporate them into their workflows. Collaboration between the AI team and end-users can lead to better adoption, reduced friction, and increased overall productivity.

Monitoring and Maintenance:

Regular monitoring and maintenance of integrated AI systems are essential for their continued success. Establish mechanisms to monitor the performance of AI systems, including data quality, model accuracy, and system reliability. Implement processes for timely detection and resolution of any issues or anomalies. Regularly assess the impact of AI integration on the overall system and refine integration approaches as needed. Additionally, stay updated with advancements in AI technology and ensure ongoing maintenance to address potential compatibility issues with future system updates or changes.

In conclusion, integrating AI systems with existing systems and processes is a critical step in maximizing the value of AI investments. By understanding existing systems, identifying integration points, ensuring data flows, addressing scalability and performance, considering security and privacy, managing change, and implementing effective monitoring and maintenance processes, organizations can achieve seamless collaboration between AI and existing infrastructure. Successful integration enables organizations to leverage the power of AI to augment decision-making, automate processes, and drive innovation while building upon the foundation of their established systems and processes.

CHAPTER 20: BIAS AND FAIRNESS IN AI ALGORITHMS

As Artificial Intelligence (AI) becomes more prevalent in various domains, it is crucial to address the issue of bias and fairness in AI algorithms. AI algorithms are designed to make decisions and predictions based on data patterns, but they can inadvertently perpetuate biases present in the data or the underlying algorithms themselves. Bias in AI algorithms can lead to unfair outcomes, perpetuate discrimination, and reinforce societal inequalities. Therefore, it is essential to understand the nature of bias, identify potential sources, and implement strategies to mitigate bias and ensure fairness in AI algorithms. Let us explore the concept of bias and fairness in AI algorithms in more detail:

Understanding Bias in AI Algorithms:

Definition of Bias:

Bias in AI algorithms refers to systematic and unfair favoritism or discrimination towards certain individuals or groups based on attributes such as race, gender, age, or socioeconomic status. Bias can arise from various sources, including biased training data, biased algorithm design, or biased interpretations of results. It is important to distinguish between intentional bias and unintended bias, as unintended bias can still have harmful effects despite being unintentional.

Sources of Bias:

Bias in AI algorithms can stem from multiple sources. One primary source is biased training data, where historical data may reflect societal biases and discrimination. If the training data is imbalanced, incomplete, or contains discriminatory patterns, the AI algorithm may learn and perpetuate those biases in its decision-making process. Biases can also be introduced during algorithm design, such as feature selection or weighting, which can inadvertently favor certain groups or attributes. Additionally, biased human judgment or subjective criteria used to label or evaluate data can introduce bias into the training process.

Types of Bias:

Bias in AI algorithms can manifest in different ways. Some common types of bias include:

a. Sample Bias: When the training data does not represent the true diversity and distribution of the population, leading to skewed results.

b. Confirmation Bias: When the AI algorithm is designed to favor information that confirms pre-existing beliefs or assumptions, disregarding contradictory evidence.

c. Stereotyping Bias: When the AI algorithm generalizes or makes assumptions about individuals or groups based on stereotypes, leading to unfair outcomes.

d. Proxy Bias: When the AI algorithm uses proxies or correlated factors that are indirectly related to sensitive attributes, which can result in discriminatory decisions.

e. Historical Bias: When the AI algorithm perpetuates biases from historical data, reinforcing societal inequalities and discrimination.

Mitigating Bias and Ensuring Fairness:

Ethical Frameworks and Guidelines:

Develop ethical frameworks and guidelines to guide the design, development, and deployment of AI algorithms. These frameworks should emphasize fairness, transparency, and accountability. They can provide principles and guidelines for data collection, model design, evaluation, and decision-making processes, promoting responsible AI practices.

Data Collection and Preprocessing:

Carefully collect, preprocess, and curate training data to ensure it is representative, diverse, and free from biases. Employ strategies such as oversampling underrepresented groups, identifying and mitigating potential biases in the data, and ensuring the inclusion of diverse perspectives during data collection.

Bias Assessment and Mitigation:

Conduct comprehensive bias assessments throughout the AI development lifecycle. Use metrics and techniques to quantify and identify biases in algorithms, data, and decision-making processes. Implement bias mitigation techniques, such as algorithmic adjustments, fairness constraints, or counterfactual fairness, to reduce the impact of biases on outcomes and ensure equitable treatment.

Explainability and Interpretability:

Promote transparency and interpretability in AI algorithms. Develop methods to explain and interpret how AI algorithms make decisions. This allows stakeholders, including end-users and regulators, to understand the reasoning behind AI-driven outcomes and detect and rectify any biases.

Diverse and Interdisciplinary Teams:

Foster diverse and interdisciplinary teams involved in AI algorithm development. Diverse teams can bring different perspectives, experiences, and cultural sensitivities to the table, helping to identify and address biases effectively. Collaboration among data scientists, domain experts, ethicists, and social scientists can contribute to more comprehensive and unbiased AI solutions.

Ongoing Monitoring and Evaluation:

Implement mechanisms for continuous monitoring and evaluation of AI algorithms in real-world settings. Regularly assess the performance and impact of AI systems to detect and mitigate biases that may emerge over time. Monitor outcomes for fairness and equity and be prepared to make adjustments and improvements, as necessary.

User Feedback and Redress:

Establish mechanisms for users and individuals affected by AI decisions to provide feedback and seek redress. This ensures that individuals can voice concerns, report biases or unfair outcomes, and request explanations for AI-driven decisions. Creating channels for user feedback fosters accountability and allows for the identification and rectification of biases in AI algorithms.

Regulatory and Policy Frameworks:

Develop regulatory and policy frameworks that address bias and fairness in AI algorithms. Governments and regulatory bodies can establish guidelines, standards, and auditing mechanisms to ensure transparency, accountability, and fairness in AI applications. Collaboration between policymakers, industry experts, and academia can help establish regulatory frameworks that balance innovation with ethical AI practices.

In conclusion, addressing bias and ensuring fairness in AI algorithms is crucial for ethical and responsible AI deployment. By understanding the sources and types of bias, implementing mitigation strategies, promoting transparency, fostering diverse teams, monitoring outcomes, and incorporating user feedback, organizations can work towards developing fair and unbiased AI algorithms. Striving for fairness in AI is not only an ethical imperative but also crucial for building trust in AI systems and mitigating the potential harm that biased algorithms can cause in society.

CHAPTER 21: TRANSPARENCY AND EXPLAINABILITY IN AI ALGORITHMS

In the realm of Artificial Intelligence (AI), transparency and explainability are critical aspects that promote trust, accountability, and ethical decision-making. As AI algorithms become increasingly complex and influential in various domains, it is essential to understand how they arrive at their decisions and to be able to explain their reasoning to stakeholders and end-users. Transparent and explainable AI algorithms empower individuals to understand, question, and challenge AI-driven outcomes, ensuring fairness, mitigating biases, and upholding ethical standards. Let us explore the significance of transparency and explainability in AI algorithms in more detail:

Transparency in AI Algorithms:

Definition of Transparency:

Transparency in AI algorithms refers to the ability to understand and examine the underlying processes, data, and decision-making logic. It involves providing clear visibility into how AI algorithms operate, the factors they consider, and the data they rely on. Transparent AI algorithms are open to scrutiny, enabling stakeholders to comprehend the inner workings and potential limitations of the algorithms.

Building Trust and Accountability:

Transparency is crucial for building trust in AI algorithms. When individuals understand how AI algorithm's function, they are more likely to trust the outcomes and rely on them for decision-making. Transparent algorithms also hold developers and organizations accountable for their actions. By allowing external examination and scrutiny, transparency reduces the risk of biased or unfair decision-making and encourages responsible AI practices.

Detecting and Addressing Biases:

Transparency facilitates the detection and mitigation of biases in AI algorithms. It allows stakeholders to examine the data sources, training processes, and model features to identify potential biases or discriminatory patterns. When biases are detected, they can be addressed, and algorithmic adjustments can be made to ensure fairness and equitable outcomes. Transparency helps organizations proactively identify and rectify any unintended biases before they lead to unfair consequences.

Regulation and Compliance:

Transparency is increasingly important for regulatory compliance in the AI domain. Government bodies and regulatory agencies may require organizations to provide transparency into AI algorithms to ensure compliance with privacy, fairness, and non-discrimination regulations. Transparent AI algorithms enable regulators to assess compliance, verify ethical practices, and hold organizations accountable for their AI-driven decision-making processes.

Explainability in AI Algorithms:

Definition of Explainability:

Explainability refers to the ability to provide understandable explanations of how AI algorithms arrive at their decisions or predictions. Explainable AI algorithms can articulate the reasoning behind their outputs in a manner that is interpretable by end-users, stakeholders, and domain experts. Explainability enables individuals to understand the factors that influenced AI-driven outcomes and to assess their reliability and accuracy.

Building Trust and Acceptance:

Explainability plays a vital role in building trust and acceptance of AI algorithms. When individuals can comprehend the factors that contributed to AI-driven decisions, they are more likely to accept and rely on those decisions. Explainability helps bridge the gap between technical AI processes and the understanding of non-technical users, fostering confidence in AI algorithms and encouraging their adoption.

Detecting and Mitigating Errors:

Explainability aids in the detection and mitigation of errors or incorrect outcomes generated by AI algorithms. When an AI algorithm produces unexpected or erroneous results, explainability allows users to trace back the decision-making process, identify the contributing factors, and assess potential sources of error. This facilitates debugging, refinement, and the improvement of AI algorithms to enhance their accuracy and reliability.

Facilitating Human-AI Collaboration:

Explainability fosters effective collaboration between humans and AI systems. When AI algorithms can explain their outputs in a human-understandable manner, it facilitates a shared decision-making process between humans and machines. Explainable AI enables end-users to question and challenge AI-driven outcomes, seek clarifications, and provide feedback, ultimately leading to more accurate and reliable decision-making.

Ethical and Legal Considerations:

Explainability is crucial for addressing ethical and legal considerations associated with AI algorithms. Ethical principles, such as the right to explanation, demand that individuals have the ability to understand and challenge decisions made by AI algorithms that affect them. In certain domains, legal requirements may mandate the provision of explanations for AI-driven decisions, such as in credit scoring or loan approvals. Explainability ensures compliance with ethical standards and legal requirements, promoting transparency and fairness in AI applications.

Techniques and Approaches for Transparency and Explainability:

Interpretable Models:

Develop AI models that inherently exhibit interpretability. Certain models, such as decision trees, linear models, or rule-based models, provide explicit rules or logic that can be easily understood and interpreted by humans. Leveraging interpretable models can enhance transparency and explainability in AI algorithms.

Post-hoc Explanation Methods:

Utilize post-hoc explanation methods that can provide insights into the decision-making process of complex AI models, such as deep neural networks. Techniques like feature importance analysis, saliency maps, or attention mechanisms can help identify the features or data points that significantly influenced the AI algorithm's output.

Rule-based Explanations:

Provide rule-based explanations that articulate the logic or rules followed by the AI algorithm in making its decisions. This involves presenting decision rules, conditional statements, or logical constraints that can be easily understood by end-users and stakeholders.

Visual Explanations:

Utilize visual representations and visualizations to explain the reasoning behind AI algorithms. Visual explanations can provide intuitive insights into how input features or data influenced the AI model's predictions or decisions. Visualizations can help individuals comprehend complex relationships or patterns within the data and enhance the interpretability of AI algorithms.

Documentation and Reporting:

Document and report the AI algorithm's design, data sources, processing steps, and decision-making processes. Clear and concise documentation provides stakeholders with a comprehensive understanding of the AI algorithm's operation and allows for external audits or reviews.

User Interaction and Feedback:

Design AI systems that allow users to interact with the algorithm, query its decision-making process, and seek further explanations. User interfaces can provide contextual information, highlight relevant features, or present alternative scenarios to enhance user understanding and facilitate meaningful human-AI collaboration.

In conclusion, transparency and explainability are vital components of responsible and ethical AI. By prioritizing transparency, organizations can build trust, mitigate biases, and promote accountability in AI algorithms. Explainability empowers individuals to understand, challenge, and collaborate with AI systems, fostering acceptance and effective decision-making. Leveraging techniques such as interpretable models, post-hoc explanations, rule-based explanations, visual representations, documentation, and user interaction can enhance transparency and explainability in AI algorithms. The integration of transparency and explainability fosters responsible AI practices and contributes to the development of trustworthy and reliable AI systems.

CHAPTER 21: PRIVACY AND DATA PROTECTION IN THE AGE OF AI

In today's digital landscape, the rapid advancement of Artificial Intelligence (AI) has raised concerns about privacy and data protection. AI systems rely on vast amounts of data to train, learn, and make decisions, making it essential to address privacy risks and safeguard individuals' personal information. Organizations must prioritize privacy and data protection to ensure compliance with regulations, build trust with users, and uphold ethical AI practices. Let us explore the significance of privacy and data protection in the context of AI:

Understanding Privacy and Data Protection:

Privacy: Privacy refers to an individual's right to control their personal information and decide how it is collected, used, stored, and shared. Privacy encompasses aspects such as data confidentiality, data minimization, purpose limitation, and user consent. With AI, privacy extends to how personal data is utilized to train AI models and make automated decisions.

Data Protection: Data protection involves safeguarding personal data from unauthorized access, use, disclosure, alteration, or destruction. It encompasses measures to ensure data integrity, security, and compliance with privacy regulations. Data protection aims to maintain the confidentiality, availability, and accuracy of personal data throughout its lifecycle.

Privacy and Data Protection Challenges in AI:

Data Collection and Consent:

AI algorithms heavily rely on diverse and extensive datasets. Ensuring proper consent and transparency regarding data collection practices is crucial. Organizations must obtain explicit consent from individuals for the collection, use, and sharing of their personal data. Consent mechanisms should clearly explain the purpose of data collection and provide options for individuals to exercise control over their data.

Data Minimization and Purpose Limitation:

Organizations must practice data minimization by collecting and using only the necessary personal data for AI purposes. Limiting data collection to relevant and specific purposes helps mitigate privacy risks and reduces the potential for unintended data exposure or misuse.

Data Security:

AI algorithms require access to vast amounts of sensitive data, making data security a top priority. Organizations must implement robust security measures to protect personal data from unauthorized access, breaches, or cyberattacks. This involves encryption, access controls, regular security assessments, and adherence to industry best practices.

Algorithmic Transparency and Privacy:

The inner workings of AI algorithms may involve processing personal data, potentially leading to privacy concerns. Organizations should ensure algorithmic transparency, providing individuals with explanations of how their data is used, how decisions are made, and the potential implications. Users should be informed about the automated profiling or decision-making processes that may impact them.

Cross-Border Data Transfers:

AI often involves the transfer of data across borders. Organizations must comply with relevant regulations and implement appropriate safeguards when transferring personal data to jurisdictions with different privacy frameworks. This may involve utilizing data transfer mechanisms such as

Standard Contractual Clauses or obtaining explicit consent from individuals.

Privacy and Data Protection Best Practices in AI:

Privacy by Design:

Adopt a privacy-by-design approach, integrating privacy and data protection measures into the design and development of AI systems from the outset. Consider privacy implications at every stage, including data collection, processing, and storage. Implement technical and organizational measures to protect privacy proactively.

Anonymization and Pseudonymization:

Apply anonymization and pseudonymization techniques to protect individual privacy. Anonymization removes personally identifiable information from datasets, ensuring that individuals cannot be re-identified. Pseudonymization replaces direct identifiers with pseudonyms, adding an extra layer of protection.

User Empowerment and Control:

Empower users with control over their personal data. Provide clear options for individuals to access, correct, delete, or restrict the use of their data. Enable users to manage their consent preferences, allowing them to make informed decisions about the use of their personal information.

Regular Data Protection Impact Assessments:

Conduct Data Protection Impact Assessments (DPIAs) to assess the potential privacy risks associated with AI projects. DPIAs evaluate the impact on individual privacy rights, identify risks, and propose mitigating measures. This process helps organizations identify and address privacy risks early in the AI development lifecycle.

Privacy Training and Awareness:

Invest in privacy training programs to ensure employees understand the importance of privacy and data protection. Promote a culture of privacy awareness, emphasizing the responsibility to handle personal data appropriately and comply with privacy regulations. Regularly update employees on privacy best practices and emerging privacy concerns.

Regular Audits and Compliance:

Perform regular audits to assess compliance with privacy regulations and internal privacy policies. Conduct internal reviews of data handling practices, data access controls, and security measures. Ensure that data processing activities align with legal requirements, and promptly address any identified compliance gaps.

Third-Party Risk Management:

Assess the privacy and data protection practices of third-party vendors or partners involved in AI projects. Implement contractual provisions and data processing agreements that require adherence to privacy and security standards. Regularly monitor and evaluate the data handling practices of third parties to ensure compliance.

Accountability and Governance:

Establish clear lines of accountability and governance for privacy and data protection within the organization. Designate a Data Protection Officer (DPO) or privacy focal point responsible for overseeing privacy practices, addressing inquiries, and ensuring compliance with privacy regulations. Establish internal policies, procedures, and guidelines to guide privacy practices and promote a culture of privacy within the organization.

In conclusion, privacy and data protection are essential considerations in AI projects. Organizations must prioritize the collection, use, and protection of personal data in alignment with privacy regulations. Implementing privacy by design, ensuring user empowerment and control, conducting regular assessments, and fostering privacy awareness contribute to the responsible and ethical use of AI. By addressing privacy challenges and adopting best practices, organizations can build trust, uphold individual privacy rights, and foster a positive environment for the development and deployment of AI systems.

CHAPTER 22: KEY PERFORMANCE INDICATORS (KPIS) FOR AI PROJECTS

Key Performance Indicators (KPIs) are crucial metrics used to assess the performance and success of projects. In the context of Artificial Intelligence (AI) projects, KPIs provide insights into the effectiveness, efficiency, and impact of AI initiatives. They help organizations measure progress, identify areas for improvement, and align AI projects with strategic goals. Let us explore some essential KPIs for AI projects:

Accuracy and Model Performance:

Accuracy is a fundamental KPI for AI models. It measures how well the model predicts or classifies data correctly. Accuracy can be assessed through metrics such as precision, recall, F1 score, or Area Under the Curve (AUC) for classification tasks. For regression tasks, metrics like Mean Absolute Error (MAE) or Root Mean Squared Error (RMSE) are used. High accuracy indicates the reliability and effectiveness of the AI model.

Speed and Efficiency:

The speed and efficiency of AI algorithms are critical KPIs, especially for real-time or time-sensitive applications. Metrics such as response time, throughput, or processing speed can be measured to evaluate the algorithm's efficiency. Faster processing times and higher throughput indicate improved performance and scalability of AI systems.

User Satisfaction and Experience:

User satisfaction and experience are crucial indicators of AI project success. User feedback, surveys, or usability testing can be used to assess user satisfaction. Metrics like user engagement, user retention, or Net Promoter Score (NPS) can provide insights into user perception and acceptance of AI-driven solutions. Positive user feedback and high satisfaction levels indicate the effectiveness and value of AI projects.

Return on Investment (ROI):

ROI measures the financial benefits generated from AI projects compared to the costs incurred. It evaluates the economic impact of AI initiatives. ROI can be calculated by comparing the costs of developing and implementing the AI system with the monetary gains achieved, such as increased revenue, cost savings, or efficiency improvements. Positive ROI indicates the success and profitability of AI projects.

Business Impact and Value:

Assessing the business impact and value of AI projects is crucial. This can be measured through metrics such as revenue growth, cost reduction, customer acquisition or retention rates, or improved operational efficiency. Quantifying the direct impact of AI on business outcomes demonstrates its value and justifies the investment in AI initiatives.

Data Quality and Availability:

Data quality and availability are essential KPIs for AI projects. Assessing the quality of input data, such as completeness, accuracy, or consistency, ensures that AI models are trained on reliable and representative data. Monitoring data availability and accessibility helps ensure that AI systems have a consistent stream of relevant and up-to-date data to generate accurate predictions or insights.

Compliance and Ethical Considerations:

Compliance with legal and ethical standards is crucial for AI projects. KPIs related to compliance can include the number of incidents or violations, adherence to privacy regulations, or the implementation of ethical guidelines. Ensuring compliance and ethical practices demonstrate responsible AI governance and mitigate potential risks or reputational damage.

Scalability and Adaptability:

Scalability measures the ability of AI systems to handle increased data volume, user demands, or expanding use cases. KPIs related to scalability can include system performance under load, resource utilization, or the ability to handle concurrent requests. Assessing scalability ensures that AI systems can adapt to changing business needs and accommodate future growth.

Learning and Continuous Improvement:

KPIs related to learning and continuous improvement reflect the agility and adaptability of AI projects. These KPIs can include the frequency of model updates, incorporation of user feedback, or the number of new features or functionalities implemented. Demonstrating a culture of continuous learning and improvement ensures that AI projects stay relevant and effective.

Alignment with Strategic Objectives:

Evaluating the alignment of AI projects with strategic objectives is crucial for measuring their impact on overall business goals. This can be assessed through KPIs such as the contribution to strategic initiatives, alignment with organizational priorities, or achievement of predefined milestones. Alignment with strategic objectives ensures that AI projects are contributing to the organization's long-term vision and objectives.

It is important to note that the choice of KPIs may vary depending on the specific AI project, industry, and organizational goals. Organizations should select KPIs that align with their strategic priorities and define clear targets or benchmarks for each KPI. Regular monitoring and analysis of KPIs enable organizations to assess project progress, identify areas for improvement, and make informed decisions to optimize AI initiatives.

CHAPTER 23: ASSESSING ROI AND VALUE CREATION IN AI PROJECTS

When implementing Artificial Intelligence (AI) projects, it is crucial to assess the return on investment (ROI) and value creation to determine the effectiveness and profitability of these initiatives. ROI measures the financial gains achieved compared to the costs incurred, while value creation examines the broader impact and benefits brought by AI projects. Assessing ROI and value creation allows organizations to make informed decisions, optimize resource allocation, and justify the investment in AI. Let us delve into the process of assessing ROI and value creation in AI projects:

ROI Assessment:

Cost Analysis:

To calculate ROI, organizations need to analyze the costs associated with the AI project. This includes expenses related to data acquisition, infrastructure, software development, hardware, training, and implementation. It is crucial to consider both upfront and ongoing costs associated with AI project maintenance and updates.

Financial Benefits:

Identify and quantify the financial benefits generated by the AI project. These can include increased revenue, cost savings, productivity gains, efficiency improvements, or reduction in operational expenses. For example, AI may enable predictive maintenance, resulting in reduced equipment downtime and maintenance costs.

Timeframe:

Establish a timeframe for ROI assessment, considering the project's expected timeline and relevant factors such as market conditions, adoption rate, and implementation challenges. ROI analysis can be conducted on a project basis or over a specific period, such as monthly, quarterly, or annually.

ROI Calculation:

Calculate ROI using the formula: (Net Profit / Total Investment) x 100. Net profit refers to the financial benefits generated minus the total costs incurred. The ROI value indicates the percentage of return on the investment made in the AI project.

Value Creation Assessment:

Strategic Alignment:

Assess the alignment of the AI project with strategic objectives and business goals. Identify the specific outcomes, improvements, or advantages that the AI project aims to deliver. This could include enhanced customer experience, increased market share, improved decision-making, or operational efficiency.

Business Impact:

Evaluate the impact of the AI project on various aspects of the organization. This can include revenue growth, customer acquisition or retention, process optimization, risk mitigation, competitive advantage, or market expansion. Measure the extent to which the AI project contributes to these areas.

Customer and User Experience:

Consider the impact of the AI project on customer satisfaction, user experience, and engagement. Assess feedback, user adoption rates, customer retention, and loyalty indicators to understand how the AI solution positively influences the experience of users or customers.

Efficiency and Productivity:

Measure the efficiency gains and productivity improvements resulting from the AI project. This could involve quantifying time savings, reduction in manual efforts, improved resource allocation, or streamlined processes. Assess the project's impact on operational workflows and resource utilization.

Decision Support and Accuracy:

Evaluate the AI project's contribution to decision-making processes. Assess the accuracy, reliability, and relevance of AI-driven insights or predictions. Determine how the AI project enables data-driven decision-making, identifies patterns or trends, and enhances the quality of decision outcomes.

Innovation and Competitive Advantage:

Consider the degree to which the AI project fosters innovation within the organization. Assess its impact on product or service differentiation, market positioning, or competitive advantage. Determine if the AI project helps the organization stay ahead of competitors and capitalize on emerging opportunities.

Societal Impact and Ethical Considerations:

Assess the societal impact and ethical implications of the AI project. Consider factors such as fairness, privacy, bias mitigation, social responsibility, and compliance with legal and regulatory requirements. Evaluating the ethical and societal value created by the AI project contributes to long-term sustainability and reputation.

Combining ROI and Value Creation Assessment:

To have a comprehensive understanding of the impact of an AI project, organizations should consider both ROI and value creation assessments together. These assessments provide a holistic view of the financial gains, as well as the broader benefits and strategic impact of the AI initiative.

It is important to note that assessing ROI and value creation in AI projects requires data collection, analysis, and ongoing monitoring. Organizations should establish clear measurement mechanisms, define relevant metrics, and periodically evaluate and update the assessments as the project progresses. Additionally, regular communication and reporting of ROI and value creation findings to stakeholders help build trust, showcase project success, and guide future decision-making.

In conclusion, assessing ROI and value creation in AI projects enables organizations to determine the financial gains, strategic impact, and broader benefits generated by these initiatives. By conducting a comprehensive analysis of costs, financial benefits, strategic alignment, business impact, customer experience, efficiency gains, decision support, innovation, and ethical considerations, organizations can make informed decisions, optimize resources, and drive successful AI implementation.

CHAPTER 24: QUANTITATIVE AND QUALITATIVE EVALUATION METHODS IN AI PROJECTS

Evaluating the performance and impact of Artificial Intelligence (AI) projects is crucial to assess their effectiveness, make informed decisions, and drive continuous improvement. Quantitative and qualitative evaluation methods are two complementary approaches used to assess different aspects of AI initiatives. Let us explore the characteristics, benefits, and examples of both quantitative and qualitative evaluation methods in AI projects:

Quantitative Evaluation Methods:

Quantitative evaluation methods involve the use of numerical data and statistical analysis to measure the performance, efficiency, and impact of AI projects. These methods provide objective and measurable insights into various aspects of AI implementation. Here are some common quantitative evaluation methods in AI projects:

Accuracy Metrics:

Quantitative evaluation often involves measuring the accuracy of AI models. Accuracy metrics, such as precision, recall, F1 score, or Area Under the Curve (AUC), are used to assess the model's ability to correctly predict or classify data. These metrics provide a quantitative measure of the model's performance and can be compared across different models or iterations.

Performance Metrics:

Performance metrics evaluate the efficiency and speed of AI algorithms. Metrics such as response time, throughput, or processing speed quantify the algorithm's performance in terms of computational efficiency. These metrics help assess the scalability and real-time capabilities of AI systems.

ROI Analysis:

Quantitative evaluation includes assessing the return on investment (ROI) of AI projects. ROI analysis quantifies the financial benefits generated by the project compared to the costs incurred. It involves calculating the monetary gains achieved, such as increased revenue, cost savings, or efficiency improvements, and comparing them to the project's total investment.

Statistical Analysis:

Statistical analysis plays a crucial role in quantitative evaluation methods. It involves analyzing data distributions, identifying correlations, conducting hypothesis testing, and performing significance tests. Statistical analysis helps identify patterns, trends, and relationships within the data, providing objective insights into the effectiveness and impact of AI projects.

Qualitative Evaluation Methods:

Qualitative evaluation methods involve collecting and analyzing non-numerical data to gain a deeper understanding of the subjective aspects, user experiences, and contextual factors related to AI projects. These methods provide rich and nuanced insights that quantitative data alone may not capture. Here are some examples of qualitative evaluation methods in AI projects:

User Surveys and Interviews:

Qualitative evaluation often includes gathering feedback from users through surveys, interviews, or focus groups. These methods capture user experiences, perceptions, and opinions regarding the AI system. User feedback provides insights into usability, satisfaction, and areas for improvement, helping to enhance user-centered design and decision-making.

User Observations and Case Studies:

Qualitative evaluation may involve observing users interacting with the AI system or conducting in-depth case studies. User observations provide insights into user behavior, decision-making processes, and challenges encountered. Case studies provide detailed contextual information, capturing the complexity and real-world impact of AI projects.

Ethnographic Research:

Ethnographic research involves immersing researchers in the context where the AI system is deployed. This method allows for a deep understanding of the social, cultural, and organizational dynamics influencing AI adoption and outcomes. Ethnographic research helps uncover hidden factors, unintended consequences, and the broader societal impact of AI projects.

Expert Evaluation and Peer Review:

Qualitative evaluation can involve expert evaluation and peer review. Experts in the field assess the AI system's performance, its alignment with best practices, and its compliance with ethical and legal standards. Peer review involves external experts reviewing the project's methodology, results, and conclusions to ensure rigor and validity.

Natural Language Processing (NLP) Analysis:

Qualitative evaluation can employ NLP techniques to analyze unstructured textual data, such as user reviews, social media posts, or customer support logs. NLP analysis helps identify sentiments, trends, and patterns in user feedback, allowing for a deeper understanding of user experiences and perceptions.

Combining Quantitative and Qualitative Evaluation:

The combination of quantitative and qualitative evaluation methods provides a comprehensive assessment of AI projects. Quantitative methods offer objective measurements and statistical insights, while qualitative methods capture the subjective aspects, user experiences, and contextual factors. The integration of both approaches allows for a more holistic understanding of AI project performance, impact, user satisfaction, and areas for improvement.

It is essential to note that the choice of evaluation methods should align with the project's objectives, data availability, and constraints. Combining different evaluation methods, using mixed-method approaches, or triangulating data from multiple sources enhances the robustness and validity of the evaluation process.

In conclusion, evaluating AI projects requires a combination of quantitative and qualitative methods. Quantitative evaluation provides objective and measurable insights into performance, efficiency, and financial impact, while qualitative evaluation captures subjective aspects, user experiences, and contextual factors. By utilizing a diverse range of evaluation methods, organizations can gain a comprehensive understanding of the effectiveness, user satisfaction, and areas for improvement in AI projects.

CHAPTER 25: THE IMPORTANCE OF CONTINUOUS LEARNING AND DEVELOPMENT

In today's rapidly evolving world, where technology and business practices are constantly changing, continuous learning and development have become essential for individuals and organizations to thrive. Continuous learning refers to the ongoing process of acquiring new knowledge, skills, and competencies throughout one's career, while development encompasses the growth and application of those acquired abilities. Let us explore the importance of continuous learning and development in personal and professional contexts:

Adaptability to Change:

Continuous learning and development foster adaptability. By staying updated on the latest industry trends, emerging technologies, and best practices, individuals can navigate changes and embrace new opportunities. Continuous learning helps individuals develop a growth mindset, enabling them to embrace challenges, overcome obstacles, and effectively respond to evolving circumstances.

Enhanced Job Performance:

Continuous learning and development enhance job performance by equipping individuals with the knowledge and skills needed to excel in their roles. As individuals acquire new competencies and stay current with industry developments, they become more efficient, effective, and innovative in their work. Continuous learning promotes mastery, enabling individuals to deliver high-quality results and drive organizational success.

Career Advancement:

Continuous learning and development are critical for career advancement. In today's competitive job market, individuals who continuously expand their knowledge and skills have a competitive edge. Learning new technologies, honing leadership capabilities, or acquiring industry-specific expertise opens doors to new opportunities and positions individuals for career growth and progression.

Innovation and Creativity:

Continuous learning stimulates innovation and creativity. By exposing oneself to diverse perspectives, emerging trends, and different domains, individuals can generate fresh ideas, challenge assumptions, and propose innovative solutions. Continuous learning fuels creativity by broadening perspectives and encouraging the exploration of new possibilities.

Personal Growth and Fulfillment:

Continuous learning and development contribute to personal growth and fulfillment. Learning new things fosters intellectual curiosity, expands horizons, and provides a sense of achievement. Acquiring new skills and knowledge enhances self-confidence and self-efficacy. Continuous learning also offers opportunities for personal exploration, self-reflection, and the pursuit of passions and interests.

Future-proofing Skills:

Continuous learning ensures that individuals remain relevant and future-proof their skills. Technology advancements, industry disruptions, and evolving job requirements can render certain skills obsolete. By embracing continuous learning, individuals can proactively update their skills and competencies to align with changing market demands. Future-proofing skills enhances employability and reduces the risk of professional stagnation.

Organizational Growth and Agility:

Continuous learning and development are vital for organizational growth and agility. Organizations that prioritize a learning culture foster innovation, adaptability, and resilience. Continuous learning initiatives, such as training programs, knowledge sharing platforms, or mentorship opportunities, nurture employee development, improve productivity, and drive organizational performance.

Knowledge Sharing and Collaboration:

Continuous learning promotes knowledge sharing and collaboration within organizations. Individuals who engage in continuous learning contribute to a culture of sharing insights, best practices, and lessons learned. This collaborative environment facilitates the dissemination of knowledge, fosters cross-functional collaboration, and accelerates organizational learning.

Change Management and Transformation:

Continuous learning and development play a crucial role in change management and organizational transformation. During periods of change, individuals need to acquire new skills, adjust their mindset, and embrace new ways of working. Continuous learning provides the foundation for successful change management, enabling individuals to navigate transitions, adopt new processes, and support organizational transformation.

Lifelong Learning Mindset:

Continuous learning fosters a lifelong learning mindset, emphasizing the importance of ongoing growth and development beyond formal education. Individuals who embrace lifelong learning are open to new experiences, seek opportunities for self-improvement, and adapt to the evolving needs of the world. A lifelong learning mindset promotes personal fulfillment, resilience, and the pursuit of excellence.

In conclusion, continuous learning and development are essential for personal growth, professional success, and organizational agility. By embracing continuous learning, individuals can adapt to change, enhance job performance, foster innovation, and future-proof their skills. Organizations that prioritize continuous learning create a culture of collaboration, innovation, and adaptability, positioning themselves for long-term success in a dynamic and competitive landscape.

CHAPTER 26: IDENTIFYING SKILL GAPS AND TRAINING NEEDS

In today's rapidly evolving and competitive landscape, organizations must regularly assess their workforce's skills to identify skill gaps and training needs. Skill gaps occur when there is a disparity between the skills required for optimal job performance and the skills possessed by employees. Identifying skill gaps and training needs is crucial for organizations to bridge those gaps, enhance employee capabilities, and drive business success. Let us explore the importance of identifying skill gaps and training needs, as well as strategies to effectively address them:

Importance of Identifying Skill Gaps and Training Needs:

Performance Optimization:

Identifying skill gaps enables organizations to optimize employee performance. By understanding the specific skills employees need to excel in their roles, organizations can provide targeted training interventions to enhance those skills. Addressing skill gaps improves productivity, efficiency, and job satisfaction, resulting in improved overall performance.

Adaptation to Technological Advancements:

Rapid technological advancements require employees to acquire new skills to remain effective in their roles. Identifying skill gaps helps organizations stay ahead of the technology curve by recognizing the emerging skills required to leverage new tools and systems. Addressing these gaps through training ensures employees can adapt to changing technological landscapes.

Succession Planning:

Identifying skill gaps is crucial for effective succession planning. By assessing the skills required for future leadership or specialized roles, organizations can identify potential gaps in the talent pipeline. Addressing these gaps through targeted training and development programs prepares employees for future responsibilities, reducing the risk of leadership or skill shortages.

Employee Engagement and Retention:

Investing in the development of employees' skills demonstrates a commitment to their growth and career progression. Identifying skill gaps and providing training opportunities shows employees that their development is valued, increasing engagement and fostering loyalty. Engaged employees are more likely to stay with the organization, reducing turnover and associated costs.

Improved Organizational Agility:

Identifying skill gaps and addressing training needs enhances organizational agility. Employees equipped with the necessary skills are more adaptable and capable of responding to changing business requirements. This agility enables organizations to seize new opportunities, navigate challenges, and remain competitive in dynamic market conditions.

Strategies for Identifying Skill Gaps and Training Needs:

Conduct Skills Assessments:

Skills assessments involve evaluating employees' existing skills against the desired competencies for their roles. This can be done through self-assessment questionnaires, manager assessments, or performance reviews. Skills assessments provide insights into individual and team proficiency levels, highlighting areas where additional training may be required.

Analyze Job Descriptions and Competency Models:

Analyzing job descriptions and competency models helps organizations identify the skills and qualifications required for specific roles. By comparing the desired skills with employees' current skill sets, skill gaps can be identified. This analysis also helps in creating competency frameworks that define the skills necessary for each role.

Seek Employee Feedback:

Engaging employees in the process of identifying skill gaps and training needs can provide valuable insights. Surveys, focus groups, or one-on-one discussions can be conducted to gather feedback on employees' perceived strengths and areas where they feel they need additional support or training.

Analyze Performance Data:

Performance data, such as Key Performance Indicators (KPIs), performance reviews, or customer feedback, can provide indicators of skill gaps. By analyzing performance data, organizations can identify patterns of underperformance or areas where employees may require further development.

Stay Current with Industry Trends:

Keeping abreast of industry trends and developments helps identify emerging skills and competencies that may be crucial for future success. Industry research, attending conferences, or networking with industry professionals can provide valuable insights into the skills that are in high demand or becoming obsolete.

Addressing Skill Gaps and Training Needs:

Develop Tailored Training Programs:

Once skill gaps are identified, organizations can design tailored training programs to address those gaps. Training programs can include instructor-led sessions, online courses, workshops, mentoring programs, or on-the-job training. The training should be aligned with employees' learning preferences and focus on developing the specific skills required.

Provide Learning Resources:

Offering a range of learning resources, such as e-learning platforms, libraries, industry publications, or access to external training providers, allows employees to pursue self-directed learning. Providing employees with resources empowers them to take ownership of their skill development and address their individual training needs.

Encourage Cross-Functional Training and Collaboration:

Encouraging cross-functional training and collaboration facilitates the transfer of knowledge and skills among employees. By providing opportunities for employees to learn from colleagues in different roles or departments, organizations can foster a culture of continuous learning and address skill gaps through peer-to-peer knowledge sharing.

Support Continuous Learning:

Promote a culture of continuous learning and skill development within the organization. Offer incentives, rewards, or recognition programs that encourage employees to engage in ongoing learning initiatives. Providing dedicated time for learning activities or establishing internal knowledge-sharing platforms can further support continuous learning efforts.

Monitor and Evaluate Progress:

Regularly monitor and evaluate the effectiveness of training programs in addressing skill gaps. Assess the application of learned skills in real work scenarios and solicit feedback from employees. Use evaluations to refine training programs and ensure they remain aligned with evolving skill requirements.

In conclusion, identifying skill gaps and training needs is crucial for optimizing employee performance, fostering adaptability, and driving organizational success. By conducting skills assessments, analyzing job descriptions, seeking employee feedback, analyzing performance data, and staying current with industry trends, organizations can pinpoint skill gaps and develop targeted training programs to address them. By investing in continuous learning and development, organizations empower their employees, enhance organizational capabilities, and remain competitive in an ever-changing business environment.

CHAPTER 27: CREATING A CULTURE OF INNOVATION AND LEARNING

In today's fast-paced and competitive business landscape, organizations must foster a culture of innovation and learning to stay ahead. A culture that values innovation and embraces continuous learning empowers employees to explore new ideas, drive creativity, adapt to change, and contribute to the organization's growth and success. Let us delve into the importance of creating a culture of innovation and learning and explore strategies to cultivate such a culture within organizations:

Importance of a Culture of Innovation and Learning:

Encourages Creativity and Problem-solving:

A culture of innovation and learning encourages employees to think creatively, explore new perspectives, and seek innovative solutions to challenges. It provides a supportive environment where employees feel empowered to take risks, experiment, and challenge the status quo. This mindset fosters problem-solving skills and nurtures a culture of continuous improvement.

Drives Adaptability to Change:

Organizations operating in a rapidly changing environment require adaptability to thrive. A culture of innovation and learning prepares employees to embrace change, see it as an opportunity, and adapt quickly to new situations. By encouraging continuous learning, organizations equip employees with the skills and mindset needed to navigate uncertainty and proactively respond to market shifts.

Enhances Employee Engagement and Satisfaction:

A culture that promotes innovation and learning enhances employee engagement and satisfaction. When employees are encouraged to contribute ideas, given opportunities for professional growth, and provided with resources for learning and development, they feel valued and empowered. Engaged and satisfied employees are more committed, productive, and likely to stay with the organization.

Fosters a Sense of Ownership and Accountability:

A culture of innovation and learning promotes a sense of ownership and accountability among employees. When individuals are encouraged to innovate, they feel a sense of ownership over their work and are motivated to deliver high-quality outcomes. Learning opportunities foster personal growth, empowering employees to take ownership of their professional development and contribute their best efforts.

Sparks Collaboration and Knowledge Sharing:

A culture that encourages innovation and learning fosters collaboration and knowledge sharing. Employees are more likely to collaborate, exchange ideas, and share expertise when they feel supported in their creative endeavors. Collaborative environments enhance problem-solving capabilities, promote cross-functional collaboration, and create opportunities for collective growth.

Strategies to Cultivate a Culture of Innovation and Learning:

Leadership Support and Role Modeling:

Leaders play a crucial role in creating a culture of innovation and learning. They need to actively support and champion innovation, demonstrate a growth mindset, and lead by example. When leaders prioritize continuous learning, take calculated risks, and reward innovative efforts, they inspire employees to do the same.

Establish a Learning and Development Framework:

Provide opportunities for continuous learning and professional development. Establish learning and development programs that offer a range of options, including training workshops, seminars, e-learning platforms, mentoring programs, and cross-functional rotations. These initiatives enable employees to acquire new skills, explore new areas of expertise, and stay updated on industry trends.

Foster Psychological Safety:

Create a psychologically safe environment where employees feel comfortable taking risks, sharing ideas, and challenging conventional thinking. Encourage open communication, active listening, and constructive feedback. When employees feel safe to voice their opinions without fear of judgment or retribution, they are more likely to contribute innovative ideas and engage in collaborative problem-solving.

Embrace Agile and Experimental Approaches:

Adopt agile methodologies that promote experimentation, iteration, and continuous improvement. Encourage employees to test new ideas, prototype, and learn from failures. Embracing a fail-forward mentality allows employees to take calculated risks and view setbacks as learning opportunities.

Promote Cross-functional Collaboration:

Facilitate cross-functional collaboration to foster innovation and learning. Encourage employees from different departments and backgrounds to collaborate on projects, share knowledge, and leverage diverse perspectives. Cross-functional teams promote interdisciplinary learning, stimulate innovation, and generate unique solutions.

Recognize and Reward Innovation:

Create mechanisms to recognize and reward innovative efforts. Acknowledge and celebrate employee contributions, whether through formal recognition programs, innovation challenges, or internal showcases of successful projects. Recognizing and rewarding innovation reinforces the importance of creativity and encourages others to actively participate in the innovation process.

Encourage Employee Autonomy:

Provide employees with the autonomy to explore new ideas and pursue their passions. Allow flexibility in work processes, allocate dedicated time for creative endeavors, and empower employees to take ownership of their learning and development. When employees have the freedom to innovate and pursue their interests, they are more likely to be motivated and creative.

Foster External Networks and Collaboration:

Encourage employees to engage in external networks, attend industry events, participate in communities of practice, or collaborate with external partners. External networks provide exposure to new ideas, emerging trends, and diverse perspectives. Encouraging employees to connect externally facilitates the transfer of knowledge, sparks innovation, and expands the organization's reach.

In conclusion, creating a culture of innovation and learning is essential for organizations seeking to stay competitive, foster employee engagement, and drive continuous improvement. By promoting creativity, supporting continuous learning, encouraging collaboration, and providing opportunities for autonomy and recognition, organizations can cultivate a culture that embraces innovation and encourages employees to unleash their full potential.

CHAPTER 28: EMERGING AI TECHNOLOGIES AND THEIR POTENTIAL IMPACT ON BUSINESSES

Artificial Intelligence (AI) continues to advance at a rapid pace, with new technologies and applications continuously emerging. These emerging AI technologies have the potential to revolutionize various industries and transform the way businesses operate. From enhanced automation and decision-making to personalized customer experiences and improved efficiency, the impact of emerging AI technologies is vast. Let us explore some of these technologies and their potential impact on businesses:

Reinforcement Learning:

Reinforcement learning is a branch of AI that enables machines to learn and make decisions through trial and error. It involves training AI models to interact with an environment, receive feedback on their actions, and optimize their decision-making processes. Reinforcement learning has the potential to revolutionize areas such as robotics, autonomous vehicles, logistics, and supply chain management. Businesses can leverage reinforcement learning to automate complex tasks, optimize resource allocation, and improve operational efficiency.

Generative Adversarial Networks (GANs):

GANs are a class of AI models that consist of two neural networks: a generator and a discriminator. The generator creates new data samples, such as images or text, while the discriminator evaluates their authenticity.

GANs have the potential to revolutionize creative industries, such as advertising, design, and entertainment. They can be used to generate realistic images, develop virtual environments, or create personalized content. GANs can enhance product design, enable virtual try-on experiences, and support the development of immersive virtual reality applications.

Edge Computing and AI:

Edge computing involves processing and analyzing data near the source of generation, rather than sending it to a centralized cloud server. When combined with AI, edge computing allows for real-time decision-making and analysis at the edge of the network. This technology has significant implications for industries that require low latency, such as healthcare, manufacturing, and autonomous vehicles. Edge computing enables AI-powered devices and systems to operate in real-time, improving response times, enhancing security, and reducing reliance on cloud connectivity.

Explainable AI:

Explainable AI focuses on developing AI systems that can provide clear explanations for their decisions and actions. This is particularly important in industries where transparency and trust are critical, such as healthcare, finance, and legal sectors. Explainable AI enables businesses to understand and interpret the reasoning behind AI-driven decisions, improving accountability and compliance. It also helps build trust with customers and stakeholders, facilitating broader adoption of AI technologies.

Natural Language Processing (NLP) Advancements:

NLP has made significant advancements in recent years, enabling machines to understand and generate human language. This technology has a transformative impact on customer service, chatbots, and virtual assistants. Businesses can leverage NLP to develop conversational AI interfaces, automate customer support, and extract insights from unstructured data. NLP advancements also have implications for sentiment analysis, language translation, and voice recognition, further enhancing customer experiences and enabling better decision-making.

Computer Vision:

Computer vision focuses on enabling machines to understand and interpret visual information. Advancements in computer vision technologies have implications for industries such as retail, manufacturing, healthcare, and security. Businesses can leverage computer vision to automate quality control processes, enable visual search capabilities, or develop augmented reality applications. Computer vision also plays a crucial role in autonomous vehicles, surveillance systems, and medical imaging, enhancing safety, accuracy, and efficiency.

Autonomous Systems:

Autonomous systems, such as autonomous vehicles and drones, have the potential to disrupt transportation, logistics, and delivery industries. These systems leverage AI technologies, including computer vision, machine learning, and sensor fusion, to navigate and make decisions independently. Autonomous systems can increase efficiency, reduce costs, and improve safety in transportation and delivery operations. They have applications in areas like last-mile delivery, warehouse management, and agriculture.

Quantum Computing:

While still in its early stages, quantum computing has the potential to revolutionize computational power and solve complex problems that are currently infeasible for classical computers. Quantum computing's impact on AI algorithms, optimization problems, and data analysis can lead to significant advancements in various fields, including drug discovery, financial modeling, and weather prediction. Quantum computing has the potential to accelerate AI training and inference processes, unlocking new possibilities for businesses.

As businesses embrace these emerging AI technologies, it is crucial to consider their ethical implications, data privacy concerns, and potential biases. Striking the right balance between innovation and responsible use of AI technologies is key to realizing their full potential and reaping the benefits they offer.

In conclusion, emerging AI technologies have the potential to revolutionize businesses across industries. From reinforcement learning and GANs to edge computing, explainable AI, NLP advancements, computer vision, autonomous systems, and quantum computing, these technologies offer new possibilities for automation, decision-making, personalization, and operational efficiency. Businesses that proactively embrace and leverage these emerging AI technologies can gain a competitive edge, drive innovation, and unlock new opportunities for growth and success.

CHAPTER 29: PREPARING FOR AI-DRIVEN CHANGES IN THE WORKFORCE

The rapid advancement of Artificial Intelligence (AI) is bringing transformative changes to the workforce, impacting the nature of jobs and the skills required to thrive in the digital age. As AI technologies continue to evolve, organizations and individuals must proactively prepare for these changes to harness the full potential of AI and navigate the future of work. Let us explore strategies for preparing for AI-driven changes in the workforce:

Embrace Lifelong Learning:

With AI automation disrupting traditional job roles, continuous learning has become essential for staying relevant in the workforce. Embrace a mindset of lifelong learning, both as individuals and organizations. Develop a culture that values and supports ongoing skill development, encouraging employees to pursue training programs, certifications, and educational opportunities that align with emerging technologies and industry trends.

Develop a Growth Mindset:

Cultivate a growth mindset that embraces change and fosters resilience. Encourage employees to view AI-driven changes as opportunities rather than threats. Emphasize the importance of adaptability, curiosity, and the willingness to acquire new skills. A growth mindset enables individuals to approach AI-driven changes with a positive attitude and a focus on continuous improvement.

Foster Creativity and Innovation:

AI excels at automating routine tasks, but creativity and innovation are uniquely human capabilities. Encourage employees to explore their creative potential and think critically. Create a supportive environment where innovative ideas are valued, and experimentation is encouraged. By fostering creativity, organizations can leverage AI as a tool to augment human creativity and problem-solving abilities.

Focus on Human-Centric Skills:

As AI automates repetitive and predictable tasks, the demand for skills that are uniquely human will increase. Emphasize the development of human-centric skills such as critical thinking, emotional intelligence, complex problem-solving, creativity, and communication. These skills, combined with AI technologies, enable individuals to excel in areas that require human judgment, empathy, and creativity.

Promote Collaboration and Teamwork:

AI-driven changes in the workforce highlight the importance of collaboration and teamwork. Encourage cross-functional collaboration and create opportunities for employees to work together on projects that leverage AI technologies. Foster a culture of knowledge sharing, teamwork, and open communication. Collaboration allows individuals to leverage their unique strengths and work synergistically with AI tools and systems.

Build Hybrid Workforce Models:

Rather than viewing AI as a replacement for human workers, organizations should focus on building hybrid workforce models that combine human capabilities with AI technologies. Identify tasks that can be automated and leverage AI tools to augment human capabilities. This approach allows organizations to optimize efficiency, improve productivity, and enhance the quality of work while maintaining a human touch.

Invest in Reskilling and Upskilling:

Invest in reskilling and upskilling programs to equip employees with the necessary skills for AI-driven roles. Identify the skills that will be in demand in the future and provide training opportunities to bridge any skill gaps. Collaborate with educational institutions, training providers, and industry experts to design programs that address emerging needs and align with organizational goals.

Develop Ethical AI Practices:

As AI becomes increasingly integrated into the workforce, organizations must develop and adhere to ethical AI practices. Ensure AI systems are transparent, explainable, and accountable. Consider the ethical implications of AI algorithms, data privacy, and bias. Promote responsible AI use and establish guidelines that prioritize ethical decision-making in the development and deployment of AI technologies.

Foster a Culture of Agility:

In the face of AI-driven changes, organizations must embrace agility. Foster a culture that values agility, embraces change, and encourages flexibility. Develop agile practices and processes that allow for quick adaptation and iterative approaches to problem-solving. Being agile enables organizations to respond swiftly to AI-driven disruptions and seize new opportunities.

Create Supportive Transition Plans:

When implementing AI technologies, proactively create transition plans to support employees affected by automation. Provide training and support to help employees transition into new roles or acquire skills that are in high demand. Implement measures such as job rotations, mentoring programs, and career development opportunities to facilitate smooth transitions and mitigate any potential negative impacts.

In conclusion, preparing for AI-driven changes in the workforce requires a proactive and strategic approach. By embracing lifelong learning, fostering a growth mindset, focusing on human-centric skills, promoting collaboration, and investing in reskilling and upskilling, organizations and individuals can adapt to the changing landscape and harness the potential of AI technologies. By combining human capabilities with AI tools, organizations can create a future-ready workforce that thrives in the AI-driven era.

CHAPTER 30: STAYING AHEAD OF THE COMPETITION THROUGH AI INNOVATION

In today's fast-paced and highly competitive business landscape, organizations must continuously innovate to stay ahead of the competition. Artificial Intelligence (AI) is one of the most powerful tools available for driving innovation and gaining a competitive edge. By harnessing the potential of AI technologies, businesses can enhance operational efficiency, deliver personalized customer experiences, uncover valuable insights, and drive strategic decision-making. Let us explore how organizations can leverage AI innovation to stay ahead of the competition:

Enhancing Operational Efficiency:

AI technologies, such as automation and robotic process automation (RPA), can streamline business processes and increase operational efficiency. By automating repetitive and rule-based tasks, organizations can optimize resource allocation, reduce errors, and improve productivity. AI-powered systems can also enhance supply chain management, inventory optimization, and production planning, leading to cost savings and improved efficiency.

Personalizing Customer Experiences:

AI enables organizations to deliver highly personalized customer experiences at scale. By leveraging machine learning algorithms and natural language processing, businesses can analyze vast amounts of customer data to gain insights into preferences, behavior patterns, and individual needs. This allows for targeted marketing campaigns, personalized recommendations, and tailored customer support, resulting in increased customer satisfaction and loyalty.

Uncovering Valuable Insights:

AI technologies excel at analyzing large volumes of data and extracting actionable insights. By employing AI-powered analytics and machine learning algorithms, businesses can uncover patterns, trends, and correlations that may be difficult to detect manually. These insights can inform strategic decision-making, drive innovation, and identify new business opportunities. AI-powered analytics can also enable predictive and prescriptive analysis, empowering organizations to anticipate customer needs, optimize operations, and mitigate risks.

Improving Decision-Making:

AI-driven insights can significantly improve decision-making processes within organizations. By augmenting human intelligence with AI technologies, businesses can access real-time data, scenario modeling, and predictive analysis, enabling informed and data-driven decision-making. AI-powered decision support systems can enhance strategic planning, risk management, and resource allocation, giving organizations a competitive advantage in fast-changing markets.

Enabling Innovative Products and Services:

AI innovation opens up new avenues for product and service development. Organizations can leverage AI to create innovative solutions that meet evolving customer demands. For example, AI-powered chatbots, virtual assistants, and voice recognition systems enable more interactive and personalized user experiences. AI can also fuel product innovation by enabling the development of smart devices, IoT solutions, and autonomous systems.

Automating and Optimizing Business Processes:

AI technologies can automate and optimize complex business processes, reducing manual effort and enabling faster and more accurate operations. Intelligent process automation, powered by AI, can streamline workflows, eliminate bottlenecks, and reduce costs. For instance, AI-driven algorithms can automate data entry, document processing, and compliance checks, freeing up employees to focus on higher-value tasks and strategic initiatives.

Embracing Predictive Analytics and Forecasting:

AI innovation empowers organizations to leverage predictive analytics and forecasting to anticipate market trends, customer behavior, and demand patterns. By analyzing historical data, AI algorithms can generate accurate predictions and forecasts, enabling businesses to make proactive decisions, optimize inventory levels, and stay ahead of market shifts. Predictive analytics also helps organizations identify opportunities for product innovation and tailored marketing strategies.

Improving Risk Management:

AI technologies play a crucial role in risk management. By leveraging machine learning algorithms, organizations can detect anomalies, identify potential fraud, and assess risk in real-time. AI-powered algorithms can continuously monitor data, flagging any unusual activities or patterns that may indicate security breaches or compliance violations. This enables organizations to proactively mitigate risks, safeguard sensitive information, and protect their reputation.

Accelerating Research and Development:

AI innovation expedites the research and development (R&D) process, enabling organizations to bring new products and services to market faster. AI algorithms can analyze vast amounts of data, conduct simulations, and generate insights that assist in R&D efforts. By automating repetitive tasks and augmenting human creativity, AI facilitates breakthrough discoveries, shortens development cycles, and accelerates innovation.

Embracing a Culture of Innovation:

To fully leverage AI innovation, organizations must foster a culture that embraces experimentation, collaboration, and continuous learning. Encouraging employees to explore new ideas, take calculated risks, and learn from failures promotes a dynamic and innovative environment. Creating cross-functional teams, organizing hackathons, and providing resources for ongoing skill development are effective strategies for fostering an innovation-driven culture.

In conclusion, AI innovation presents immense opportunities for businesses to gain a competitive advantage and stay ahead of the competition. By leveraging AI technologies to enhance operational efficiency, personalize customer experiences, uncover insights, improve decision-making, drive innovation, and optimize business processes, organizations can position themselves as industry leaders. Embracing a culture of innovation, investing in AI talent, and staying abreast of emerging AI trends are crucial for organizations seeking to harness the full potential of AI and maintain a competitive edge in today's digital landscape.

Chapter 31: Encouraging Experimentation and Risk-Taking

In today's rapidly evolving business landscape, organizations need to foster a culture of experimentation and risk-taking to drive innovation and stay competitive. Encouraging employees to explore new ideas, take calculated risks, and learn from failures can lead to breakthrough innovations, improved problem-solving, and a more agile and resilient organization. Let us explore the importance of encouraging experimentation and risk-taking and discuss strategies for cultivating this culture within organizations:

Promoting Innovation and Creativity:

Encouraging experimentation and risk-taking is essential for promoting innovation and creativity within organizations. By creating an environment where employees feel empowered to explore new ideas and challenge the status quo, organizations can unlock the potential for breakthrough innovations. Employees are more likely to think outside the box, propose novel solutions, and generate new opportunities when they feel supported in taking risks and experimenting with different approaches.

Driving Continuous Improvement:

Experimentation and risk-taking are closely tied to continuous improvement. Encouraging employees to test new ideas, processes, and technologies enables organizations to identify areas for improvement and optimize their operations. By embracing a mindset of continuous learning and experimentation, organizations can foster a culture of continuous improvement, allowing them to adapt to changing market conditions, identify innovative solutions, and enhance their competitive advantage.

Nurturing a Learning Organization:

Encouraging experimentation and risk-taking nurtures a learning organization. When employees are empowered to experiment and learn from both successes and failures, they gain valuable insights and knowledge. This culture of learning enables employees to develop new skills, acquire a growth mindset, and continuously enhance their capabilities. It also promotes knowledge sharing and collaboration, as employees are more likely to share their learnings and experiences when experimentation is valued.

Building Resilience and Adaptability:

In a rapidly changing business environment, organizations must be resilient and adaptable. Encouraging experimentation and risk-taking helps build resilience by fostering an organizational mindset that embraces change and uncertainty. When employees are encouraged to take risks and learn from failures, they become more resilient in the face of setbacks and more adaptable to new challenges and opportunities. This adaptability enables organizations to respond quickly to market shifts, innovate, and maintain a competitive edge.

Embracing a Fail-Forward Mentality:

To encourage experimentation and risk-taking, organizations must embrace a fail-forward mentality. This means viewing failures as opportunities for learning and growth rather than as setbacks. When employees are not afraid of failure, they are more likely to take calculated risks, try new approaches, and explore innovative ideas. Organizations should create a safe environment where employees feel supported and encouraged to learn from failures, share lessons learned, and iterate on their ideas.

Allocating Resources for Experimentation:

To foster experimentation and risk-taking, organizations should allocate dedicated resources, such as time, funding, and expertise, for employees to pursue innovative projects. This demonstrates a commitment to innovation and sends a clear message that experimentation is valued. Providing employees with the necessary resources and support increases their motivation and ability to explore new ideas and take risks.

Recognizing and Rewarding Innovation:

Recognizing and rewarding innovation is crucial for fostering a culture of experimentation and risk-taking. Organizations should celebrate and acknowledge employees who take calculated risks, propose innovative ideas, and drive positive change. Recognitions can take the form of monetary rewards, promotions, public recognition, or opportunities for career advancement. By rewarding and celebrating innovation, organizations reinforce the value of experimentation and encourage others to follow suit.

Leading by Example:

Leaders play a critical role in setting the tone for experimentation and risk-taking. They should lead by example and demonstrate a willingness to take risks, learn from failures, and embrace new ideas. When leaders openly share their experiences, including failures and lessons learned, it creates a culture of psychological safety and encourages employees to do the same. Leaders should provide guidance, support, and resources to empower employees to experiment and take calculated risks.

Creating Collaborative Spaces and Platforms:

Creating collaborative spaces and platforms for idea sharing and experimentation can foster a culture of innovation and risk-taking. This can include physical spaces designed for brainstorming, ideation sessions, and prototyping, as well as digital platforms that facilitate idea exchange and collaboration. By providing employees with platforms to share ideas, collaborate, and receive feedback, organizations can encourage experimentation and enable cross-functional collaboration.

Promoting a Growth Mindset:

Encouraging a growth mindset is crucial for fostering experimentation and risk-taking. A growth mindset emphasizes the belief that abilities and intelligence can be developed through dedication and hard work. By promoting a growth mindset, organizations encourage employees to see failures as opportunities for growth and improvement. This mindset encourages them to take risks, learn from mistakes, and persevere in the face of challenges.

In conclusion, encouraging experimentation and risk-taking is vital for driving innovation, fostering a culture of continuous improvement, and staying competitive in today's dynamic business landscape. By promoting innovation and creativity, nurturing a learning organization, building resilience, embracing a fail-forward mentality, allocating resources, recognizing and rewarding innovation, leading by example, creating collaborative spaces, and promoting a growth mindset, organizations can cultivate a culture that encourages employees to explore new ideas, take calculated risks, and drive positive change. This culture of experimentation and risk-taking empowers organizations to adapt to change, embrace innovation, and seize new opportunities.

Chapter 33: Fostering Cross-Functional Collaboration

In today's complex and rapidly evolving business environment, fostering cross-functional collaboration has become essential for organizations to achieve their goals and stay competitive. Cross-functional collaboration brings together individuals from different departments, disciplines, and backgrounds to work towards a common objective, leveraging diverse perspectives, expertise, and skills. By breaking down silos and promoting collaboration across functions, organizations can drive innovation, enhance problem-solving capabilities, improve decision-making, and achieve better outcomes. Let us explore the importance of fostering cross-functional collaboration and strategies for creating a collaborative culture within organizations:

Harnessing Diverse Perspectives and Expertise:

Cross-functional collaboration enables organizations to harness the power of diverse perspectives and expertise. When individuals from different functions collaborate, they bring unique insights, experiences, and knowledge to the table. This diversity of thought sparks creativity, fosters innovation, and promotes more comprehensive problem-solving. By breaking down departmental barriers and encouraging collaboration, organizations can tap into the collective intelligence of their workforce, leading to better decision-making and improved outcomes.

Solving Complex Problems:

Complex business problems often require a multidimensional approach. By fostering cross-functional collaboration, organizations can assemble teams with a range of skills and expertise necessary to tackle these challenges effectively. Cross-functional teams can bring together individuals with different functional backgrounds, such as marketing, finance, operations, and technology, to analyze problems from various angles and develop holistic solutions. This collaborative problem-solving approach enhances the organization's ability to address complex challenges and adapt to dynamic market conditions.

Improving Communication and Knowledge Sharing:

Cross-functional collaboration facilitates open communication and knowledge sharing across departments. When individuals from different functions collaborate, they exchange ideas, share best practices, and learn from one another's experiences. This collaboration helps break down communication barriers, promote a culture of transparency, and improve information flow within the organization. Improved communication and knowledge sharing enhance coordination, alignment, and organizational agility, enabling teams to work more efficiently and effectively.

Breaking Down Silos:

One of the primary barriers to effective collaboration is the existence of departmental silos within organizations. Silos hinder communication, impede information sharing, and limit collaboration opportunities. Fostering cross-functional collaboration breaks down these silos by encouraging individuals to work together towards common goals, regardless of their functional roles. By creating opportunities for cross-functional interaction and collaboration, organizations can facilitate a more integrated and cohesive work environment, leading to improved performance and innovation.

Enhancing Innovation and Creativity:

Cross-functional collaboration is a catalyst for innovation and creativity. When individuals from diverse backgrounds collaborate, they bring together different perspectives, experiences, and knowledge, which can spark creative ideas and generate innovative solutions. By fostering an environment that encourages cross-functional collaboration, organizations create the conditions necessary for disruptive thinking, fresh insights, and breakthrough innovations. This collaborative approach empowers employees to think beyond their traditional roles and explore new possibilities.

Accelerating Decision-Making:

Effective decision-making is critical for organizational success. Cross-functional collaboration accelerates the decision-making process by facilitating information sharing and involving stakeholders from various functions in the decision-making process. By bringing together individuals with different perspectives, organizations can benefit from a more comprehensive assessment of options, increased buy-in, and faster decision-making. This collaborative decision-making approach enhances organizational agility and enables quicker responses to market changes.

Building Trust and Collaboration Skills:

Cross-functional collaboration promotes trust, as it requires individuals to rely on each other's expertise and contributions. Collaborating across functions builds relationships, enhances understanding, and fosters mutual respect among team members. This trust forms the foundation for effective collaboration and lays the groundwork for future collaborations. Additionally, cross-functional collaboration helps develop collaboration skills among employees, such as active listening, empathy, and effective communication, which can be transferred to other areas of their work.

Providing Diverse Development Opportunities:

Cross-functional collaboration offers employees diverse development opportunities by exposing them to different functional areas, roles, and responsibilities. It broadens their understanding of the business and allows them to gain new skills and perspectives. By encouraging employees to collaborate across functions, organizations support their professional growth, expand their capabilities, and enhance their career prospects. This cross-functional exposure can also foster a sense of belonging and engagement among employees.

Strategies for Fostering Cross-Functional Collaboration:

To foster cross-functional collaboration within organizations, consider the following strategies:

Set Clear Objectives: Clearly define the objectives, outcomes, and expectations of cross-functional collaboration initiatives to ensure alignment and focus.

Create Shared Goals: Establish shared goals that require collaboration across functions to encourage mutual accountability and cooperation.

Establish Collaborative Spaces: Create physical or virtual spaces that facilitate cross-functional interaction, such as common areas, project collaboration tools, or cross-functional task forces.

Promote Communication Channels: Implement communication channels, such as chat platforms, online forums, or regular cross-functional meetings, to encourage information sharing and open dialogue.

Provide Training and Development: Offer training programs that enhance collaboration skills, promote understanding of different functions, and build empathy among employees.

Recognize and Reward Collaboration: Recognize and reward individuals and teams that demonstrate effective cross-functional collaboration to reinforce its value and encourage further collaboration.

Foster a Culture of Trust: Develop a culture that values trust, transparency, and cooperation, where employees feel comfortable reaching out to colleagues from other functions and sharing their expertise.

Lead by Example: Leaders should lead by example, collaborating across functions, and actively promoting cross-functional collaboration as a core value within the organization.

In conclusion, fostering cross-functional collaboration is crucial for organizations seeking to drive innovation, solve complex problems, improve decision-making, and stay ahead of the competition. By harnessing diverse perspectives and expertise, breaking down silos, improving communication, and promoting a collaborative culture, organizations can unleash the full potential of their workforce and foster a collaborative environment that propels growth and success. Embracing cross-functional collaboration allows organizations to tap into the collective intelligence of their teams and gain a competitive advantage in today's dynamic business landscape.

CHAPTER 34: NURTURING A DATA-DRIVEN MINDSET ACROSS THE ORGANIZATION

In the digital age, data has become a valuable asset that can drive informed decision-making, fuel innovation, and provide a competitive edge. Nurturing a data-driven mindset across the organization is crucial for organizations to unlock the full potential of their data and leverage it effectively. A data-driven mindset encourages employees at all levels to make decisions based on data, use data to gain insights, and continuously seek opportunities to improve processes and strategies. Let us explore the importance of nurturing a data-driven mindset and discuss strategies for fostering it within organizations:

Making Informed Decisions:

A data-driven mindset empowers employees to make decisions based on evidence and insights derived from data. Instead of relying solely on intuition or past experiences, employees learn to gather and analyze relevant data to inform their decision-making process. By fostering a data-driven mindset, organizations enable employees to make informed decisions that are more accurate, objective, and aligned with organizational goals.

Leveraging Data for Insights:

Data-driven organizations recognize the value of data in uncovering actionable insights. Encouraging employees to leverage data for insights fosters a culture of curiosity and continuous learning. By providing employees with the necessary tools, skills, and access to data, organizations empower them to derive meaningful insights that drive improvements in various areas, such as operations, customer experience, and product development.

Encouraging Data Literacy:

Nurturing a data-driven mindset involves promoting data literacy across the organization. Data literacy refers to the ability to read, interpret, and communicate data effectively. Providing training and resources to enhance employees' data literacy skills enables them to understand and derive insights from data, ask relevant questions, and communicate their findings to others. This empowers employees to engage with data and use it as a basis for decision-making.

Fostering a Culture of Experimentation:

A data-driven mindset embraces experimentation and learning from data. Organizations should encourage employees to test hypotheses, run experiments, and collect data to validate assumptions and drive continuous improvement. By creating a safe environment where failures are viewed as opportunities for learning, organizations foster a culture that embraces data-driven experimentation and innovation.

Aligning Incentives with Data-Driven Practices:

To nurture a data-driven mindset, organizations should align incentives and performance metrics with data-driven practices. Recognizing and rewarding employees who actively seek data to inform decision-making or demonstrate innovative data-driven solutions encourages the adoption of a data-driven mindset. This helps embed data-driven practices as part of the organizational culture and reinforces the importance of data in driving business outcomes.

Providing Access to Data and Analytics Tools:

To foster a data-driven mindset, organizations need to provide employees with access to data and user-friendly analytics tools. This accessibility empowers employees to explore data, perform analyses, and derive insights independently. Organizations should invest in data infrastructure and analytics platforms that make it easy for employees to access and analyze data, regardless of their technical expertise.

Establishing Data Governance and Quality Standards:

Nurturing a data-driven mindset requires establishing data governance and quality standards. Clear guidelines for data collection, storage, security, and privacy ensure that employees have confidence in the data they use for decision-making. Organizations should establish data governance frameworks, data quality control processes, and regular data audits to maintain data accuracy, reliability, and integrity.

Promoting Data Collaboration and Knowledge Sharing:

Encouraging collaboration and knowledge sharing around data enhances the data-driven mindset within the organization. Cross-functional data teams, communities of practice, and data-sharing platforms can facilitate collaboration, allowing employees to learn from each other's experiences, share best practices, and collaborate on data-driven projects. This collaborative approach fosters a sense of collective ownership and promotes a culture where data is viewed as a valuable resource for everyone.

Leadership as Data Advocates:

Leadership plays a crucial role in nurturing a data-driven mindset. Leaders should champion data-driven decision-making, set an example by using data in their own decision-making processes, and communicate the importance of data to the organization's success. By actively promoting and supporting a data-driven mindset, leaders can create a cultural shift and motivate employees to embrace data-driven practices.

Continuous Learning and Development:

To nurture a data-driven mindset, organizations should prioritize continuous learning and development. Offering training programs, workshops, and resources on data literacy, analytics, and data-driven decision-making equips employees with the necessary skills to engage with data effectively. Encouraging employees to pursue data-related certifications or attend industry conferences and webinars keeps them up to date with emerging trends and advancements in data-driven practices.

In conclusion, nurturing a data-driven mindset across the organization is essential for organizations to effectively leverage data and drive business success. By making informed decisions, leveraging data for insights, encouraging data literacy, fostering a culture of experimentation, aligning incentives, providing access to data and analytics tools, establishing data governance standards, promoting collaboration and knowledge sharing, showcasing leadership support, and prioritizing continuous learning and development, organizations can foster a data-driven mindset and create a culture where data is valued, trusted, and utilized to drive innovation and growth.

CHAPTER 35: DEVELOPING AI GOVERNANCE FRAMEWORKS AND POLICIES

As Artificial Intelligence (AI) continues to advance and become more integrated into various aspects of society, the need for robust governance frameworks and policies becomes increasingly important. AI governance frameworks and policies are designed to ensure that AI technologies are developed, deployed, and used in a responsible, ethical, and accountable manner. They provide guidelines, principles, and rules for the responsible use of AI, addressing concerns related to fairness, transparency, privacy, bias, accountability, and societal impact. Let us explore the key considerations and steps involved in developing AI governance frameworks and policies:

Understand the Context and Risks:

Developing effective AI governance frameworks and policies begins with a deep understanding of the context and risks associated with AI technologies. This includes understanding the potential impact of AI on individuals, society, and various sectors, as well as the risks related to bias, fairness, transparency, privacy, security, and accountability. Conducting thorough risk assessments and considering the ethical implications of AI applications are crucial steps in developing an appropriate governance framework.

Define Clear Objectives and Principles:

Establish clear objectives and principles that underpin the AI governance framework. These objectives should align with the organization's mission, values, and ethical considerations. The principles should outline the desired outcomes and the core values that guide AI development, deployment, and use. Examples of principles include fairness, transparency, accountability, privacy, and human-centric design.

Involve Stakeholders:

Effective AI governance requires collaboration and input from various stakeholders, including industry experts, policymakers, academia, civil society organizations, and the public. Engage in a multi-stakeholder approach to gather diverse perspectives, identify potential risks, and ensure that the governance framework considers the needs and concerns of all stakeholders. This collaborative process helps build trust, legitimacy, and consensus around the governance framework.

Establish Ethical Guidelines:

Ethics play a central role in AI governance. Develop clear ethical guidelines that address the responsible development, deployment, and use of AI technologies. These guidelines should encompass considerations such as fairness, non-discrimination, privacy protection, accountability, transparency, explainability, safety, and human rights. Ethical guidelines provide a foundation for decision-making and help organizations navigate complex ethical dilemmas related to AI.

Promote Transparency and Explainability:

Transparency and explainability are vital for AI governance. Organizations should strive to make AI systems and algorithms transparent to the extent possible, ensuring that users and stakeholders have a clear understanding of how AI operates and makes decisions. Implement mechanisms for explaining the reasoning behind AI decisions and provide avenues for recourse or appeal when AI systems have adverse impacts.

Establish Data Governance and Privacy Policies:

AI relies on data, and therefore, it is essential to have robust data governance and privacy policies. Establish guidelines for data collection, storage, sharing, and protection to ensure compliance with applicable laws and regulations, as well as respect for individuals' privacy rights. Implement appropriate data anonymization and security measures to mitigate the risk of data breaches and unauthorized access.

Address Bias and Discrimination:

Bias in AI algorithms can lead to unfair or discriminatory outcomes. Establish guidelines and procedures to detect and mitigate bias throughout the AI development lifecycle. This includes ensuring diverse and representative training datasets, regularly monitoring and auditing AI systems for bias, and implementing mechanisms for addressing bias when identified. Organizations should strive for fairness and inclusivity in AI applications to avoid perpetuating existing biases and discrimination.

Establish Accountability Mechanisms:

Accountability is a key aspect of AI governance. Organizations should define roles and responsibilities for the development, deployment, and use of AI technologies. Establish mechanisms for oversight, auditing, and accountability to ensure compliance with the established governance framework and policies. Hold individuals and organizations accountable for any misuse or unethical practices related to AI.

Implement Continuous Monitoring and Evaluation:

AI governance frameworks and policies should be dynamic and adaptive to evolving risks and challenges. Implement continuous monitoring and evaluation mechanisms to assess the effectiveness of the governance framework, identify areas for improvement, and address emerging ethical and societal concerns related to AI. Regularly review and update the governance framework to keep pace with technological advancements and societal expectations.

Promote Awareness and Education:

Developing AI governance frameworks and policies is not sufficient on its own. Promote awareness and education among employees, stakeholders, and the public about the principles, guidelines, and procedures outlined in the governance framework. Provide training and resources to ensure that individuals involved in AI development, deployment, and use understand their roles, responsibilities, and ethical considerations.

Engage in Regulatory and Policy Discussions:

Engage with regulatory bodies and policymakers to contribute to the development of AI regulations and policies at the national and international levels. Participate in discussions and collaborate with relevant stakeholders to shape the regulatory landscape and ensure that regulations align with ethical standards and societal expectations.

In conclusion, developing AI governance frameworks and policies is crucial for ensuring the responsible and ethical development, deployment, and use of AI technologies. By understanding the context and risks, defining clear objectives and principles, involving stakeholders, establishing ethical guidelines, promoting transparency and explainability, addressing bias and discrimination, establishing accountability mechanisms, implementing continuous monitoring and evaluation, promoting awareness and education, and engaging in regulatory and policy discussions, organizations can develop comprehensive governance frameworks that mitigate risks, uphold ethical standards, and foster trust in AI technologies.

CHAPTER 36: ENSURING COMPLIANCE WITH DATA PROTECTION AND PRIVACY REGULATIONS

In today's data-driven world, organizations face increasing regulatory scrutiny and public expectations regarding the protection of personal data and privacy. Compliance with data protection and privacy regulations is not only a legal obligation but also a fundamental aspect of maintaining trust and reputation with customers and stakeholders. To ensure compliance, organizations must establish robust processes, policies, and safeguards to protect personal data and respect individuals' privacy rights. Let us explore key considerations and strategies for ensuring compliance with data protection and privacy regulations:

Understand the Regulatory Landscape:

The first step in ensuring compliance is to have a comprehensive understanding of the regulatory landscape. Familiarize yourself with relevant data protection and privacy regulations applicable to your industry and geographical location. Key regulations include the General Data Protection Regulation (GDPR) in the European Union, the California Consumer Privacy Act (CCPA) in the United States, and other country-specific regulations such as the Personal Data Protection Act (PDPA) in Singapore or the Personal Information Protection and Electronic Documents Act (PIPEDA) in Canada.

Appoint a Data Protection Officer (DPO):

Designate a Data Protection Officer (DPO) or a privacy professional responsible for overseeing compliance with data protection and privacy regulations. The DPO should have expertise in privacy laws, regulations, and best practices and serve as a point of contact for individuals and regulatory authorities regarding data protection matters.

Conduct Data Protection Impact Assessments (DPIAs):

Perform Data Protection Impact Assessments (DPIAs) to identify and assess potential risks to individuals' privacy rights and ensure that appropriate measures are in place to mitigate these risks. DPIAs are particularly important when implementing new systems or processes that involve the processing of personal data.

Establish Data Protection Policies and Procedures:

Develop and implement robust data protection policies and procedures that align with relevant regulations. These policies should cover data collection, storage, processing, retention, sharing, and disposal practices. They should also address data subject rights, consent management, data breach notification, and other key aspects of data protection and privacy.

Obtain Lawful Basis for Data Processing:

Ensure that you have a valid lawful basis for processing personal data under applicable regulations. Depending on the purpose of data processing, lawful bases can include the necessity of processing for the performance of a contract, compliance with legal obligations, consent from individuals, legitimate interests pursued by the organization, or other specific legal grounds.

Implement Privacy by Design and Default:

Adopt a Privacy by Design and Default approach, which involves integrating privacy considerations into the design and development of products, services, and business processes. By default, only collect and process personal data that is necessary for the intended purpose and retain it for the minimum required period.

Implement Security Measures:

Implement appropriate technical and organizational security measures to protect personal data from unauthorized access, loss, or destruction. This includes encryption, access controls, regular security assessments, and staff training on data security best practices. Implement incident response plans to effectively respond to and mitigate the impact of data breaches or security incidents.

Maintain Data Subject Rights:

Respect individuals' data subject rights as outlined in data protection regulations. Establish processes for handling data subject requests, including requests for access, rectification, erasure, restriction of processing, data portability, and objection to processing. Respond to such requests within the specified timeframes and ensure that individuals can exercise their rights easily.

Establish Data Sharing and Data Processing Agreements:

When sharing personal data with third parties or engaging with data processors, ensure that appropriate data sharing or data processing agreements are in place. These agreements should include provisions for data protection, security, confidentiality, and compliance with applicable regulations.

Provide Privacy Notices and Obtain Consent:

Provide individuals with clear and concise privacy notices that explain how their personal data is collected, used, shared, and protected. Obtain valid consent for data processing activities when required by applicable regulations and ensure that individuals have the option to withdraw consent at any time.

Regularly Audit and Update Data Protection Practices:

Conduct regular audits and assessments of data protection practices to ensure ongoing compliance with regulations. Stay up to date with changes in data protection and privacy laws and adapt your practices accordingly.

Maintain documentation of data processing activities, policies, procedures, and compliance efforts.

Train and Raise Awareness:

Educate employees about data protection and privacy regulations, their responsibilities, and the importance of compliance. Provide regular training on data protection practices, security awareness, and handling personal data. Foster a privacy-aware culture within the organization by promoting awareness and accountability at all levels.

In conclusion, ensuring compliance with data protection and privacy regulations is vital for organizations to protect personal data, maintain trust, and meet legal obligations. By understanding the regulatory landscape, appointing a Data Protection Officer, conducting DPIAs, establishing data protection policies and procedures, obtaining lawful basis for data processing, implementing privacy by design and default, implementing security measures, respecting data subject rights, establishing data sharing agreements, providing privacy notices and obtaining consent, auditing and updating practices, training employees, and raising awareness, organizations can build a strong foundation for data protection and privacy compliance. These efforts not only mitigate the risk of regulatory penalties but also enhance customer trust and contribute to the responsible and ethical use of personal data.

CHAPTER 37: AUDITING AI SYSTEMS AND PROCESSES

As Artificial Intelligence (AI) becomes increasingly integrated into various aspects of organizations, auditing AI systems and processes is essential to ensure their effectiveness, fairness, transparency, and compliance with ethical and regulatory standards. AI auditing involves evaluating the design, development, deployment, and ongoing performance of AI systems to identify potential risks, biases, or ethical concerns. Let us explore the importance of auditing AI systems and processes and discuss key considerations and strategies for conducting effective AI audits:

Ensuring Accountability and Compliance:

AI audits play a crucial role in ensuring accountability and compliance with legal, regulatory, and ethical standards. By conducting audits, organizations can demonstrate their commitment to responsible AI practices and adherence to applicable laws and regulations. Auditing helps identify any potential non-compliance issues, such as biases, discrimination, or privacy infringements, and enables organizations to take corrective actions.

Evaluating AI System Performance:

AI audits assess the performance of AI systems to ensure they deliver the intended outcomes accurately and reliably. Auditing helps identify any performance gaps, such as low accuracy, false positives/negatives, or inconsistencies, allowing organizations to refine and improve their AI models, algorithms, or processes. Evaluating AI system performance is essential to maintain trust in the technology and optimize its impact on organizational goals.

Identifying Biases and Fairness Concerns:

Auditing AI systems helps detect biases and fairness concerns that may arise from data or algorithmic decisions. Bias in AI algorithms can result in unfair or discriminatory outcomes, perpetuating societal biases or exacerbating inequalities. Through auditing, organizations can assess whether AI systems exhibit biases and take appropriate steps to mitigate them, such as refining training data, enhancing algorithmic fairness, or considering alternative models.

Assessing Data Quality and Integrity:

AI systems heavily rely on data, and auditing helps assess the quality, integrity, and representativeness of the data used in training and inference processes. Audits examine data sources, data collection processes, data cleaning methods, and data storage practices to ensure data accuracy, relevance, and compliance with privacy and security standards. Ensuring high-quality data is essential for reliable and ethical AI outcomes.

Promoting Transparency and Explainability:

Auditing AI systems and processes promotes transparency and explainability, which are critical for building trust and addressing concerns related to AI decision-making. Audits assess the level of transparency and explainability in AI systems, including whether decision-making processes can be understood and justified. Organizations can employ techniques like algorithmic explainability, documentation, or external audits to enhance transparency and explainability.

Mitigating Legal and Regulatory Risks:

AI audits help organizations mitigate legal and regulatory risks associated with AI deployments. Auditing ensures compliance with relevant regulations, such as data protection, privacy, consumer protection, or sector-specific requirements. By conducting audits, organizations can identify potential legal or regulatory gaps and take appropriate measures to address them, minimizing the risk of non-compliance.

Assessing Ethical Considerations:

AI audits include an evaluation of ethical considerations, such as the alignment of AI systems with ethical guidelines, societal values, and organizational principles. Auditing enables organizations to identify any potential ethical concerns, evaluate the impact of AI on stakeholders, and ensure that AI systems operate in an ethically responsible manner. Organizations can establish ethical review boards or guidelines to guide AI audits and decision-making processes.

Evaluating Human-AI Interaction and Oversight:

AI audits should consider the interaction between humans and AI systems. Assessing the human-AI interface helps identify opportunities to improve usability, user experience, or decision-making collaboration. Auditing should also evaluate the level of human oversight and intervention in AI systems to ensure accountability, risk management, and the ability to intervene when necessary.

Implementing Robust Security Measures:

Auditing AI systems involves evaluating security measures to protect AI systems from malicious attacks, unauthorized access, or data breaches. Audits assess the security of AI infrastructure, data storage, model updates, and access controls. Organizations should implement security best practices and regularly assess the effectiveness of security measures to protect AI systems from potential threats.

Ongoing Monitoring and Review:

AI audits should be performed periodically and as part of ongoing monitoring and review processes. Regular audits help organizations stay updated with changes in AI systems, data sources, regulatory requirements, or organizational goals. Ongoing monitoring allows organizations to identify emerging risks, adapt to evolving challenges, and continuously improve their AI systems and processes.

In conclusion, auditing AI systems and processes is essential to ensure accountability, compliance, performance, fairness, transparency, and ethical use of AI technologies. By conducting comprehensive AI audits, organizations can identify and address potential risks, biases, or compliance gaps, thereby enhancing the reliability, trustworthiness, and responsible use of AI. Auditing should be an iterative process, conducted periodically, and integrated into organizational governance frameworks to support ongoing monitoring and continuous improvement of AI systems.

CHAPTER 38: IDENTIFYING AND MITIGATING AI-RELATED SECURITY THREATS

As organizations increasingly adopt Artificial Intelligence (AI) technologies, it is crucial to address the potential security threats associated with AI systems. AI-related security threats can have serious consequences, including unauthorized access, data breaches, manipulation of AI models, adversarial attacks, or malicious use of AI algorithms. Identifying and mitigating these threats is essential to protect sensitive data, maintain trust in AI systems, and ensure the integrity of organizational operations. Let us explore key considerations and strategies for identifying and mitigating AI-related security threats:

Understanding AI-Specific Threats:

Start by understanding the unique security threats that are specific to AI systems. These threats can include model poisoning, adversarial attacks, data poisoning, model theft, inference attacks, and privacy breaches. Understanding these threats and their potential impact on AI systems is essential for developing effective security measures.

Conducting Risk Assessments:

Perform comprehensive risk assessments to identify potential vulnerabilities and threats to AI systems. Assess the potential impact of security breaches, data breaches, or unauthorized access to AI models and data. Evaluate the likelihood of these threats occurring and prioritize them based on their severity and potential impact on business operations, reputation, and privacy.

Securing AI Infrastructure:

Ensure the security of the underlying AI infrastructure, including servers, networks, storage systems, and data centers. Implement strong access controls, encryption mechanisms, and intrusion detection systems to safeguard AI infrastructure from unauthorized access or tampering. Regularly update and patch software and hardware components to address vulnerabilities and stay protected against emerging threats.

Protecting Training Data:

AI models heavily rely on training data, and securing the integrity and confidentiality of this data is crucial. Implement appropriate data protection measures such as data encryption, access controls, and secure data storage. Prevent unauthorized access, tampering, or exfiltration of training data by implementing robust data governance practices and security protocols.

Ensuring Model Integrity:

Protect the integrity of AI models throughout their lifecycle. Implement measures to prevent unauthorized modifications, tampering, or manipulation of models. This includes securing model development environments, version control, and access controls to prevent unauthorized modifications to the models. Implement robust testing and validation procedures to ensure that only trusted and validated models are deployed.

Guarding Against Adversarial Attacks:

Adversarial attacks aim to manipulate or deceive AI models by introducing subtle changes or perturbations to input data. Implement techniques such as adversarial training, input sanitization, or anomaly detection to detect and mitigate adversarial attacks. Regularly test AI models against known adversarial attacks and adopt defensive mechanisms to enhance model robustness.

Implementing Data Anonymization Techniques:

Anonymize sensitive data used for AI training to protect individuals' privacy. Apply techniques such as differential privacy, data masking, or synthetic data generation to minimize the risk of re-identification or unauthorized use of personal information. Implement strong data anonymization protocols and review data sharing agreements to ensure compliance with privacy regulations.

Continuous Monitoring and Threat Detection:

Implement robust monitoring and threat detection mechanisms to identify potential security breaches or anomalies in AI systems. Utilize techniques such as anomaly detection, behavior analytics, or intrusion detection systems to monitor AI infrastructure, data access, and model performance. Promptly investigate and respond to any detected anomalies or suspicious activities.

Conducting Penetration Testing:

Regularly perform penetration testing and vulnerability assessments on AI systems. This involves simulating real-world attacks to identify potential vulnerabilities and weaknesses in the system's security architecture. Penetration testing helps uncover potential entry points for attackers and allows organizations to address these vulnerabilities before they are exploited.

Ensuring Secure Model Deployment and Runtime:

Pay attention to the security of AI models during deployment and runtime. Securely configure AI systems, including access controls, network segmentation, and user permissions. Regularly update and patch AI frameworks, libraries, and dependencies to address any identified security vulnerabilities.

Educating and Training Personnel:

Raise awareness among employees and stakeholders about AI-related security threats and best practices. Educate personnel about phishing attacks, social engineering, secure coding practices, and the importance of following security protocols. Encourage employees to report any suspicious activities or potential security breaches promptly.

Collaborating with Security Experts:

Engage security experts and consultants who specialize in AI security to conduct external audits, provide guidance, and validate the security measures in place. Collaborate with external security experts to stay updated on the latest AI security threats and best practices.

In conclusion, identifying and mitigating AI-related security threats is crucial to protect sensitive data, maintain the integrity of AI systems, and ensure the trustworthiness of AI-driven operations. By understanding AI-specific threats, conducting risk assessments, securing AI infrastructure, protecting training data, ensuring model integrity, guarding against adversarial attacks, anonymizing data, implementing continuous monitoring, conducting penetration testing, ensuring secure model deployment and runtime, educating personnel, and collaborating with security experts, organizations can effectively mitigate AI-related security threats and build resilient and secure AI systems. Proactive security measures and ongoing vigilance are essential to stay one step ahead of emerging security challenges in the evolving landscape of AI.

CHAPTER 39: IMPLEMENTING ROBUST ACCESS CONTROLS AND MONITORING

In the era of digital transformation and increasing cybersecurity threats, implementing robust access controls and monitoring is crucial for organizations to protect sensitive data, prevent unauthorized access, and ensure the integrity of their systems and information assets. Access controls involve defining and enforcing policies and procedures to grant or restrict access to resources, while monitoring involves the continuous observation and logging of system activities to detect and respond to potential security incidents. Let us explore the importance of implementing robust access controls and monitoring and discuss key considerations and strategies for effective implementation:

Protecting Confidentiality and Data Privacy:

Access controls play a critical role in protecting the confidentiality of sensitive data and ensuring compliance with data privacy regulations. Implementing strong authentication mechanisms, such as multi-factor authentication, and role-based access controls help ensure that only authorized individuals can access sensitive information. Additionally, encrypting data at rest and in transit adds an extra layer of protection.

Preventing Unauthorized Access:

Robust access controls prevent unauthorized users from gaining access to systems, applications, and data. By implementing strong password policies, user account management processes, and privileged access management, organizations can minimize the risk of unauthorized access. It is essential to regularly review and update access control lists, revoke access when no longer required, and implement separation of duties to reduce the risk of insider threats.

Enforcing Least Privilege Principle:

The principle of least privilege ensures that users have only the necessary permissions required to perform their job functions. Implementing least privilege access controls minimizes the potential impact of compromised accounts or insider threats. By granting access rights on a need-to-know basis, organizations can reduce the attack surface and mitigate the risk of unauthorized activities.

Implementing Secure Authentication Mechanisms:

Strong authentication mechanisms, such as biometrics, smart cards, or token-based authentication, enhance the security of access controls. Implement multi-factor authentication to require users to provide multiple types of credentials, such as something they know (password), something they have (smart card), or something they are (biometric), to authenticate their identity. This helps prevent unauthorized access even if one factor is compromised.

Role-Based Access Controls (RBAC):

RBAC is a widely adopted access control model that assigns permissions to users based on their roles and responsibilities within the organization. By implementing RBAC, organizations can streamline access management, enforce security policies consistently, and simplify user provisioning and deprovisioning processes. RBAC ensures that users have access only to the resources necessary to perform their duties.

Continuous Monitoring and Logging:

Monitoring system activities and logging events is crucial for detecting and responding to security incidents promptly. Implement a robust logging mechanism to record access attempts, system changes, and other relevant events. Regularly review log files to identify any suspicious or anomalous activities that may indicate potential security breaches or unauthorized access attempts.

Security Information and Event Management (SIEM):

Implementing a SIEM system helps centralize and correlate log data from various systems and applications, enabling real-time monitoring and proactive threat detection. SIEM tools provide advanced analytics, alerting capabilities, and automated response mechanisms to identify and respond to security incidents promptly. SIEM can also aid in compliance reporting and incident response management.

User Behavior Analytics (UBA):

Leverage user behavior analytics to detect anomalous behavior patterns and identify potential insider threats or compromised accounts. UBA solutions use advanced machine learning algorithms to establish baseline behavior profiles for users and detect deviations that may indicate malicious activities. By monitoring user behavior, organizations can detect and respond to security incidents in a timely manner.

Regular Security Audits and Penetration Testing:

Conduct regular security audits and penetration testing to identify vulnerabilities and assess the effectiveness of access controls. Security audits help identify gaps in the access control implementation and ensure compliance with organizational policies and regulatory requirements. Penetration testing involves simulating real-world attacks to identify weaknesses and address them before malicious actors exploit them.

Employee Education and Awareness:

Education and awareness programs are crucial for promoting a security-conscious culture within the organization. Regularly educate employees about the importance of access controls, password hygiene, and safe computing practices. Raise awareness about the potential risks of sharing credentials, falling victim to phishing attacks, or using unauthorized software or devices.

Incident Response and Remediation:

Develop an incident response plan that outlines the steps to be followed in the event of a security incident. Establish clear protocols for detecting, reporting, and responding to security breaches. Regularly test and update the incident response plan to ensure its effectiveness. Additionally, conduct post-incident reviews to learn from security incidents and improve access controls and monitoring processes.

Regular Access Control Reviews:

Perform regular reviews of access controls to ensure their ongoing effectiveness and alignment with changing business needs. Conduct periodic audits of user accounts, access rights, and permission levels. Remove unnecessary or unused accounts, reassess user roles, and conduct access control reviews to address any identified issues or potential security risks.

In conclusion, implementing robust access controls and monitoring is essential for organizations to protect sensitive data, prevent unauthorized access, and ensure the integrity of their systems. By implementing strong authentication mechanisms, enforcing the least privilege principle, implementing role-based access controls, implementing secure authentication mechanisms, continuous monitoring and logging, employing SIEM and UBA, conducting security audits and penetration testing, promoting employee education and awareness, establishing incident response plans, and conducting regular access control reviews, organizations can enhance their security posture and minimize the risk of security breaches. A comprehensive approach to access controls and monitoring is crucial in today's rapidly evolving threat landscape.

CHAPTER 40: DEVELOPING INCIDENT RESPONSE PLANS FOR AI-RELATED BREACHES

As organizations increasingly rely on Artificial Intelligence (AI) technologies, it is crucial to develop robust incident response plans specifically tailored to address AI-related breaches. AI-related breaches can have significant consequences, including data breaches, algorithmic manipulation, adversarial attacks, or unauthorized access to sensitive information. Developing incident response plans for AI-related breaches helps organizations effectively detect, respond to, and mitigate the impact of security incidents, ensuring the integrity and security of AI systems and data. Let us explore the key considerations and strategies for developing incident response plans for AI-related breaches:

Formulating an AI Incident Response Team:

Establish a dedicated AI incident response team comprising experts from various relevant domains, including AI, cybersecurity, legal, IT, and communication. This team should have the necessary skills and knowledge to handle AI-related breaches promptly and effectively. Define roles and responsibilities, designate a team leader, and ensure clear communication channels within the team.

Identify AI-Specific Incident Scenarios:

Identify potential incident scenarios specific to AI systems and applications. This may include unauthorized access to AI models, data breaches, adversarial attacks, model poisoning, or manipulation of training data. By understanding the unique threats and risks associated with AI, organizations can tailor their incident response plans to address these specific scenarios.

Establish Incident Response Procedures:

Develop comprehensive incident response procedures specifically addressing AI-related breaches. These procedures should outline the steps to be taken in the event of an incident, including detection, containment, eradication, recovery, and post-incident analysis. Ensure that the procedures are aligned with industry best practices, regulatory requirements, and organizational policies.

Implement Incident Detection and Monitoring Mechanisms:

Deploy robust detection and monitoring mechanisms to identify AI-related security incidents promptly. Implement real-time monitoring of AI systems, network traffic, log files, and access controls to detect anomalies, suspicious activities, or unauthorized access attempts. Utilize security information and event management (SIEM) tools, anomaly detection systems, or user behavior analytics (UBA) to enhance incident detection capabilities.

Define Communication and Reporting Protocols:

Establish clear communication and reporting protocols to ensure effective coordination and communication during incident response. Define internal and external communication channels, identify key stakeholders, and establish procedures for notifying relevant parties, such as executive management, legal teams, data protection authorities, or affected individuals. Clearly outline the roles and responsibilities of the incident response team members in communication and reporting.

Coordinate with Legal and Compliance Teams:

Involve legal and compliance teams in the development of incident response plans to ensure compliance with applicable laws, regulations, and contractual obligations. Consider the requirements of data breach notification laws and privacy regulations, and develop procedures to meet reporting obligations. Legal experts can provide guidance on handling evidence, preserving data integrity, and managing potential legal implications.

Conduct Tabletop Exercises and Simulations:

Regularly conduct tabletop exercises and simulations to test the effectiveness of incident response plans and ensure preparedness. Simulate AI-related breach scenarios to evaluate the incident response team's ability to detect, respond, and mitigate the impact of incidents. Identify areas for improvement and refine incident response procedures based on lessons learned from these exercises.

Collaborate with External Partners:

Establish relationships with external partners, such as incident response service providers, forensic experts, or legal counsel, to enhance incident response capabilities. These partners can provide specialized expertise and resources during AI-related breach incidents, assisting with incident analysis, containment, forensic investigations, or legal aspects.

Preserve Evidence and Conduct Forensic Analysis:

In the event of an AI-related breach, it is crucial to preserve evidence and conduct thorough forensic analysis. Implement processes to capture and retain relevant logs, data samples, or system snapshots for forensic investigations. Work closely with forensic experts to identify the root cause of the incident, understand the impact, and gather evidence for legal or regulatory purposes.

Learn and Improve:

Conduct post-incident analysis and learning reviews to identify areas for improvement in incident response procedures. Analyze the incident response process, effectiveness of controls, and effectiveness of communication and collaboration. Incorporate the lessons learned from previous incidents into incident response plans to continuously enhance the organization's incident response capabilities.

Update and Test Incident Response Plans Regularly:

Incident response plans should be regularly reviewed, updated, and tested to account for changes in the threat landscape, technology advancements, or organizational changes. Ensure that incident response plans remain relevant and effective by incorporating feedback from incidents, audits, or regulatory changes. Conduct periodic reviews and tests to validate the effectiveness of the plans.

In conclusion, developing robust incident response plans for AI-related breaches is crucial for organizations to effectively detect, respond to, and mitigate the impact of security incidents. By formulating an AI incident response team, identifying AI-specific incident scenarios, establishing incident response procedures, implementing detection and monitoring mechanisms, defining communication and reporting protocols, collaborating with legal and compliance teams, conducting tabletop exercises, collaborating with external partners, preserving evidence, conducting forensic analysis, learning from incidents, and regularly updating and testing the plans, organizations can ensure a proactive and effective response to AI-related breaches. The ability to respond swiftly and efficiently is essential in maintaining the security, trust, and integrity of AI systems and data.

CHAPTER 41: DESIGNING AI SYSTEMS FOR GROWTH AND ADAPTABILITY

In today's rapidly evolving technological landscape, designing AI systems for growth and adaptability is crucial for organizations to stay competitive and leverage the full potential of artificial intelligence (AI) technologies. AI systems that are designed to scale, evolve, and adapt to changing business needs enable organizations to maximize their return on investment, respond to emerging challenges, and capitalize on new opportunities. Let us explore the key considerations and strategies for designing AI systems that are primed for growth and adaptability:

Scalability and Performance:

Design AI systems with scalability and performance in mind. Consider the potential growth in data volume, user base, or computational requirements. Ensure that the system architecture, infrastructure, and algorithms can handle increasing workloads and process data efficiently. Leverage cloud computing, distributed computing, or parallel processing techniques to scale AI systems as needed.

Flexibility in Data Handling:

Build flexibility into AI systems to handle diverse and evolving data sources. Consider different data types, formats, and integration points. Implement data preprocessing and transformation pipelines that can accommodate new data sources without requiring significant modifications to the underlying AI models. This flexibility enables organizations to leverage a wide range of data sources to drive insights and decision-making.

Modular and Reusable Components:

Design AI systems with a modular and component-based architecture. Break down complex systems into smaller, reusable components that can be easily combined or replaced as needed. This approach facilitates system updates, enhancements, or the integration of new technologies without disrupting the overall system. Modular components also promote code reusability and facilitate collaboration among development teams.

Open Standards and Interoperability:

Adopt open standards and promote interoperability between AI systems and other technologies or platforms. Use standardized data formats, APIs, and communication protocols to enable seamless integration with existing systems or third-party solutions. Open standards facilitate data sharing, interconnectivity, and collaboration, ensuring that AI systems can adapt and evolve within the broader technological ecosystem.

Continuous Learning and Adaptation:

Design AI systems that can continuously learn and adapt to new information, trends, or user feedback. Implement feedback loops and mechanisms for capturing new data, monitoring model performance, and updating models as new information becomes available. This iterative approach allows AI systems to improve over time, adapt to changing circumstances, and deliver more accurate and relevant results.

Ethical Considerations:

Integrate ethical considerations into the design of AI systems from the outset. Ensure that AI systems comply with legal and regulatory requirements, protect user privacy, and avoid biases or discrimination. Consider the ethical implications of data usage, algorithmic decision-making, and potential societal impacts. Design AI systems that align with ethical guidelines and promote responsible and transparent use of AI technologies.

Modelling for Uncertainty and Variability:

Account for uncertainty and variability in AI systems by using probabilistic models or incorporating uncertainty estimates into predictions. Recognize that real-world data may have inherent noise or unpredictability, and design AI systems that can handle and adapt to such variability. By incorporating uncertainty modeling, organizations can make informed decisions while accounting for potential risks and uncertainties.

Collaboration between AI and Human Experts:

Facilitate collaboration between AI systems and human experts. Design AI systems that augment human capabilities, provide interpretable insights, and support decision-making processes. Enable human experts to provide feedback, validate AI-generated results, and fine-tune models. The collaboration between AI and human experts leads to more effective and trustworthy outcomes.

Future-Proofing:

Anticipate future advancements and trends in AI technologies. Stay informed about emerging research, algorithms, or frameworks that could enhance the capabilities of AI systems. Design AI systems with flexibility, extensibility, and adaptability to incorporate future innovations seamlessly. Future-proofing AI systems enables organizations to stay ahead of the curve and leverage the latest advancements.

Agile Development and Iterative Improvement:

Adopt agile development methodologies and iterative improvement cycles for AI system design. Break down development into smaller iterations, test new features, collect feedback, and iterate based on user needs and evolving requirements. This iterative approach allows for continuous learning, improvement, and adaptation of AI systems based on real-world feedback and market dynamics.

Robust Documentation and Knowledge Management:

Maintain comprehensive documentation and knowledge management practices throughout the AI system design process. Document design decisions, system architecture, algorithms, and data sources. This documentation facilitates knowledge sharing, enables effective collaboration, and supports future system enhancements or maintenance.

In conclusion, designing AI systems for growth and adaptability is essential for organizations to unlock the full potential of AI technologies and thrive in dynamic business environments. By focusing on scalability, flexibility, modularity, continuous learning, ethical considerations, collaboration with human experts, future-proofing, iterative improvement, robust documentation, and knowledge management, organizations can develop AI systems that can evolve, scale, and adapt to changing business needs. The ability to leverage AI systems that can grow, adapt, and align with emerging technologies and evolving requirements empowers organizations to remain innovative, competitive, and responsive in the AI-driven era.

CHAPTER 42: OPTIMIZING AI MODELS AND ALGORITHMS FOR PERFORMANCE

In the field of Artificial Intelligence (AI), optimizing models and algorithms for performance is crucial for achieving accurate and efficient results. High-performing AI models and algorithms enable organizations to process large volumes of data, make real-time predictions, and deliver optimal outcomes. By fine-tuning and optimizing AI models and algorithms, organizations can enhance their efficiency, reduce computational costs, and improve the overall performance of AI systems. Let us explore key considerations and strategies for optimizing AI models and algorithms for performance:

Data Preprocessing and Feature Engineering:

Data preprocessing and feature engineering are fundamental steps in optimizing AI models. Clean, normalize, and transform data to ensure its quality and compatibility with the model. Feature engineering involves selecting relevant features, creating new features, or reducing the dimensionality of the data to focus on the most informative aspects. Well-prepared data improves model performance and reduces unnecessary computational overhead.

Algorithm Selection and Architecture Design:

Choose the most suitable algorithm and model architecture for the specific task at hand. Consider factors such as the complexity of the problem, available data, computational resources, and performance requirements.

Compare different algorithms and architectures to identify the most efficient and accurate option. Deep learning algorithms, such as convolutional neural networks (CNNs) or recurrent neural networks (RNNs), are often used for complex tasks involving images, text, or sequential data.

Hyperparameter Tuning:

Optimize model performance by fine-tuning hyperparameters. Hyperparameters are adjustable parameters that govern the behavior and performance of AI models, such as learning rate, batch size, regularization strength, or network depth. Use techniques like grid search, random search, or Bayesian optimization to explore different hyperparameter combinations and find the optimal configuration that maximizes model performance.

Regularization and Dropout:

Regularization techniques help prevent overfitting, where the model performs well on training data but fails to generalize to new data. Techniques such as L1 or L2 regularization, dropout, or early stopping can be applied to avoid overfitting and improve the model's ability to generalize to unseen data. Regularization balances model complexity and prevents the model from memorizing noise or irrelevant patterns in the training data.

Model Compression:

Model compression techniques aim to reduce the size and computational requirements of AI models while maintaining their performance. Techniques like pruning, quantization, or knowledge distillation can be applied to reduce the number of parameters, compress model representations, or transfer knowledge from larger models to smaller ones. Model compression enables faster inference, reduces memory requirements, and allows deployment on resource-constrained devices.

Parallelization and Hardware Acceleration:

Leverage parallel processing and hardware acceleration techniques to improve AI model performance. Parallelization techniques, such as data parallelism or model parallelism, distribute computations across multiple processing units or devices, allowing for faster training or inference. Hardware accelerators, like graphics processing units (GPUs) or tensor processing units (TPUs), are optimized for AI workloads and can significantly speed up computations.

Batch Processing and Minibatch Training:

Batch processing and minibatch training techniques improve computational efficiency by processing data in batches rather than individually. Minibatch training allows for more frequent weight updates and reduces memory requirements compared to processing the entire dataset at once. Batch processing and minibatch training improve the efficiency of training algorithms and accelerate the convergence of models.

Transfer Learning and Pretrained Models:

Leverage transfer learning and pretrained models to boost performance and reduce training time. Transfer learning involves utilizing knowledge learned from one task or domain to improve performance on a different but related task. Pretrained models, trained on large-scale datasets, can serve as a starting point for training new models, allowing for faster convergence and improved generalization.

Model Monitoring and Maintenance:

Continuously monitor and maintain AI models to ensure their ongoing performance. Monitor model accuracy, precision, recall, or other relevant metrics to detect performance degradation or drift. Retrain models periodically or when necessary, using updated data or fine-tuning techniques. Regularly evaluate model performance and iterate on the optimization process to keep models performing at their best.

Efficient Data Pipelines and Infrastructure:

Optimize data pipelines and infrastructure to minimize data processing and model inference time. Efficiently manage data storage, retrieval, and transformation to ensure smooth and fast data processing. Utilize distributed computing, caching mechanisms, or data streaming techniques to handle large-scale data and improve overall system performance.

Continuous Improvement and Experimentation:

Embrace a culture of continuous improvement and experimentation to drive performance optimization. Encourage experimentation with new algorithms, architectures, or optimization techniques. Use A/B testing or controlled experiments to evaluate the impact of changes on model performance. Regularly update and evolve AI models and algorithms to leverage new research advancements and emerging technologies.

In conclusion, optimizing AI models and algorithms for performance is vital to achieve accurate, efficient, and scalable AI systems. By focusing on data preprocessing, algorithm selection, hyperparameter tuning, regularization, model compression, parallelization, transfer learning, monitoring, efficient data pipelines, and continuous improvement, organizations can optimize AI models for enhanced performance. Optimal performance enables organizations to make data-driven decisions, deliver fast and accurate predictions, and maximize the value derived from AI technologies.

CHAPTER 43: LEVERAGING CLOUD COMPUTING AND EDGE COMPUTING FOR AI SCALABILITY

As organizations increasingly adopt Artificial Intelligence (AI) technologies, the need for scalable infrastructure becomes paramount. Cloud computing and edge computing are two powerful paradigms that organizations can leverage to enhance the scalability and efficiency of their AI systems. Cloud computing provides on-demand access to computing resources over the internet, while edge computing brings computing power closer to the data source. Let us explore how organizations can leverage cloud computing and edge computing to achieve AI scalability:

Cloud Computing for Scalability:

Cloud computing offers virtually unlimited computing resources, making it an ideal platform for scaling AI workloads. Organizations can take advantage of the following features and services provided by cloud providers:

a. Elastic Computing: Cloud platforms enable organizations to scale their computing resources up or down based on demand. With auto-scaling capabilities, AI systems can dynamically adjust resource allocation to handle fluctuating workloads.

b. Data Storage and Processing: Cloud providers offer scalable storage solutions that allow organizations to store and process large volumes of data required for training and inference. Services like Amazon S3, Google Cloud Storage, or Microsoft Azure Blob Storage provide cost-effective and scalable options for storing AI data.

c. Machine Learning as a Service (MLaaS): Cloud providers offer managed machine learning services that abstract away the complexities of infrastructure management. MLaaS platforms like Amazon SageMaker, Google Cloud AI Platform, or Microsoft Azure Machine Learning enable organizations to build, train, and deploy AI models at scale with minimal operational overhead.

d. Distributed Computing: Cloud platforms facilitate distributed computing, enabling organizations to distribute AI workloads across multiple instances or nodes. Services like Amazon EC2, Google Compute Engine, or Microsoft Azure Virtual Machines allow organizations to run AI computations in parallel, significantly reducing training and inference times.

e. Serverless Computing: Serverless computing models, such as AWS Lambda, Google Cloud Functions, or Azure Functions, enable organizations to execute code without provisioning or managing servers. This pay-per-execution model allows for cost-efficient and scalable execution of AI functions.

Edge Computing for Low Latency and Offline Capabilities:

Edge computing brings computing power closer to the data source, reducing network latency and enabling real-time decision-making. By processing AI workloads at the edge, organizations can leverage the following benefits:

a. Low Latency: Edge computing reduces the round-trip time between data generation and processing, enabling real-time or near real-time AI applications. This is particularly important in scenarios where low latency is critical, such as autonomous vehicles, industrial automation, or real-time video analytics.

b. Offline Capabilities: Edge computing allows AI models to operate offline or with limited connectivity. This is advantageous in scenarios where continuous internet connectivity is not guaranteed or where low latency is essential, such as in remote locations or IoT devices.

c. Data Localization and Privacy: Edge computing enables organizations to keep sensitive data localized and processed at the edge, minimizing data transfer and addressing privacy concerns. This is particularly important for organizations operating in industries with strict data regulations or for scenarios where data cannot leave specific geographical boundaries.

d. Bandwidth Optimization: By processing AI workloads at the edge, organizations can reduce the amount of data sent to the cloud, optimizing bandwidth usage and reducing operational costs. This is beneficial for applications that generate large amounts of data but only require a subset of that data to be transmitted to the cloud.

e. Enhanced Security: Edge computing can enhance security by processing AI workloads locally, reducing the attack surface and minimizing the risk of data breaches during data transmission. Additionally, edge devices can incorporate security measures like encryption and access control, further protecting sensitive AI data.

Hybrid Approaches:

Organizations can combine cloud computing and edge computing in a hybrid approach to leverage the advantages of both paradigms. This approach allows organizations to process AI workloads at the edge for low latency and offline capabilities while utilizing the cloud for scalability, centralized management, and advanced analytics. Hybrid approaches offer flexibility, enabling organizations to optimize their AI infrastructure based on specific use cases, network conditions, or compliance requirements.

Data Synchronization and Management:

When using both cloud computing and edge computing, organizations need to ensure efficient data synchronization and management. Data generated at the edge must be synchronized with the cloud for centralized storage, training, and analysis. Technologies like data replication, data caching, or data streaming can be utilized to manage data synchronization and ensure data integrity and consistency across edge and cloud environments.

Cost Considerations:

Organizations should consider the cost implications of leveraging cloud computing and edge computing for AI scalability. While cloud computing offers scalability and flexibility, organizations should be mindful of operational costs, data transfer fees, and ongoing resource management. Edge computing, on the other hand, may involve upfront costs for deploying edge devices and maintaining local infrastructure. A cost-benefit analysis should be conducted to determine the most cost-effective approach based on the organization's specific requirements and workload patterns.

In conclusion, leveraging cloud computing and edge computing provides organizations with powerful tools to enhance the scalability of their AI systems. Cloud computing offers virtually unlimited resources, elastic scaling, and managed services for AI workloads, while edge computing enables low latency, offline capabilities, data localization, and enhanced security. By adopting hybrid approaches, optimizing data synchronization, and considering cost implications, organizations can create a scalable and efficient AI infrastructure that meets their specific needs. The combination of cloud computing and edge computing empowers organizations to process AI workloads effectively, derive timely insights, and drive real-time decision-making.

CHAPTER 44: ENHANCING CUSTOMER INTERACTIONS WITH AI-POWERED CHATBOTS AND VIRTUAL ASSISTANTS

In today's digital age, organizations are increasingly leveraging Artificial Intelligence (AI) technologies to enhance customer interactions and deliver personalized experiences. AI-powered chatbots and virtual assistants are transforming the way businesses engage with customers by providing instant, intelligent, and efficient support. Let us explore how organizations can enhance customer interactions using AI-powered chatbots and virtual assistants:

24/7 Availability and Instant Responses:

AI-powered chatbots and virtual assistants are available round the clock, providing instant responses to customer inquiries. Unlike human agents, chatbots can handle multiple conversations simultaneously, ensuring prompt assistance and reducing wait times. This availability enhances customer satisfaction by offering timely support regardless of the time zone or business hours.

Personalized and Contextual Conversations:

AI-powered chatbots can gather and analyze customer data to deliver personalized interactions. By leveraging natural language processing (NLP) and machine learning techniques, chatbots can understand customer intents, preferences, and context, allowing for tailored conversations. Personalization creates a more engaging and customized experience for customers, increasing their satisfaction and loyalty.

Efficient Customer Support:

Chatbots and virtual assistants streamline customer support processes by automating routine inquiries and tasks. They can handle frequently asked questions, provide self-service options, or guide customers through step-by-step processes. By automating repetitive tasks, organizations can free up human agents' time, enabling them to focus on complex or high-value customer interactions.

Seamless Multichannel Support:

AI-powered chatbots can be integrated across multiple channels, including websites, messaging platforms, mobile apps, and social media. This multichannel support ensures a seamless and consistent customer experience across various touchpoints. Customers can initiate conversations through their preferred channels, and chatbots can maintain context and conversation history, allowing for continuity and convenience.

Natural Language Understanding and Language Support:

AI-powered chatbots leverage natural language understanding (NLU) to comprehend and respond to customer queries in a conversational manner. They can understand and interpret customer intents, handle different languages, and provide relevant and accurate responses. Language support is especially valuable for organizations with a global customer base, enabling them to serve customers in their preferred languages.

Intelligent Routing and Escalation:

AI-powered chatbots can intelligently route conversations based on customer needs. They can assess the complexity or urgency of inquiries and determine whether they can be handled by the chatbot or require human intervention. In cases that require human support, chatbots can seamlessly escalate conversations to human agents, providing a smooth transition and ensuring timely resolution.

Continuous Learning and Improvement:

AI-powered chatbots can learn from customer interactions and improve over time. They can analyze conversational data, identify trends, and update their knowledge base to provide more accurate and relevant responses. Machine learning algorithms enable chatbots to continuously enhance their language understanding, conversational abilities, and problem-solving skills, leading to improved customer interactions.

Integration with Backend Systems:

AI-powered chatbots can be integrated with backend systems, such as customer relationship management (CRM) platforms, knowledge bases, or inventory management systems. This integration allows chatbots to access real-time information, provide up-to-date product or service details, and offer personalized recommendations. Seamless integration enhances the efficiency and effectiveness of customer interactions.

Handling Complex Queries with Human Assistance:

While chatbots can handle many inquiries, there are instances where complex or sensitive issues require human intervention. AI-powered chatbots can seamlessly transfer conversations to human agents, providing them with relevant context and conversation history. This collaboration between chatbots and human agents ensures a smooth handover, reducing customer frustration and improving issue resolution.

Data-driven Insights and Analytics:

AI-powered chatbots generate valuable data and insights from customer interactions. Organizations can analyze this data to gain actionable insights into customer preferences, pain points, or frequently asked questions. These insights can inform business decisions, improve products or services, and drive continuous improvement in customer interactions.

Continuous Monitoring and Maintenance:

Organizations should continuously monitor chatbot performance, collect user feedback, and conduct regular maintenance. By monitoring conversations and analyzing user feedback, organizations can identify areas for improvement and address any issues promptly. Regular maintenance ensures that chatbots remain up-to-date, accurate, and aligned with changing customer needs.

In conclusion, AI-powered chatbots and virtual assistants offer significant potential to enhance customer interactions and deliver personalized experiences. Their 24/7 availability, instant responses, personalization capabilities, efficient customer support, seamless multichannel experience, natural language understanding, continuous learning, integration with backend systems, collaboration with human agents, data-driven insights, and continuous monitoring contribute to improved customer satisfaction, increased efficiency, and enhanced brand loyalty. By embracing AI-powered chatbots and virtual assistants, organizations can revolutionize their customer interactions, provide exceptional support, and gain a competitive edge in today's digital landscape.

CHAPTER 45: PERSONALIZING CUSTOMER EXPERIENCES THROUGH AI-DRIVEN INSIGHTS

In today's digital era, customer expectations are evolving, and personalized experiences have become a key differentiator for businesses. Leveraging Artificial Intelligence (AI) technologies, organizations can gain valuable insights from customer data to deliver tailored and relevant experiences. AI-driven insights enable organizations to understand customer preferences, anticipate needs, and personalize interactions at scale. Let us explore how organizations can personalize customer experiences through AI-driven insights:

Data Collection and Integration:

To personalize customer experiences, organizations need to collect and integrate customer data from various sources. This data may include demographic information, purchase history, browsing behavior, social media interactions, customer support interactions, and more. AI-driven technologies help organizations aggregate and unify this data, creating a comprehensive view of each customer.

Customer Segmentation and Profiling:

AI enables organizations to segment and profile customers based on common characteristics, preferences, or behaviors. By employing machine learning algorithms, organizations can identify distinct customer segments, such as high-value customers, frequent buyers, or first-time visitors. These segments form the foundation for personalization strategies, as organizations can tailor experiences based on specific segment attributes and preferences.

Predictive Analytics:

AI-driven predictive analytics helps organizations forecast customer behaviors, such as purchasing patterns, churn likelihood, or future preferences. By analyzing historical data, organizations can identify patterns, correlations, and trends that provide insights into customer behavior. Predictive analytics enables organizations to proactively anticipate customer needs, offer personalized recommendations, and tailor experiences accordingly.

Real-time Personalization:

With AI-driven insights, organizations can personalize customer experiences in real time. By analyzing customer interactions and behaviors in the moment, AI algorithms can dynamically adapt content, offers, or recommendations to match individual preferences. Real-time personalization allows organizations to deliver relevant and timely experiences, increasing engagement and conversion rates.

Recommendation Engines:

AI-powered recommendation engines leverage customer data and behavioral patterns to suggest relevant products, services, or content. By analyzing past purchases, browsing history, and customer preferences, organizations can present personalized recommendations to customers. These recommendations improve cross-selling and upselling opportunities, driving customer satisfaction and loyalty.

Dynamic Content Optimization:

AI enables dynamic content optimization, tailoring website or application content based on individual customer attributes or behavior. By leveraging

AI algorithms, organizations can present personalized product recommendations, customized messages, or targeted offers to each customer. This level of personalization enhances engagement, conversion rates, and customer satisfaction.

Chatbots and Virtual Assistants:

AI-powered chatbots and virtual assistants can provide personalized assistance and support to customers. By leveraging natural language processing and machine learning algorithms, chatbots can understand customer queries, provide relevant responses, and offer personalized recommendations. Chatbots create conversational experiences that mimic human interactions, delivering personalized support at scale.

Sentiment Analysis:

AI-driven sentiment analysis enables organizations to understand customer sentiments and emotions from various channels, such as social media, customer reviews, or support interactions. By analyzing text or speech data, organizations can gauge customer satisfaction, identify issues, and take proactive measures to address concerns. Sentiment analysis helps personalize responses and improve customer sentiment.

Multichannel Personalization:

AI enables organizations to personalize customer experiences across multiple channels, including websites, mobile applications, email marketing, social media, and more. By leveraging AI-driven insights, organizations can ensure consistent and personalized interactions regardless of the customer touchpoint. This cohesive multichannel personalization enhances the overall customer journey and strengthens brand loyalty.

A/B Testing and Optimization:

AI facilitates A/B testing and optimization of personalized experiences. Organizations can use AI algorithms to analyze customer responses and behaviors to different variations of personalized content or offers. This iterative testing process allows organizations to refine their personalization strategies and optimize customer experiences for maximum impact.

Privacy and Data Ethics:

Organizations must prioritize privacy and data ethics when leveraging AI-driven insights for personalization. They should ensure compliance with data protection regulations, obtain appropriate consent for data usage, and establish robust security measures to protect customer data. Transparency and responsible data handling practices build trust and confidence among customers.

In conclusion, personalizing customer experiences through AI-driven insights empowers organizations to understand customer preferences, anticipate needs, and deliver tailored interactions. By leveraging data collection, customer segmentation, predictive analytics, real-time personalization, recommendation engines, dynamic content optimization, chatbots, sentiment analysis, multichannel personalization, A/B testing, and privacy considerations, organizations can create engaging and memorable customer experiences. Personalization strengthens customer relationships, drives customer satisfaction, increases loyalty, and ultimately contributes to business growth and success in today's highly competitive marketplace.

CHAPTER 46: LEVERAGING AI FOR PREDICTIVE ANALYTICS AND CUSTOMER SEGMENTATION

In today's data-driven business landscape, organizations are turning to Artificial Intelligence (AI) to extract meaningful insights from vast amounts of data. Two powerful applications of AI in this context are predictive analytics and customer segmentation. By leveraging AI algorithms and techniques, organizations can gain a deeper understanding of their customers, identify patterns and trends, and make data-driven decisions. Let us explore how organizations can effectively leverage AI for predictive analytics and customer segmentation:

Predictive Analytics:

Predictive analytics involves using historical data, statistical models, and machine learning algorithms to make predictions about future events or outcomes. AI plays a crucial role in predictive analytics by enabling organizations to:

a. Data Collection and Integration: AI technologies facilitate the collection and integration of diverse data sources, including structured and unstructured data. This data may include customer interactions, transaction history, social media activity, website behavior, and more. AI algorithms can process and analyze this data to identify patterns and trends.

b. Data Preprocessing and Feature Engineering: Before applying predictive models, AI helps in data preprocessing and feature engineering. It involves cleaning, transforming, and normalizing the data, as well as selecting and engineering relevant features. AI techniques automate these processes, reducing the manual effort required and enhancing data quality.

c. Predictive Modeling: AI algorithms, such as regression, decision trees, random forests, or neural networks, can be applied to build predictive models. These models can analyze historical data and identify relationships between variables to predict future outcomes. Predictive models can be used for a variety of applications, such as sales forecasting, demand prediction, churn prediction, or fraud detection.

d. Model Evaluation and Refinement: AI enables organizations to evaluate the performance of predictive models using various metrics like accuracy, precision, recall, or F1-score. By iteratively refining the models and incorporating new data, organizations can improve their predictive accuracy over time.

e. Real-time Predictions: AI enables organizations to make real-time predictions by deploying predictive models in production environments. This capability allows organizations to respond quickly to changing market conditions, customer needs, or emerging trends. Real-time predictions are particularly valuable in dynamic industries such as e-commerce, finance, or healthcare.

f. Anomaly Detection: AI algorithms can identify anomalies or outliers in data, which can be indicative of unusual or potentially fraudulent behavior. Anomaly detection helps organizations detect and mitigate risks, such as fraudulent transactions, network intrusions, or equipment failures, before they cause significant damage.

Customer Segmentation:

Customer segmentation involves dividing a customer base into distinct groups based on shared characteristics, behaviors, or preferences. AI can significantly enhance customer segmentation efforts by:

a. Data-driven Segmentation: AI leverages machine learning algorithms to automatically identify patterns and group customers based on their similarities. By analyzing various attributes like demographic information, purchase history, browsing behavior, or social media activity, AI algorithms can cluster customers into segments without relying on predefined rules or assumptions.

b. Micro-Segmentation: AI allows organizations to perform micro-segmentation, where customers are divided into fine-grained segments based on highly specific criteria. This level of segmentation enables organizations to deliver personalized marketing campaigns, offers, or recommendations to each segment, leading to higher engagement and conversion rates.

c. Dynamic Segmentation: AI enables organizations to dynamically update customer segments in real time as new data becomes available. By continuously analyzing customer behavior and preferences, organizations can adapt their segmentation strategies to reflect evolving customer needs and preferences.

d. Predictive Segmentation: AI algorithms can predict the likelihood of customers belonging to different segments based on their characteristics or behaviors. By leveraging predictive segmentation, organizations can identify potential target segments for new products, tailor marketing messages, or personalize customer experiences.

e. Lifetime Value Analysis: AI algorithms can analyze customer behavior and historical data to predict customer lifetime value. By understanding the value that each customer brings to the organization over their entire relationship, organizations can prioritize their marketing efforts, allocate resources effectively, and design customer retention strategies.

f. Personalization and Targeted Marketing: Customer segmentation powered by AI enables organizations to deliver personalized marketing messages, offers, and recommendations to specific customer segments. By tailoring marketing campaigns to each segment's preferences and interests, organizations can enhance customer engagement, conversion rates, and overall customer satisfaction.

In conclusion, leveraging AI for predictive analytics and customer segmentation provides organizations with powerful tools to gain actionable insights from their data. Through AI-enabled data collection, preprocessing, predictive modeling, real-time predictions, anomaly detection, and AI-driven customer segmentation, organizations can make data-driven decisions, personalize customer experiences, and optimize marketing strategies. By harnessing the power of AI, organizations can gain a competitive advantage, improve customer satisfaction, and drive business growth in today's data-driven business landscape.

CHAPTER 47: STAYING INFORMED ON AI TRENDS AND EMERGING TECHNOLOGIES

Artificial Intelligence (AI) is a rapidly evolving field with constant advancements and new technologies emerging regularly. To stay ahead of the curve and harness the full potential of AI, it is crucial for organizations and professionals to stay informed about the latest AI trends and emerging technologies. Let us explore why staying informed is important and discuss effective strategies for staying updated on AI trends and emerging technologies:

Importance of Staying Informed:

Competitive Advantage: By staying informed on AI trends and emerging technologies, organizations can gain a competitive edge. They can identify innovative solutions, leverage new AI capabilities, and apply them to improve processes, products, and customer experiences. Staying ahead of the competition enables organizations to be proactive, innovative, and agile in their AI strategies.

Strategic Decision Making: Staying informed about AI trends helps organizations make informed and strategic decisions. They can assess the relevance and potential impact of emerging technologies on their business models, operational processes, and customer engagement. With up-to-date knowledge, organizations can make better decisions about investments, partnerships, and resource allocation related to AI initiatives.

Business Opportunities: Being aware of AI trends and emerging technologies opens doors to new business opportunities. Organizations can identify potential applications of AI in their industry, explore new markets, and develop innovative AI-driven products or services. Staying informed allows organizations to align their strategies with emerging market demands and seize opportunities for growth and expansion.

Talent Acquisition and Retention: In the competitive AI landscape, skilled professionals are in high demand. By staying informed about AI trends, organizations can understand the skills, knowledge, and expertise required in the industry. This knowledge helps in attracting and retaining top talent, building teams with the right skillsets, and fostering a culture of innovation and learning.

Strategies for Staying Informed:

Engage in Continuous Learning: AI is a rapidly evolving field, and continuous learning is essential to stay informed. Professionals should invest time in reading industry publications, research papers, and academic journals to understand the latest AI advancements. Online learning platforms, webinars, conferences, and workshops offer opportunities to acquire new knowledge, upskill, and stay updated on AI trends.

Follow Thought Leaders and Influencers: Identify thought leaders, experts, and influencers in the AI field and follow their work. These individuals often share valuable insights, research findings, and opinions on AI trends and emerging technologies. Engaging with their content through blogs, podcasts, social media, or attending their presentations can provide valuable insights and fresh perspectives.

Join AI Communities and Forums: Participate in AI communities, online forums, and discussion groups to connect with peers, share knowledge, and discuss AI trends. Platforms like GitHub, Kaggle, or Stack Overflow provide opportunities to collaborate, learn from others, and stay updated on the latest developments in AI. Engaging in conversations and sharing experiences with like-minded professionals helps in staying informed and building a strong network.

Collaborate with Academia and Research Institutions: Partnering with academic institutions, research labs, and universities can provide access to cutting-edge AI research and emerging technologies. Collaborating on research projects, attending seminars, or participating in industry-academia events fosters knowledge exchange and keeps organizations informed about the latest breakthroughs in AI.

Monitor Industry News and Publications: Regularly follow industry news, publications, and AI-focused websites to stay updated on the latest trends. Publications like AI Magazine, MIT Technology Review, Forbes AI, or AI Business offer insights into AI applications, market trends, and emerging technologies. Subscribing to newsletters, RSS feeds, or setting up Google alerts can provide curated updates delivered directly to your inbox.

Network and Attend AI Conferences and Events: Attend AI conferences, industry events, and meetups to connect with industry leaders, professionals, and experts. These events provide opportunities to learn from keynote speakers, participate in panel discussions, and engage in networking activities. Attending conferences keeps organizations at the forefront of AI trends and provides exposure to real-world use cases and success stories.

Foster Partnerships and Collaborations: Establish partnerships with AI technology providers, startups, and research organizations. Collaborating with external entities allows organizations to access expertise, gain insights into emerging technologies, and explore innovative AI solutions. Partnerships enable organizations to stay informed about the latest AI trends and potentially influence the direction of AI development.

In conclusion, staying informed on AI trends and emerging technologies is crucial for organizations and professionals seeking to leverage AI effectively. By understanding the potential impact of AI on their industry, embracing continuous learning, following thought leaders, engaging in communities, collaborating with academia, monitoring industry news, attending conferences, and fostering partnerships, organizations can navigate the evolving AI landscape with confidence, make informed decisions, and capitalize on new opportunities. Staying informed ensures that organizations are well-prepared to harness the transformative power of AI in a rapidly changing business environment.

CHAPTER 48: ADAPTING TO REGULATORY CHANGES AND INDUSTRY STANDARDS IN THE ERA OF AI

The rapid advancement of Artificial Intelligence (AI) technologies brings forth new challenges and considerations related to regulatory frameworks and industry standards. As AI continues to evolve and integrate into various sectors, it is crucial for organizations to proactively adapt to regulatory changes and comply with industry standards. Let us explore why adapting to regulatory changes and industry standards is important and discuss effective strategies for ensuring compliance in the AI landscape:

Importance of Adapting to Regulatory Changes and Industry Standards:

Legal Compliance: Adhering to regulatory changes is essential to ensure legal compliance. Governments and regulatory bodies are actively working to develop frameworks that address ethical concerns, data protection, privacy, bias, fairness, transparency, and accountability in AI systems. Compliance with these regulations helps organizations avoid legal penalties, reputational damage, and potential legal disputes.

Risk Mitigation: Adapting to regulatory changes and industry standards mitigates potential risks associated with AI deployments. Regulations are designed to protect individuals, sensitive data, and prevent AI systems from causing harm. By adhering to these regulations, organizations can minimize risks related to security breaches, data misuse, biased algorithms, or unintended consequences, thereby safeguarding their reputation and customer trust.

Enhanced Trust and Transparency: Compliance with regulatory changes and industry standards builds trust among customers, stakeholders, and the public. Demonstrating a commitment to ethical AI practices, data protection, and responsible use of AI technologies fosters transparency and instills confidence in the organization's AI-driven solutions. Trust is essential for widespread adoption of AI and building long-term relationships with customers.

Competitive Advantage: Adapting to regulatory changes and industry standards can provide a competitive edge. Organizations that are proactive in complying with regulations position themselves as responsible and trustworthy partners, differentiating themselves from competitors. Compliance enhances an organization's reputation and can attract customers who prioritize ethical practices and data protection.

Strategies for Adapting to Regulatory Changes and Industry Standards:

Stay Informed and Engage in Policy Discussions: Stay updated on regulatory developments and actively engage in policy discussions related to AI. Monitor government initiatives, regulatory bodies, and industry associations involved in shaping AI regulations. Participate in public consultations, share expertise, and provide input to ensure that regulations align with the practical considerations of AI implementation.

Conduct Regulatory Impact Assessments: Evaluate the impact of regulatory changes on existing AI systems and future projects. Conducting regulatory impact assessments helps organizations identify potential compliance gaps, ensure alignment with legal requirements, and plan for necessary modifications or adjustments. This assessment includes reviewing data protection practices, algorithmic fairness, explainability, and compliance with specific industry regulations.

Implement Ethical AI Frameworks: Develop and implement internal ethical AI frameworks that align with regulatory requirements and industry best practices. These frameworks should include guidelines for responsible data collection and use, algorithmic fairness, transparency, explainability, and accountability. Ethical AI frameworks provide a foundation for ensuring compliance and guiding ethical decision-making throughout the AI development lifecycle.

Enhance Data Governance and Privacy Practices: Strengthen data governance and privacy practices to ensure compliance with data protection regulations. Implement robust data management processes, secure data storage, and implement privacy-enhancing techniques such as anonymization and encryption. Ensure that data collection, storage, and processing activities are aligned with privacy laws and user consent requirements.

Integrate Privacy by Design: Incorporate privacy by design principles into AI systems from the early stages of development. Privacy by design involves considering privacy and data protection implications throughout the entire AI system's lifecycle. It includes conducting privacy impact assessments, implementing privacy-enhancing technologies, and applying data minimization and purpose limitation principles.

Establish Ethical Review Boards or Committees: Create internal review boards or committees to evaluate and monitor the ethical implications of AI systems. These boards can provide guidance on regulatory compliance, algorithmic fairness, privacy concerns, and ethical decision-making. They ensure that AI deployments align with ethical guidelines, industry standards, and regulatory requirements.

Collaborate with Regulatory Authorities and Industry Bodies: Collaborate with regulatory authorities, industry associations, and standard-setting bodies to understand evolving regulations, share best practices, and shape industry standards. Engage in dialogue with these entities to provide feedback, share insights, and contribute to the development of responsible AI practices.

Invest in Employee Training and Awareness: Provide regular training and awareness programs to employees on AI-related regulations, ethical considerations, and industry standards. Equip employees with the knowledge and skills necessary to comply with regulations and adhere to ethical practices when developing and deploying AI systems.

Conduct Independent Audits and Assessments: Periodically conduct independent audits and assessments to evaluate compliance with regulatory requirements and industry standards. External audits provide objective evaluations of an organization's AI systems, data protection practices, and adherence to ethical guidelines. These audits help identify areas for improvement, validate compliance efforts, and ensure ongoing regulatory compliance.

Monitor International and Cross-Border Regulations: Stay informed about international regulations and cross-border considerations, particularly if the organization operates in multiple jurisdictions. Understand the legal obligations and compliance requirements in each relevant jurisdiction to ensure consistency in AI practices across different regions.

In conclusion, adapting to regulatory changes and industry standards is vital for organizations embracing AI technologies. By ensuring legal compliance, mitigating risks, building trust, and gaining a competitive advantage, organizations can navigate the evolving regulatory landscape while fostering ethical AI practices. By staying informed, engaging in policy discussions, conducting impact assessments, implementing ethical frameworks, enhancing data governance, collaborating with regulatory authorities, investing in employee training, conducting audits, and monitoring international regulations, organizations can effectively adapt to regulatory changes and drive responsible AI adoption.

CHAPTER 49: CONTINUOUSLY REFINING AND EVOLVING YOUR AI STRATEGY FOR LONG-TERM SUCCESS

As Artificial Intelligence (AI) continues to advance and shape various industries, organizations must recognize that developing an AI strategy is not a one-time endeavor. To ensure long-term success, organizations need to continuously refine and evolve their AI strategy. This iterative approach allows organizations to adapt to changing business needs, emerging technologies, and evolving market dynamics. Let us explore why continuous refinement of the AI strategy is essential and discuss effective strategies for its evolution:

Importance of Continuous Refinement:

Keep Pace with Technological Advancements: AI is a rapidly evolving field, with new technologies, algorithms, and frameworks emerging regularly. Continuous refinement of the AI strategy enables organizations to leverage these advancements and stay at the forefront of technological innovation. By staying up to date with the latest AI developments, organizations can enhance their competitiveness and drive innovation.

Adapt to Changing Business Landscape: Business needs and market dynamics evolve over time. Continuous refinement of the AI strategy ensures that organizations align their AI initiatives with changing business objectives. It allows them to identify new use cases, prioritize projects based on strategic goals, and realign resources as needed. Adapting to the changing business landscape enables organizations to remain agile and responsive to market demands.

Address Lessons Learned: Through the implementation of AI projects, organizations gain valuable insights and learn from their experiences. Continuous refinement of the AI strategy enables organizations to incorporate these lessons learned into future initiatives. By identifying successes, challenges, and areas for improvement, organizations can optimize their AI strategy and drive better outcomes in subsequent projects.

Optimize Resource Allocation: Continuous refinement allows organizations to optimize resource allocation for AI initiatives. By evaluating the performance and impact of ongoing projects, organizations can determine resource requirements, prioritize investments, and allocate budgets effectively. This optimization ensures that resources are directed towards the most promising AI projects that align with business objectives and deliver maximum value.

Strategies for Evolving the AI Strategy:

Establish a Feedback Loop: Implement a feedback mechanism to capture insights and feedback from stakeholders, end-users, and project teams. Regularly solicit input on AI initiatives, their impact, and potential areas for improvement. This feedback loop helps identify gaps, address concerns, and generate ideas for enhancing the AI strategy.

Monitor Key Performance Indicators (KPIs): Define and monitor KPIs to assess the effectiveness and impact of AI initiatives. Regularly track and analyze performance metrics related to project outcomes, operational efficiency, customer satisfaction, and business value. This data-driven approach enables organizations to evaluate the success of their AI projects and make data-backed decisions for refining the AI strategy.

Foster Cross-functional Collaboration: Encourage collaboration between business units, IT teams, data scientists, and other stakeholders involved in AI initiatives. By fostering a collaborative environment, organizations can leverage diverse perspectives and expertise to refine the AI strategy. Collaborative efforts help identify synergies, align AI initiatives with business goals, and ensure that the AI strategy reflects the needs of the entire organization.

Embrace an Agile Approach: Apply agile methodologies to AI projects to enable flexibility and iterative development. Agile practices such as scrum or Kanban allow organizations to break down complex AI initiatives into smaller, manageable tasks. This iterative approach facilitates continuous feedback, promotes adaptability, and enables organizations to respond to evolving requirements and emerging opportunities.

Stay Informed on AI Trends: Stay updated on the latest AI trends, emerging technologies, and industry best practices. Regularly monitor research publications, attend conferences, engage with AI communities, and collaborate with experts to gain insights into new AI advancements. This knowledge helps organizations identify opportunities for innovation, refine their AI strategy, and make informed decisions about adopting new technologies.

Invest in Continuous Learning and Development: Encourage continuous learning and professional development for employees involved in AI initiatives. Provide training programs, workshops, and resources to enhance technical skills, domain knowledge, and understanding of AI ethics. Building a culture of continuous learning ensures that the organization's workforce is equipped with the necessary skills to drive the evolution of the AI strategy.

Emphasize Ethical Considerations: As AI applications become more prevalent, ethical considerations play a crucial role in the evolution of the

AI strategy. Regularly reassess ethical guidelines, privacy policies, and data governance practices to ensure compliance with evolving regulations and industry standards. Incorporate ethical considerations into the AI strategy to build trust, maintain transparency, and uphold ethical principles in AI-driven initiatives.

Embrace Experimentation and Innovation: Encourage experimentation and innovation within the organization to foster a culture of continuous improvement. Allocate resources for exploring new AI technologies, piloting projects, and testing new approaches. Embracing experimentation allows organizations to explore new possibilities, uncover hidden opportunities, and discover novel applications of AI that can shape the future of the business.

In conclusion, continuously refining and evolving the AI strategy is essential for organizations to achieve long-term success in the rapidly changing AI landscape. By keeping pace with technological advancements, adapting to the changing business landscape, addressing lessons learned, optimizing resource allocation, and embracing feedback, collaboration, agility, and continuous learning, organizations can refine their AI strategy to drive innovation, deliver business value, and maintain a competitive advantage.

CHAPTER 50: IDENTIFYING AND ADDRESSING COMMON ROADBLOCKS IN AI PROJECTS

Artificial Intelligence (AI) projects have the potential to revolutionize businesses, but they also come with their fair share of challenges and roadblocks. Identifying and addressing these roadblocks is crucial for the successful implementation of AI projects. By understanding the common obstacles that organizations face during AI initiatives and implementing strategies to overcome them, organizations can enhance their chances of achieving desired outcomes. Let us explore some of the common roadblocks in AI projects and discuss effective approaches to address them:

Lack of Data Quality and Accessibility:

One of the primary roadblocks in AI projects is the availability and quality of data. Insufficient or poor-quality data can hinder the training and performance of AI models. To address this roadblock, organizations should:

Perform a comprehensive data audit: Assess the quality, completeness, and relevance of available data. Identify data gaps and take steps to fill them.

Implement data cleansing and preprocessing: Utilize data cleaning techniques to eliminate errors, outliers, and inconsistencies. Preprocess data to make it suitable for AI model training.

Invest in data collection and enrichment: If data is insufficient, consider collecting additional data or enriching existing data through external sources or partnerships.

Lack of AI Expertise and Talent:

AI projects require skilled professionals who possess expertise in areas such as data science, machine learning, and AI algorithms. However, there is often a shortage of AI talent. To address this roadblock:

Build a multidisciplinary team: Assemble a team with diverse skills, including data scientists, AI engineers, domain experts, and project managers. Foster collaboration and knowledge-sharing within the team.

Invest in training and upskilling: Provide training programs and professional development opportunities to existing employees to enhance their AI skills. Encourage continuous learning and stay updated with the latest AI techniques and methodologies.

Collaborate with external experts: Consider partnering with AI consultants, universities, or research institutions to leverage their expertise and bridge the talent gap.

Complexity of AI Algorithms and Models:

AI algorithms and models can be complex and require significant computational resources. Handling the complexity can be a roadblock for organizations. To address this challenge:

Start with simpler models: Begin with simpler algorithms and models to gain familiarity and build a foundation. Gradually progress to more advanced techniques as the organization's AI capabilities mature.

Leverage pre-trained models: Utilize pre-trained models or frameworks available in the AI community to reduce development complexity and accelerate project timelines.

Invest in scalable infrastructure: Ensure that the organization has the necessary computational resources, such as cloud computing or high-performance computing, to handle the computational requirements of AI algorithms.

Ethical and Regulatory Considerations:

Ethical considerations, privacy concerns, and compliance with regulations are crucial roadblocks that organizations must navigate during AI projects. To address these challenges:

Establish an ethics framework: Develop guidelines and policies that address ethical considerations, fairness, transparency, and accountability in AI projects. Consider the impact of AI on privacy, bias, and discrimination.

Stay updated with regulations: Continuously monitor regulatory requirements related to data protection, privacy, and AI-specific regulations. Adapt AI projects to comply with applicable laws and regulations.

Implement privacy-preserving techniques: Utilize techniques such as differential privacy, secure multi-party computation, or federated learning to protect sensitive data and ensure privacy compliance.

Resistance to Change and Organizational Culture:

Resistance to change and a lack of a supportive organizational culture can hinder the successful implementation of AI projects. To address this roadblock:

Foster a culture of innovation: Create an environment that encourages experimentation, risk-taking, and learning. Emphasize the potential benefits of AI and provide incentives for employees to adopt and embrace AI initiatives.

Communicate the value proposition: Clearly communicate the goals, benefits, and potential impact of AI projects to stakeholders at all levels. Demonstrate how AI can contribute to the organization's strategic objectives and drive positive outcomes.

Provide change management support: Offer training, resources, and support to help employees adapt to new AI systems and processes. Address concerns, clarify misconceptions, and provide guidance to ensure a smooth transition.

Lack of Scalability and Integration:

Ensuring that AI solutions can scale and seamlessly integrate with existing systems and processes can be a significant roadblock. To address this challenge:

Design for scalability: Consider scalability from the early stages of AI project planning. Develop modular and flexible architectures that can accommodate future growth and increasing demands.

Prioritize interoperability: Choose AI tools and platforms that support integration with existing systems and technologies. Invest in APIs, data connectors, and standard protocols to facilitate seamless data exchange and interoperability.

Conduct comprehensive testing and validation: Thoroughly test AI systems for scalability, reliability, and performance. Validate the integration of AI solutions with existing systems to ensure smooth operation and minimal disruption.

In conclusion, identifying and addressing common roadblocks in AI projects is essential for achieving successful outcomes. By addressing challenges related to data quality, talent, algorithm complexity, ethics, organizational culture, scalability, and integration, organizations can navigate the complexities of AI initiatives and unlock the transformative potential of AI. By implementing effective strategies and adopting a proactive and adaptable approach, organizations can overcome roadblocks and pave the way for successful AI projects.

CHAPTER 51: ENSURING STAKEHOLDER BUY-IN AND SUPPORT IN AI PROJECTS

The success of AI projects heavily relies on obtaining buy-in and support from key stakeholders within an organization. Stakeholder buy-in ensures that AI initiatives receive the necessary resources, support, and collaboration to thrive. It also helps create a positive organizational culture that embraces AI technologies and fosters innovation. Let us explore why stakeholder buy-in is crucial and discuss effective strategies to ensure buy-in and support for AI projects:

Importance of Stakeholder Buy-In:

Resource Allocation: Stakeholder buy-in is essential for securing the necessary resources, including budget, personnel, and infrastructure, to execute AI projects successfully. When stakeholders understand the potential benefits and value of AI, they are more likely to allocate the required resources to support the initiative.

Cross-Functional Collaboration: AI projects often involve multiple teams and departments within an organization. Stakeholder buy-in promotes collaboration and facilitates the exchange of knowledge, expertise, and resources across different functions. It helps break down silos, encourages cross-functional communication, and ensures alignment of AI initiatives with broader organizational goals.

Decision-Making Support: Stakeholder buy-in provides a strong foundation for decision-making. When stakeholders are engaged and supportive, they actively participate in discussions, provide insights, and contribute to the decision-making process. Their involvement helps validate the project's direction, enhances decision quality, and increases the likelihood of successful outcomes.

Change Management: AI projects often introduce changes to existing processes, workflows, and roles within the organization. Stakeholder buy-in helps manage the change effectively by creating a sense of ownership, reducing resistance, and fostering a smooth transition. Engaged stakeholders act as change champions, promoting acceptance and adoption of AI initiatives among employees.

Strategies to Ensure Stakeholder Buy-In and Support:

Communication and Education:

Effectively communicate the vision, goals, and potential benefits of AI projects to stakeholders. Tailor the message to address the specific interests and concerns of each stakeholder group. Use clear and concise language, avoiding technical jargon, to ensure understanding across all levels of the organization. Provide educational resources, such as workshops, training sessions, and documentation, to increase stakeholders' knowledge and confidence in AI technologies.

Early Involvement and Collaboration:

Involve stakeholders early in the AI project lifecycle. Seek their input during the planning and scoping stages to ensure their perspectives and requirements are considered. Encourage collaboration and active participation through workshops, brainstorming sessions, and cross-functional meetings. Engage stakeholders in shaping the project scope, identifying use cases, and setting realistic expectations. Foster an environment that values their contributions and empowers them to take ownership of the project.

Demonstrate Value and Success Stories:

Illustrate the value of AI through concrete examples and success stories. Showcase how AI can solve specific business challenges, improve operational efficiency, enhance customer experiences, or drive revenue growth. Provide tangible evidence of AI's impact by sharing case studies, metrics, and testimonials from similar projects. Demonstrating the value and potential return on investment helps stakeholders understand the significance of AI initiatives and strengthens their support.

Address Concerns and Risks:

Proactively address stakeholders' concerns and risks associated with AI projects. Conduct risk assessments, communicate mitigation strategies, and provide transparency regarding data privacy, security, and ethical considerations. Address potential job displacement concerns by emphasizing the augmentation role of AI and highlighting opportunities for upskilling and reskilling employees. Engage stakeholders in open and honest discussions to build trust, alleviate fears, and address any misconceptions.

Build a Coalition of AI Advocates:

Identify influential stakeholders who are supportive of AI and can serve as advocates within the organization. Engage these advocates in championing the benefits of AI, addressing resistance, and sharing their positive experiences. Leverage their influence to drive broader stakeholder buy-in and support. Consider establishing an AI governance committee or advisory board consisting of diverse stakeholders to provide ongoing guidance and oversight.

Track and Communicate Progress:

Regularly communicate the progress, milestones, and achievements of AI projects to stakeholders. Provide updates on key performance indicators, success metrics, and lessons learned. Celebrate successes and acknowledge the contributions of stakeholders. This transparent communication builds trust, reinforces stakeholders' commitment, and demonstrates the project's impact on the organization's goals.

Continuous Engagement and Feedback:

Maintain ongoing engagement with stakeholders throughout the project lifecycle. Seek their feedback, suggestions, and concerns at different stages of the project. Actively listen to their input and incorporate valuable insights into decision-making. This continuous engagement creates a sense of ownership and collaboration, making stakeholders feel valued and invested in the project's success.

In conclusion, ensuring stakeholder buy-in and support is vital for the successful execution of AI projects. By effectively communicating the project vision, involving stakeholders early, demonstrating value, addressing concerns, building coalitions of advocates, tracking progress, and maintaining continuous engagement, organizations can secure the necessary support and collaboration to drive AI initiatives forward. Establishing a culture that embraces AI technologies and fosters innovation becomes possible when stakeholders are aligned and committed to leveraging AI's potential for transformative impact.

CHAPTER 52: MANAGING ORGANIZATIONAL CHANGE DURING AI ADOPTION

Introducing Artificial Intelligence (AI) into an organization brings about significant technological and operational changes. Successfully navigating this change is essential for ensuring a smooth and effective AI adoption process. Managing organizational change during AI adoption involves addressing the concerns and resistance of employees, aligning the organization's culture with AI principles, providing adequate training and support, and fostering a culture of continuous learning and adaptability. Let us explore some key strategies for managing organizational change during AI adoption:

Create a Vision and Communicate:

Develop a clear vision for AI adoption that aligns with the organization's strategic goals. Communicate this vision to employees and stakeholders to foster understanding and gain their support. Explain how AI can bring positive changes, improve productivity, and enhance the organization's competitiveness. Emphasize the benefits and opportunities that AI adoption can bring, such as increased efficiency, improved decision-making, and new growth avenues.

Address Employee Concerns and Fears:

Change can often create resistance and anxiety among employees. Address their concerns by providing open and transparent communication. Explain the impact of AI on their roles and responsibilities, and highlight the potential for new opportunities and skill development. Create forums for dialogue and actively listen to employee feedback. Address misconceptions and provide reassurance that AI is meant to augment and support employees, rather than replace them.

Provide Training and Support:

Offer comprehensive training programs to employees to build their AI-related skills and knowledge. Provide both technical training on AI technologies and non-technical training on AI ethics, implications, and best practices. Encourage employees to participate in workshops, seminars, and online courses. Support them in obtaining relevant certifications. Additionally, establish support mechanisms such as AI help desks or dedicated AI champions who can provide guidance and answer questions.

Foster Collaboration and Cross-Functional Teams:

Promote collaboration and teamwork across different departments and functions. Encourage employees to work together to explore AI opportunities and share their expertise. Create cross-functional teams that bring together employees from different areas of the organization to collaborate on AI initiatives. Foster a culture of sharing ideas and knowledge, enabling employees to learn from each other and leverage collective intelligence.

Lead by Example:

Leadership plays a critical role in managing organizational change during AI adoption. Leaders should lead by example, showcasing their own commitment to AI initiatives and embracing AI technologies themselves. Demonstrate the value of AI through pilot projects and success stories. Involve leaders in the AI adoption process and encourage their active participation. Their visible support and enthusiasm will inspire and motivate employees to embrace AI.

Empower Employees and Involve Them in Decision-Making:

Empower employees by involving them in the decision-making process. Seek their input and ideas for AI adoption, and involve them in the planning and implementation stages. This fosters a sense of ownership and increases their engagement and commitment to the change process. Encourage employees to experiment with AI technologies, propose innovative ideas, and contribute to the organization's AI roadmap.

Monitor Progress and Celebrate Achievements:

Regularly monitor and evaluate the progress of AI adoption. Establish key performance indicators (KPIs) to measure the impact of AI initiatives. Celebrate achievements and recognize employees' efforts and contributions. Highlight success stories and share the positive outcomes of AI adoption to motivate and inspire others.

Continuously Learn and Adapt:

AI technologies and their applications continue to evolve rapidly. Encourage a culture of continuous learning and adaptation. Stay abreast of the latest developments in AI and share knowledge and insights with employees. Foster a mindset of experimentation and learning from failures. Encourage employees to provide feedback, share lessons learned, and suggest improvements to the AI adoption process.

Evaluate and Adjust:

Regularly evaluate the effectiveness of AI adoption initiatives and adjust strategies as needed. Monitor employee satisfaction, adoption rates, and the impact of AI on business outcomes. Identify any challenges or roadblocks and take corrective actions. Be flexible and adaptive in refining the AI adoption strategy based on the organization's needs and evolving industry trends.

In conclusion, managing organizational change during AI adoption requires a thoughtful and comprehensive approach. By creating a compelling vision, addressing employee concerns, providing training and support, fostering collaboration, leading by example, empowering employees, monitoring progress, and fostering a culture of continuous learning, organizations can effectively manage the change process and maximize the benefits of AI adoption. Successful change management ensures a smooth transition, minimizes resistance, and sets the foundation for a successful AI-powered future.

CHAPTER 53: ENHANCING DATA-DRIVEN DECISION-MAKING WITH AI INSIGHTS

In today's data-driven world, organizations are increasingly turning to Artificial Intelligence (AI) to extract valuable insights from vast amounts of data. AI technologies, such as machine learning and predictive analytics, offer the potential to transform data into actionable intelligence, enabling more informed and effective decision-making. Let us explore how AI insights enhance data-driven decision-making and the key benefits organizations can expect from leveraging AI in this context:

Uncovering Patterns and Trends:

AI algorithms excel at analyzing large volumes of data, identifying patterns, and uncovering hidden trends that may not be apparent to human analysts. By applying machine learning techniques to diverse datasets, AI can reveal correlations, causations, and anomalies that are crucial for making data-driven decisions. These insights can provide a deeper understanding of customer behavior, market dynamics, operational processes, and other factors that impact business outcomes.

Predictive Analytics and Forecasting:

AI enables organizations to move beyond descriptive analytics and embrace predictive analytics. By leveraging historical data and applying machine learning algorithms, AI can forecast future trends, behaviors, and outcomes. Predictive analytics enables organizations to anticipate customer needs, optimize resource allocation, mitigate risks, and make proactive decisions. It empowers businesses to stay ahead of the competition and seize opportunities in a dynamic marketplace.

Real-Time Insights for Timely Decision-Making:

Traditional data analysis methods often involve manual data processing, which can be time-consuming and hinder real-time decision-making. AI-powered analytics solutions offer the capability to process and analyze data in real-time, enabling organizations to make timely and agile decisions. By accessing real-time insights, businesses can respond swiftly to changing market conditions, customer preferences, or emerging opportunities, gaining a competitive edge.

Enhanced Accuracy and Reduced Bias:

AI algorithms can reduce human biases and subjective interpretations when making data-driven decisions. AI-based systems analyze data objectively, focusing on patterns and correlations without the influence of personal biases. This can lead to more accurate and consistent decision-making, minimizing the risks associated with human error and cognitive biases. AI can help organizations make data-driven decisions based on objective insights, improving the overall quality and reliability of decision-making processes.

Automated Data Processing and Analysis:

AI technologies automate the processing and analysis of large datasets, significantly reducing the time and effort required for data preparation and analysis. This automation allows organizations to handle and analyze massive volumes of data more efficiently, leading to faster decision-making processes. By automating repetitive tasks, AI frees up valuable human resources to focus on more strategic and value-added activities, driving innovation and growth.

Enhanced Risk Management:

AI insights contribute to more effective risk management strategies. By analyzing historical data, AI can identify patterns and signals that indicate potential risks or anomalies. Organizations can leverage these insights to proactively mitigate risks, optimize risk assessments, and enhance risk management processes. AI can also provide real-time monitoring and alerts, enabling organizations to respond quickly to emerging risks or threats.

Personalized Customer Experiences:

AI insights enable organizations to deliver personalized customer experiences by leveraging customer data and preferences. By analyzing customer behavior, purchase history, and interactions, AI can provide tailored recommendations, personalized marketing messages, and customized offers. This level of personalization enhances customer satisfaction, drives customer loyalty, and increases the effectiveness of marketing and sales strategies.

Improved Operational Efficiency:

AI insights can optimize operational processes and resource allocation by identifying inefficiencies, bottlenecks, or areas for improvement. AI-powered analytics can identify patterns that impact operational performance and suggest optimization strategies. This enables organizations to streamline processes, reduce costs, enhance productivity, and make data-driven decisions for resource allocation, supply chain management, inventory optimization, and more.

Continuous Learning and Adaptation:

AI systems have the capability to continuously learn and adapt based on new data and changing conditions. By continuously analyzing data and adjusting models, AI can provide updated insights and recommendations over time. This adaptability ensures that decision-making processes remain aligned with the evolving business landscape, enabling organizations to stay agile and responsive to market dynamics.

In conclusion, leveraging AI insights enhances data-driven decision-making by uncovering patterns, predicting outcomes, providing real-time insights, reducing bias, automating analysis, improving risk management, enabling personalization, optimizing operational efficiency, and fostering continuous learning. Organizations that embrace AI technologies and effectively integrate AI insights into their decision-making processes gain a competitive advantage, drive innovation, and achieve better business outcomes in an increasingly data-centric world.

CHAPTER 54: LEVERAGING AI FOR COMPETITIVE INTELLIGENCE AND MARKET ANALYSIS

In today's highly competitive business landscape, organizations must gain a deep understanding of their market, competitors, and customers to make informed decisions and maintain a competitive edge. Traditional market analysis and competitive intelligence methods can be time-consuming and resource-intensive, often unable to keep up with the rapidly evolving business environment. Artificial Intelligence (AI) offers a transformative approach to market analysis and competitive intelligence by automating data collection, analysis, and interpretation. Let us explore how organizations can leverage AI to gain valuable insights, make informed decisions, and stay ahead of the competition:

Data Collection and Processing:

AI technologies can automate the collection of vast amounts of data from diverse sources, such as social media, news articles, industry reports, and public databases. AI algorithms can aggregate, process, and filter this data, enabling organizations to gather comprehensive and up-to-date information about their market, competitors, and customers. This automation streamlines the data collection process, saving time and resources compared to manual methods.

Sentiment Analysis and Brand Monitoring:

AI-powered sentiment analysis techniques enable organizations to monitor and analyze customer sentiment, opinions, and feedback. By analyzing customer reviews, social media posts, and online discussions, AI can identify positive and negative sentiment towards a brand, product, or service. This information helps organizations understand customer perceptions, monitor brand reputation, and make data-driven decisions to improve their products or services.

Competitive Benchmarking:

AI can assist in comparing and benchmarking an organization's performance against competitors. By analyzing competitors' marketing strategies, pricing models, product features, and customer feedback, AI algorithms can provide valuable insights into the competitive landscape. Organizations can identify gaps and opportunities, adjust their strategies, and differentiate themselves to gain a competitive advantage.

Predictive Market Analysis:

AI algorithms can leverage historical data, market trends, and other variables to generate predictive insights. By analyzing patterns and correlations, AI can forecast market dynamics, customer behavior, demand fluctuations, and industry trends. This predictive analysis enables organizations to anticipate market shifts, identify emerging opportunities, and make proactive decisions to capitalize on market trends before their competitors.

Pricing and Demand Forecasting:

AI algorithms can analyze historical pricing data, market demand, customer preferences, and other factors to forecast pricing strategies and demand patterns. This helps organizations optimize pricing decisions, determine price elasticity, and identify the ideal pricing points for maximizing revenue and profitability. Accurate demand forecasting allows businesses to optimize inventory levels, improve supply chain efficiency, and enhance customer satisfaction.

Competitor Analysis and Strategy:

AI-powered competitor analysis goes beyond simply gathering information. AI algorithms can analyze competitors' strengths, weaknesses, market positioning, and strategic moves. By processing large amounts of data, including financial reports, news articles, social media updates, and patents, AI can identify competitor strategies and predict potential future actions. These insights empower organizations to develop effective counter-strategies, identify market gaps, and differentiate themselves from competitors.

Customer Segmentation and Targeting:

AI enables organizations to segment their customer base effectively by identifying patterns and similarities among customers. By analyzing customer demographics, purchase behavior, browsing history, and interactions, AI algorithms can identify distinct customer segments. This allows organizations to tailor their marketing campaigns, personalize customer experiences, and target specific segments with relevant offers, increasing the effectiveness of their marketing efforts.

Market Trend Analysis:

AI algorithms can analyze a vast amount of data from various sources to identify and monitor emerging market trends. By tracking news articles, social media trends, industry reports, and consumer conversations, AI can provide real-time insights into evolving customer preferences, technological advancements, regulatory changes, and emerging market opportunities. This information enables organizations to adapt their strategies, launch new products, and position themselves as industry leaders in rapidly evolving markets.

Competitive Price Monitoring:

AI can automate the monitoring of competitors' prices, discounts, and promotions. By comparing prices across different channels and identifying pricing patterns, AI algorithms can help organizations adjust their pricing strategies in response to competitor movements. This ensures that organizations remain competitive while maximizing profitability.

In conclusion, leveraging AI for competitive intelligence and market analysis empowers organizations to make informed decisions, gain a deeper understanding of their market and competitors, and identify new opportunities. By automating data collection, analyzing sentiment, benchmarking performance, predicting market dynamics, optimizing pricing and demand, conducting competitor analysis, segmenting customers, monitoring market trends, and tracking competitive pricing, organizations can stay ahead of the competition and drive business growth in an increasingly dynamic business environment. Embracing AI in competitive intelligence and market analysis is no longer a luxury but a necessity for organizations aiming to thrive and succeed.

CHAPTER 55: IMPLEMENTING AI-POWERED DASHBOARDS AND VISUALIZATION TOOLS

In today's data-driven world, organizations are generating and collecting vast amounts of data from various sources. To derive actionable insights from this data and make informed decisions, businesses need effective tools for data visualization and analysis. Artificial Intelligence (AI)-powered dashboards and visualization tools have emerged as valuable solutions to simplify complex data and enable users to understand information more intuitively. Let us explore the benefits of implementing AI-powered dashboards and visualization tools and key considerations for successful implementation:

Benefits of AI-Powered Dashboards and Visualization Tools:

Enhanced Data Understanding:

AI-powered dashboards and visualization tools provide a visual representation of complex data sets, making it easier for users to understand trends, patterns, and relationships within the data. Visualizations enable users to identify insights quickly, spot anomalies, and make data-driven decisions in real-time.

Real-Time Data Monitoring:

AI-powered dashboards can be connected to live data sources, enabling real-time data monitoring and analysis. This allows organizations to track key performance indicators (KPIs), monitor business metrics, and identify emerging trends as they happen. Real-time insights enable proactive decision-making and rapid response to changing business conditions.

Interactive and Intuitive User Experience:

AI-powered dashboards and visualization tools offer interactive and user-friendly interfaces. Users can customize visualizations, drill down into specific data points, apply filters, and interact with the data in real-time. This interactivity enhances user engagement and empowers users to explore the data from different angles, enabling deeper insights and analysis.

Data Integration and Centralized View:

AI-powered dashboards can integrate data from various sources, including internal databases, third-party applications, and external APIs. This integration allows organizations to consolidate data into a centralized view, providing a holistic picture of business performance. Users can access comprehensive insights without the need to navigate multiple systems or siloed data sources.

Automated Data Analysis and Insights:

AI-powered dashboards can leverage machine learning algorithms to automatically analyze data and generate insights. These insights can include anomaly detection, trend analysis, predictive analytics, and recommendations. By automating data analysis, AI-powered dashboards save time and empower users with valuable insights without the need for manual data crunching.

Data Visualization for Stakeholder Communication:

Visual representations of data are highly effective for communicating complex information to stakeholders. AI-powered dashboards provide visually appealing and interactive charts, graphs, and other visual elements that can be easily understood by stakeholders. This enhances communication and facilitates data-driven discussions and decision-making across teams and departments.

Key Considerations for Implementing AI-Powered Dashboards and Visualization Tools:

Define Clear Objectives and KPIs:

Before implementing AI-powered dashboards, organizations should clearly define their objectives and identify the key performance indicators (KPIs) they want to monitor. This ensures that the dashboard focuses on delivering actionable insights aligned with business goals and priorities.

Identify Relevant Data Sources:

Identify the relevant data sources required for the dashboard. These can include internal databases, external APIs, cloud-based applications, or third-party data providers. Ensure that the necessary data integration processes are in place to connect and retrieve data from these sources.

Data Quality and Governance:

Data quality is crucial for accurate and meaningful visualizations. Implement data quality processes, including data cleansing, validation, and standardization, to ensure that the data used for visualization is accurate, consistent, and reliable. Establish data governance policies to maintain data integrity and security.

Select the Right Visualization Techniques:

Choose visualization techniques that best represent the data and insights you want to communicate. Consider different chart types, graphs, maps, and interactive elements that align with the data characteristics and user requirements. Keep the visualizations simple, intuitive, and relevant to the specific information being conveyed.

Ensure Scalability and Performance:

Consider the scalability and performance requirements of the AI-powered dashboards. As data volumes and user demands increase, the dashboard should be capable of handling the growing workload without compromising performance. Evaluate the scalability and responsiveness of the underlying infrastructure and technologies.

User-Friendly Interface and Accessibility:

Design the dashboard interface to be user-friendly, intuitive, and accessible to users with varying levels of technical expertise. Consider the needs of different user roles and provide the necessary training and support to ensure users can effectively navigate and utilize the dashboard's features.

Security and Privacy:

Ensure that appropriate security measures are in place to protect the data displayed on the dashboard. Implement access controls, data encryption, and user authentication mechanisms to safeguard sensitive information. Adhere to data privacy regulations and best practices to maintain confidentiality and compliance.

Regular Maintenance and Updates:

Maintain the AI-powered dashboards regularly to ensure data accuracy, system stability, and optimal performance. Address any technical issues promptly and provide ongoing support and training to users. Continuously update and enhance the dashboard based on user feedback and evolving business requirements.

In conclusion, implementing AI-powered dashboards and visualization tools offers organizations a powerful means to unlock insights, monitor real-time data, and facilitate data-driven decision-making. By providing enhanced data understanding, real-time monitoring, interactive user experiences, automated analysis, centralized views, and effective stakeholder communication, AI-powered dashboards empower organizations to leverage their data assets effectively and gain a competitive advantage in the market. However, successful implementation requires careful planning, data quality assurance, user-friendly design, scalability, security measures, and ongoing maintenance to maximize the value and impact of AI-powered dashboards.

CHAPTER 56: IDENTIFYING UNIQUE AI OPPORTUNITIES WITHIN YOUR INDUSTRY

Artificial Intelligence (AI) has the potential to revolutionize various industries by enabling automation, optimizing processes, and uncovering valuable insights from vast amounts of data. However, each industry has its own unique characteristics, challenges, and opportunities. Identifying the specific AI opportunities within your industry requires a systematic approach that considers industry-specific use cases, pain points, and potential areas of improvement. Here are key steps to help you identify unique AI opportunities within your industry:

Understand Industry Challenges and Pain Points:

Start by gaining a deep understanding of the challenges and pain points faced by your industry. This can involve researching industry trends, speaking with industry experts, and engaging in discussions with key stakeholders. Identify the areas where existing processes, systems, or technologies fall short, and where AI has the potential to make a significant impact. Common challenges in various industries include operational inefficiencies, data overload, manual processes, customer experience gaps, regulatory compliance, or emerging market demands.

Assess Industry-Specific Use Cases:

Analyze industry-specific use cases where AI can provide valuable solutions. Consider the areas where AI techniques such as machine learning, natural language processing, computer vision, or predictive analytics can be applied effectively. For example, in healthcare, AI can be used for medical imaging analysis, patient diagnosis, or drug discovery. In finance, AI can assist with fraud detection, algorithmic trading, or customer risk profiling. Explore use cases in your industry that align with your organization's goals, resources, and expertise.

Analyze Data Availability and Quality:

Evaluate the availability and quality of data within your industry. AI thrives on large, diverse, and high-quality datasets. Determine if your industry has access to relevant data sources, both internal and external, that can be utilized for AI applications. Assess the data's volume, variety, velocity, and veracity. If data is lacking or insufficient, explore strategies to collect, clean, and augment the data to meet AI requirements. Additionally, consider data privacy and security regulations that may impact data collection and usage.

Engage with Industry Experts and Partners:

Collaborate with industry experts, researchers, and technology partners to gain insights into emerging AI opportunities within your industry. Attend conferences, seminars, and industry-specific events to stay updated on the latest AI developments and innovations. Engage in discussions with technology providers, startups, or research institutions that specialize in AI for your industry. Such partnerships can provide valuable insights, access to expertise, and potential collaboration opportunities to drive AI initiatives forward.

Evaluate Competitor and Market Landscape:

Assess the AI initiatives and deployments of your competitors and peers within the industry. Investigate how AI is being utilized to gain a competitive advantage or address industry challenges. Analyze case studies, success stories, or research papers to understand the AI strategies and applications adopted by others. This analysis can provide inspiration, help identify gaps, and highlight areas where you can differentiate your organization through AI implementation.

Prioritize Opportunities and Feasibility:

Based on your research and analysis, prioritize the AI opportunities that align with your organization's strategic objectives and resources. Evaluate the feasibility of implementing AI solutions in terms of technology readiness, resource requirements, and potential impact. Consider factors such as ROI, time to market, data availability, organizational capabilities, and regulatory constraints. It may be helpful to conduct a cost-benefit analysis or proof-of-concept projects to validate the feasibility and potential benefits of specific AI opportunities.

Develop an AI Roadmap:

Create an AI roadmap that outlines the identified AI opportunities, prioritized initiatives, and implementation plan. Define the required resources, technology infrastructure, and skill sets needed for successful execution. Identify potential risks and mitigation strategies. Break down the roadmap into phases or milestones, considering the scalability and complexity of each opportunity. Establish key performance indicators (KPIs) and metrics to measure the success and impact of AI implementation within your industry.

Foster a Culture of Innovation:

To fully capitalize on the identified AI opportunities, foster a culture of innovation within your organization. Encourage collaboration, knowledge-sharing, and experimentation. Provide training and upskilling opportunities for employees to develop AI-related skills. Embrace agile methodologies and iterative approaches to AI implementation, allowing for continuous learning and improvement. Emphasize the importance of embracing change and exploring new possibilities to drive industry-specific AI innovation.

In conclusion, identifying unique AI opportunities within your industry requires a combination of industry understanding, collaboration, data analysis, market assessment, and strategic prioritization. By analyzing industry-specific challenges, assessing use cases, evaluating data availability, engaging with experts, monitoring competitors, and developing an AI roadmap, you can identify and leverage the AI opportunities that have the potential to transform your industry and drive your organization's success.

CHAPTER 58: ADAPTING AI STRATEGIES TO INDUSTRY-SPECIFIC CHALLENGES AND OPPORTUNITIES

Artificial Intelligence (AI) is not a one-size-fits-all solution. Each industry has its unique set of challenges, opportunities, and dynamics that require tailored AI strategies for maximum impact. Adapting AI strategies to industry-specific challenges and opportunities enables organizations to address critical pain points, capitalize on industry trends, and gain a competitive advantage. Let us explore key considerations and approaches to adapt AI strategies to industry-specific contexts:

Understand Industry-Specific Challenges:

Start by gaining a deep understanding of the specific challenges faced by your industry. Identify pain points, bottlenecks, or inefficiencies that hinder productivity, growth, or customer satisfaction. For example, healthcare organizations may face challenges related to patient data management and analysis, while manufacturing companies may struggle with quality control or supply chain optimization. By identifying these challenges, you can align your AI strategies to address them effectively.

Leverage Industry-Specific Data:

Each industry generates unique data sets, and leveraging this data is crucial for AI success. Understand the nature, volume, and quality of industry-specific data available. For example, the retail industry may have transactional data, customer behavior data, and inventory data, while the transportation industry may have geolocation data and vehicle sensor data. Identify the relevant data sources and explore techniques to collect, clean, and enrich the data for AI applications.

Identify Industry-Specific Use Cases:

Identify and prioritize industry-specific use cases where AI can have the most significant impact. Work closely with stakeholders, domain experts, and end-users to identify pain points and areas where AI can provide value. For instance, in finance, use cases may include fraud detection, algorithmic trading, or credit risk assessment. In marketing, use cases may involve customer segmentation, personalized recommendations, or sentiment analysis. Tailor your AI strategies to address these use cases and deliver tangible business outcomes.

Collaborate with Industry Experts:

Engage with industry experts, consultants, and research organizations that specialize in your industry. Collaborating with these experts can provide valuable insights, domain knowledge, and industry-specific best practices. Industry experts can help you identify untapped opportunities, validate your AI strategies, and navigate industry-specific challenges. By leveraging their expertise, you can ensure that your AI strategies align with industry standards and emerging trends.

Consider Regulatory and Compliance Factors:

Different industries have specific regulatory and compliance requirements that must be considered when implementing AI strategies. Understand the legal and ethical implications of AI adoption within your industry. For example, healthcare organizations must comply with patient privacy regulations, while financial institutions need to adhere to anti-money laundering and know-your-customer regulations. Ensure that your AI strategies adhere to these requirements and consider privacy, security, and transparency concerns.

Build Industry-Specific Partnerships:

Forge partnerships with industry-specific technology providers, startups, or research institutions that specialize in AI applications for your industry. These partnerships can provide access to cutting-edge technologies, domain expertise, and collaborative opportunities. By working together, you can leverage industry-specific knowledge and resources to accelerate the implementation and adoption of AI strategies tailored to your industry.

Address Industry-Specific Talent Needs:

Building a team with the right skill set is essential for successful AI implementation. Identify the specific skills and expertise required to execute your AI strategies within your industry. This may include data scientists, domain experts, AI engineers, and subject matter specialists. Invest in training programs, recruit talent with industry-specific knowledge, and foster a culture of continuous learning and innovation.

Monitor Industry Trends and Innovations:

Stay abreast of industry trends, technological advancements, and AI innovations relevant to your industry. Attend industry conferences, participate in industry forums, and follow thought leaders to stay informed. Understanding emerging technologies, market shifts, and evolving customer expectations will help you adapt and refine your AI strategies to stay ahead of the competition and embrace future opportunities.

In conclusion, adapting AI strategies to industry-specific challenges and opportunities is crucial for maximizing the value and impact of AI within your industry. By understanding industry-specific challenges, leveraging relevant data, identifying use cases, collaborating with industry experts, considering regulatory factors, building partnerships, addressing talent needs, and monitoring industry trends, you can develop AI strategies tailored to your industry's unique characteristics. This adaptability allows organizations to unlock the full potential of AI and drive transformational change in their respective industries.

CHAPTER 59: ENHANCING NETWORK AND DATA SECURITY WITH AI-POWERED TOOLS

In today's digital landscape, organizations face increasingly sophisticated cyber threats that can compromise network infrastructure and sensitive data. To strengthen their security posture, businesses are turning to advanced technologies like Artificial Intelligence (AI) to detect, prevent, and respond to security incidents effectively. AI-powered tools offer unique capabilities to enhance network and data security, enabling organizations to proactively protect their systems and safeguard critical information. Let us explore how AI-powered tools can enhance network and data security:

Threat Detection and Prevention:

AI-powered tools can analyze vast amounts of network data, logs, and user behavior patterns to detect and identify potential security threats. Machine learning algorithms can learn from historical data to identify anomalous activities and indicators of compromise. By continuously monitoring network traffic and applying behavioral analytics, AI tools can identify suspicious patterns, malware, or unauthorized access attempts, allowing security teams to respond promptly and mitigate risks.

Advanced Threat Intelligence:

AI-powered tools leverage machine learning algorithms to analyze threat intelligence feeds, open-source data, and dark web sources. By processing and correlating large volumes of threat data, AI can identify emerging threats, predict attack trends, and provide actionable insights to security teams. This enables organizations to proactively defend against known and emerging threats, enhancing their ability to detect and respond to potential risks.

User and Entity Behavior Analytics (UEBA):

AI-powered tools can analyze user behavior and access patterns to identify anomalous activities and potential insider threats. By establishing baselines of normal behavior, AI algorithms can detect deviations and trigger alerts when unusual or risky activities occur. UEBA systems can help identify compromised accounts, unauthorized access attempts, or malicious insider activities, enabling security teams to take appropriate actions.

Automated Security Incident Response:

AI-powered tools can automate security incident response processes, reducing the time to detect and respond to security incidents. AI algorithms can analyze security alerts, prioritize incidents based on risk, and automatically initiate predefined response actions. This automation streamlines incident handling, reduces manual effort, and enables security teams to focus on more complex and critical security tasks.

Fraud Detection and Prevention:

AI-powered tools can detect patterns and anomalies in financial transactions, customer interactions, or user behavior to identify potential fraud activities. By applying machine learning algorithms to analyze large volumes of transactional data, AI can identify suspicious activities, flag fraudulent transactions, and minimize false positives. This helps organizations mitigate financial losses, protect customer data, and maintain trust and confidence in their services.

Network Intrusion Detection and Prevention:

AI-powered tools can enhance network intrusion detection and prevention capabilities. By continuously monitoring network traffic, analyzing packet-level data, and applying AI algorithms, these tools can detect and block malicious activities, such as network intrusions, distributed denial-of-service (DDoS) attacks, or unauthorized access attempts. AI-powered intrusion detection systems can provide real-time threat intelligence and help organizations respond quickly to emerging threats.

Vulnerability Management:

AI-powered tools can assist in identifying vulnerabilities in network systems and applications. By analyzing security scan results, system configurations, and historical vulnerability data, AI can prioritize vulnerabilities based on risk severity, business impact, and exploitability. This enables organizations to focus their resources on addressing the most critical vulnerabilities and reducing the attack surface.

Adaptive Access Control:

AI-powered tools can enhance access control mechanisms by providing adaptive and contextual authentication. By analyzing user behavior, device information, and contextual data, AI algorithms can evaluate the risk level of access requests and enforce appropriate security measures. This can include multi-factor authentication, dynamic access policies, or adaptive access controls based on user profiles and behavior patterns.

Predictive Security Analytics:

AI-powered tools can leverage predictive analytics to identify potential security risks and proactively mitigate them. By analyzing historical security data, AI algorithms can detect patterns, predict potential threats, and provide actionable insights to security teams. This enables organizations to anticipate and prevent security incidents before they occur, reducing the impact of attacks and enhancing overall security resilience.

Security Operations Optimization:

AI-powered tools can automate and optimize security operations, improving efficiency and reducing response time. By automating routine security tasks, such as log analysis, incident triage, or threat hunting, AI can free up security personnel to focus on more complex and strategic security initiatives. This allows organizations to leverage their resources effectively and respond to security incidents more efficiently.

While AI-powered tools offer significant benefits for network and data security, it is important to consider potential limitations and challenges. AI tools rely on accurate and reliable data for effective operation, and they may face challenges with false positives, adversarial attacks, or privacy concerns. Organizations must carefully evaluate and validate the effectiveness of AI-powered security tools in their specific environments and ensure that they are deployed as part of a comprehensive security strategy that includes human expertise and oversight.

In conclusion, AI-powered tools have the potential to significantly enhance network and data security capabilities. By leveraging AI algorithms for threat detection, advanced threat intelligence, user behavior analytics, automated incident response, fraud detection, network intrusion prevention, vulnerability management, adaptive access control, predictive security analytics, and security operations optimization, organizations can strengthen their security posture and protect critical assets. However, it is important to carefully evaluate and integrate AI-powered tools within a holistic security framework to address industry-specific challenges and ensure effective protection against evolving cyber threats.

CHAPTER 60: LEVERAGING AI FOR PROACTIVE THREAT DETECTION AND RESPONSE

In today's increasingly complex and dynamic cybersecurity landscape, organizations face sophisticated and evolving threats that require proactive measures for detection and response. Traditional security approaches often fall short in keeping up with the speed and complexity of these threats. Artificial Intelligence (AI) offers a powerful solution by leveraging machine learning algorithms and advanced analytics to enhance threat detection capabilities, automate incident response, and enable organizations to stay one step ahead of cybercriminals. Let us explore how AI can be leveraged for proactive threat detection and response:

Advanced Threat Detection:

AI-powered systems can analyze large volumes of data, including logs, network traffic, and user behavior, to identify patterns, anomalies, and indicators of compromise that may go unnoticed by traditional security tools. Machine learning algorithms can learn from historical data and identify unknown threats or zero-day attacks. By continuously monitoring and analyzing data, AI can detect emerging threats and potential vulnerabilities, allowing organizations to take proactive measures before they are exploited.

Behavioral Analytics:

AI can employ behavioral analytics to establish baselines of normal user behavior and network activities. By continuously monitoring and analyzing patterns, AI algorithms can detect deviations from these baselines that may indicate malicious activities or insider threats. Behavioral analytics help identify suspicious behavior, such as unauthorized access attempts or abnormal data transfers, enabling security teams to respond promptly and prevent potential breaches.

Threat Intelligence and Hunting:

AI can leverage vast amounts of threat intelligence data from internal and external sources to proactively identify potential threats. By processing and correlating this data in real-time, AI can detect indicators of compromise, emerging attack techniques, and trends in cybercriminal activities. AI-powered threat hunting can help identify hidden threats and provide valuable insights to security teams for proactive threat mitigation.

Automated Incident Response:

AI can automate incident response processes, enabling organizations to respond rapidly to security incidents and minimize the impact of breaches. AI-powered systems can analyze security alerts, prioritize incidents based on severity and risk, and initiate predefined response actions. Automated incident response reduces response time, minimizes human error, and allows security teams to focus on critical tasks, such as investigating complex threats and improving overall security posture.

Malware Detection and Prevention:

AI can enhance malware detection and prevention capabilities by analyzing file behavior, network traffic, and system anomalies. AI-powered systems can identify known malware based on signature analysis and detect previously unknown malware using behavioral analysis. By continuously updating their knowledge and learning from new threats, AI-based malware detection systems can proactively block and mitigate malware infections.

Insider Threat Detection:

AI algorithms can analyze user behavior, access patterns, and data interactions to detect potential insider threats. By monitoring user activities and identifying unusual or suspicious behavior, AI-powered systems can flag potential insider threats, such as data exfiltration, unauthorized access, or abnormal usage of privileges. This proactive approach allows organizations to prevent data breaches or financial loss caused by internal actors.

Predictive Analytics:

AI can leverage predictive analytics to identify potential security risks and anticipate emerging threats. By analyzing historical data, security trends, and threat intelligence, AI algorithms can detect patterns and predict the likelihood of future security incidents. This proactive approach enables organizations to implement preventive measures, such as patching vulnerable systems, strengthening access controls, or improving security awareness training.

Threat Hunting and Adversarial Detection:

AI can assist security teams in proactive threat hunting by identifying hidden threats and advanced persistent threats (APTs). AI-powered systems can analyze vast amounts of data and search for indicators of compromise or signs of malicious activities that may have bypassed traditional security controls. By combining machine learning algorithms and human expertise, organizations can proactively detect and respond to sophisticated threats that evade traditional security defenses.

Real-Time Security Monitoring:

AI can provide real-time security monitoring and alerts, allowing organizations to respond promptly to security incidents. AI-powered systems can continuously monitor network traffic, log data, system events, and user activities, analyzing them in real-time for signs of unauthorized access, abnormal behavior, or malicious activities. Real-time monitoring helps organizations detect and respond to security incidents before they cause significant damage.

Continuous Improvement and Adaptability:

AI systems can learn from their experiences, continuously improving their threat detection capabilities over time. By analyzing feedback, adapting to new attack techniques, and incorporating new threat intelligence, AI-powered systems become more effective at detecting and responding to emerging threats. This adaptive nature allows organizations to stay ahead of evolving threats and improve their overall security posture.

In conclusion, leveraging AI for proactive threat detection and response is a crucial aspect of modern cybersecurity strategies. By harnessing the power of AI algorithms, organizations can enhance threat detection, automate incident response, detect insider threats, leverage threat intelligence, and proactively hunt for hidden threats. Embracing AI technologies empowers organizations to detect and respond to security incidents faster, minimize the impact of breaches, and stay resilient in the face of evolving cyber threats.

CHAPTER 61: IMPLEMENTING AI-DRIVEN CYBERSECURITY TRAINING AND AWARENESS PROGRAMS

In the ever-evolving landscape of cybersecurity threats, organizations must prioritize training and awareness programs to educate employees about potential risks and equip them with the knowledge and skills to protect against cyberattacks. Artificial Intelligence (AI) can play a significant role in enhancing cybersecurity training and awareness programs, enabling organizations to deliver targeted and effective educational initiatives. Let us explore how AI can be implemented to drive cybersecurity training and awareness:

Personalized Training Content:

AI can analyze individual user behavior, knowledge gaps, and learning preferences to deliver personalized cybersecurity training content. By leveraging machine learning algorithms, AI can adapt training materials to the specific needs of each employee. Personalized content ensures that employees receive the most relevant and engaging training materials, enhancing their understanding of cybersecurity best practices and increasing their commitment to security.

Simulated Phishing Attacks:

AI-powered tools can simulate phishing attacks to test employee awareness and response. These tools can create realistic phishing scenarios and measure employees' ability to identify and report suspicious emails. AI algorithms can analyze the results to identify patterns, assess vulnerability levels, and provide targeted training to individuals or teams that require additional guidance. Simulated phishing attacks help employees recognize phishing indicators, develop a sense of vigilance, and improve their ability to mitigate phishing threats.

Gamification and Interactive Learning:

AI can enhance cybersecurity training programs by incorporating gamification and interactive elements. Gamification techniques, such as leaderboards, badges, and rewards, motivate employees to actively participate in training activities and foster healthy competition. AI can also power interactive learning modules, quizzes, and simulations that engage employees and reinforce learning through real-world scenarios. These approaches increase employee engagement, retention of cybersecurity knowledge, and the practical application of secure practices.

Continuous Monitoring and Assessment:

AI-powered tools can continuously monitor employee behavior, systems, and networks to detect security anomalies and potential insider threats. By analyzing patterns, AI algorithms can identify unusual activities that may indicate malicious intent or policy violations. Continuous monitoring provides valuable insights into security risks and enables organizations to address vulnerabilities promptly. It also facilitates ongoing assessment and evaluation of employees' adherence to cybersecurity policies, allowing targeted interventions and customized training as needed.

Adaptive Learning Paths:

AI can adapt training paths based on individual progress and knowledge levels. By continuously assessing employees' cybersecurity knowledge and skills, AI algorithms can recommend specific modules or training materials that address their areas of weakness or interest. This adaptive learning approach ensures that employees receive training that is relevant to their current skill level, maximizing the effectiveness of the program and optimizing time spent on training activities.

Threat Intelligence Integration:

AI can integrate real-time threat intelligence feeds into training programs, providing employees with up-to-date information about the latest cyber threats and attack techniques. By leveraging AI algorithms to analyze threat intelligence data, training programs can be tailored to focus on current and emerging threats, ensuring employees are equipped with the necessary knowledge to recognize and respond to these threats effectively. This integration enhances the relevance and timeliness of cybersecurity training, allowing organizations to stay ahead of evolving threats.

Virtual Assistants and Chatbots:

AI-powered virtual assistants and chatbots can provide on-demand support and guidance for employees regarding cybersecurity best practices. These assistants can answer questions, provide training materials, or offer real-time assistance during potentially risky situations. AI-powered virtual assistants ensure consistent delivery of training information, reduce the burden on security teams, and create a self-service learning environment that empowers employees to make informed security decisions.

Behavioral Analytics and Reporting:

AI algorithms can analyze employee behavior, training performance, and security incidents to identify trends, assess training effectiveness, and generate insightful reports. Behavioral analytics can highlight areas where employees may require additional training or where policy enforcement should be strengthened. These reports help measure the impact of cybersecurity training programs, identify areas for improvement, and inform decision-making processes to enhance overall security posture.

Mobile and Microlearning:

AI can facilitate mobile learning and microlearning formats, making training materials easily accessible and digestible. AI-powered mobile apps can deliver bite-sized training modules, quizzes, or reminders to employees' mobile devices, allowing them to engage with training content at their convenience. Microlearning formats improve knowledge retention, accommodate diverse learning styles, and provide just-in-time training resources that can be accessed when needed.

Benchmarking and Continuous Improvement:

AI can compare the organization's security posture, training effectiveness, and employee performance against industry benchmarks and best practices. By analyzing aggregated data and benchmarking metrics, AI algorithms can identify areas of strength and weakness, highlight improvement opportunities, and guide decision-making for future enhancements of the cybersecurity training and awareness programs.

In conclusion, implementing AI-driven cybersecurity training and awareness programs is essential for organizations to combat evolving cyber threats and build a strong security culture. By leveraging AI to personalize training content, simulate phishing attacks, incorporate gamification and interactive learning, enable continuous monitoring and assessment, integrate threat intelligence, utilize virtual assistants and chatbots, apply behavioral analytics, facilitate mobile and microlearning, and benchmark progress, organizations can empower employees to become the first line of defense against cyberattacks. AI-driven cybersecurity training and awareness programs enable organizations to develop a proactive security posture, foster a security-conscious workforce, and significantly reduce the risk of successful cyber breaches.

CHAPTER 62: INTEGRATING AI AND IOT FOR ENHANCED DATA ANALYSIS AND INSIGHTS

The convergence of Artificial Intelligence (AI) and the Internet of Things (IoT) presents a powerful opportunity for organizations to leverage the vast amounts of data generated by IoT devices and extract valuable insights. By integrating AI with IoT, businesses can enhance data analysis capabilities, gain actionable insights, and drive informed decision-making. Let us explore how the integration of AI and IoT can enable enhanced data analysis and insights:

Data Collection and Aggregation:

IoT devices generate massive volumes of data from various sources, such as sensors, wearables, machinery, and environmental monitoring systems. AI can be employed to collect, aggregate, and process this data efficiently. AI algorithms can handle the complexities of data collection, filtering, and normalization, ensuring the quality and reliability of the IoT data used for analysis.

Real-time Data Processing:

AI algorithms can analyze IoT data in real-time, allowing organizations to derive insights and make timely decisions. By integrating AI with IoT, businesses can process and analyze data streams as they are generated, enabling proactive and immediate responses. Real-time data processing facilitates instant anomaly detection, predictive maintenance, and real-time monitoring of critical systems.

Advanced Analytics and Predictive Modeling:

AI algorithms can uncover patterns, trends, and correlations within IoT data that may not be apparent through traditional analytics methods. By leveraging machine learning algorithms, organizations can perform complex analyses, predictive modeling, and anomaly detection to gain deeper insights into their IoT data. AI enables businesses to identify potential issues, predict outcomes, optimize operations, and make data-driven decisions based on actionable insights.

Edge Computing and AI:

The integration of AI and IoT can be enhanced by deploying AI algorithms at the edge of the network, where IoT devices generate and process data. Edge computing enables real-time data analysis and decision-making, minimizing latency and reducing the need for transferring large volumes of IoT data to central servers. AI-powered edge devices can autonomously analyze data locally, enabling faster responses, lower network bandwidth requirements, and improved security and privacy.

Predictive Maintenance and Condition Monitoring:

AI algorithms can analyze IoT sensor data to predict equipment failures, identify maintenance needs, and optimize maintenance schedules. By detecting patterns and anomalies in sensor data, AI can enable predictive maintenance, reducing downtime, and improving operational efficiency. Condition monitoring with AI can identify deviations from normal operating parameters, triggering alerts or initiating maintenance actions when necessary.

Enhanced Resource Optimization:

Integrating AI with IoT enables businesses to optimize resource allocation based on real-time data and AI-driven insights. For example, in smart buildings, AI can analyze occupancy data collected by IoT sensors to optimize energy consumption, heating, and cooling. In supply chain management, AI-powered analytics can analyze IoT data to optimize logistics, inventory management, and demand forecasting, leading to cost savings and operational efficiencies.

Intelligent Automation and Control:

The combination of AI and IoT allows for intelligent automation and control of connected devices and systems. AI algorithms can analyze IoT data, learn from historical patterns, and make real-time decisions to automate processes or control devices. For example, in manufacturing, AI can optimize production workflows, adjust machine settings, or perform quality control checks based on real-time IoT data, reducing human intervention and improving overall efficiency.

Enhanced Safety and Security:

Integrating AI with IoT can enhance safety and security by leveraging AI algorithms to analyze IoT data for potential risks or security threats. AI-powered systems can identify abnormal patterns, detect intrusion attempts, and initiate automated security protocols. This proactive approach strengthens the security posture of IoT deployments, protecting against potential cyber-attacks or physical security breaches.

Data Monetization:

The integration of AI and IoT opens up opportunities for organizations to monetize their IoT data. By leveraging AI algorithms to extract valuable insights, businesses can develop data-driven products or services, create new revenue streams, or optimize existing business models. For example, in the agriculture industry, AI-powered analytics can analyze IoT data to optimize crop yields, water usage, and resource allocation, enabling farmers to provide data-driven services to other stakeholders.

Enhanced User Experience and Personalization:

Integrating AI and IoT can enable personalized experiences and improved user interactions. AI algorithms can analyze IoT data to understand user preferences, behaviors, and context, allowing businesses to deliver personalized recommendations, targeted advertisements, or tailored services. For example, in smart homes, AI can learn individual users' preferences and adjust lighting, temperature, and entertainment systems accordingly.

In conclusion, integrating AI and IoT offers organizations a powerful platform to enhance data analysis capabilities, gain valuable insights, and make data-driven decisions. By leveraging AI algorithms for real-time data processing, advanced analytics, predictive modeling, edge computing, and intelligent automation, businesses can unlock the full potential of their IoT data. The integration of AI and IoT drives innovation, improves operational efficiency, enhances safety and security, and enables organizations to deliver personalized experiences to their customers. Embracing the integration of AI and IoT is key to remaining competitive in today's data-driven world.

CHAPTER 63: LEVERAGING AI-DRIVEN ANALYTICS FOR PREDICTIVE MAINTENANCE AND ASSET MANAGEMENT

In today's fast-paced business environment, organizations rely on the smooth operation of their assets to maintain productivity and efficiency. Traditional approaches to maintenance and asset management, such as reactive or scheduled maintenance, often result in costly downtime and inefficient resource allocation. However, the integration of Artificial Intelligence (AI) with analytics has transformed maintenance practices, enabling organizations to implement predictive maintenance and optimize asset management. Let us explore how AI-driven analytics can revolutionize predictive maintenance and asset management:

Data Collection and Integration:

AI-driven analytics for predictive maintenance and asset management rely on the collection and integration of vast amounts of data from various sources. This includes sensor data from Internet of Things (IoT) devices, historical maintenance records, operational data, and external data sources. AI algorithms can integrate these disparate data sources, transforming raw data into actionable insights.

Machine Learning Algorithms for Anomaly Detection:

AI-powered analytics leverage machine learning algorithms to detect anomalies in the collected data. By analyzing patterns and trends, AI algorithms can identify deviations from normal operating conditions and flag potential issues or failures. This enables organizations to predict when maintenance will be required, allowing for proactive intervention before a critical failure occurs.

Real-Time Monitoring and Condition-Based Maintenance:

AI-driven analytics enable real-time monitoring of asset performance using sensor data. By continuously analyzing the streaming data, AI algorithms can assess the current condition of assets and identify early warning signs of degradation or failure. This data-driven approach allows organizations to shift from scheduled maintenance to condition-based maintenance, intervening only when necessary, and optimizing resource allocation.

Predictive Models for Failure Prediction:

AI-driven analytics can build predictive models based on historical and real-time data to forecast the probability of asset failure. These models consider factors such as operating conditions, usage patterns, environmental factors, and historical maintenance records. By combining these variables, AI algorithms can predict when an asset is likely to fail, allowing organizations to plan and schedule maintenance activities proactively.

Optimal Resource Allocation:

AI-driven analytics enable organizations to allocate resources optimally by predicting the maintenance requirements of assets. By using AI algorithms to analyze asset data and predict failure probabilities, organizations can prioritize maintenance activities based on the criticality and potential impact of each asset. This optimization of resource allocation reduces downtime, improves asset performance, and minimizes maintenance costs.

Asset Performance Analysis and Optimization:

AI-driven analytics provide organizations with in-depth insights into asset performance. By analyzing historical and real-time data, organizations can identify patterns and trends that impact asset performance and efficiency. AI algorithms can uncover hidden correlations between variables, enabling organizations to optimize asset performance, reduce energy consumption, and extend asset lifespan.

Prescriptive Maintenance Recommendations:

AI-driven analytics can generate prescriptive maintenance recommendations based on the analysis of asset data. By combining historical maintenance records, real-time sensor data, and predictive models, AI algorithms can recommend the most effective maintenance strategies, including timing, required resources, and the appropriate actions to prevent failures. These recommendations empower maintenance teams to make informed decisions and take proactive measures to avoid asset downtime.

Integration with Enterprise Systems:

AI-driven analytics can be integrated with existing enterprise systems, such as Enterprise Resource Planning (ERP) or Computerized Maintenance Management Systems (CMMS), to streamline maintenance workflows and enable seamless data exchange. By integrating AI-driven analytics with these systems, organizations can automate maintenance scheduling, track maintenance activities, and ensure the availability of historical maintenance records for analysis.

Continuous Learning and Improvement:

AI-driven analytics can continuously learn and adapt to changing operational conditions and asset performance data. By analyzing new data, refining predictive models, and incorporating feedback, AI algorithms become more accurate over time. This iterative learning process ensures that predictive maintenance strategies evolve and improve, leading to increased efficiency and effectiveness.

Cost Savings and Increased Efficiency:

By leveraging AI-driven analytics for predictive maintenance and asset management, organizations can achieve significant cost savings and increased operational efficiency. By minimizing unplanned downtime, reducing unnecessary maintenance activities, optimizing resource allocation, and extending asset lifespan, organizations can achieve cost reductions, improved productivity, and enhanced customer satisfaction.

In conclusion, leveraging AI-driven analytics for predictive maintenance and asset management revolutionizes traditional maintenance practices. By combining machine learning algorithms, real-time data analysis, predictive modeling, and prescriptive recommendations, organizations can shift from reactive or scheduled maintenance to a proactive, condition-based approach. This enables organizations to optimize asset performance, reduce maintenance costs, increase efficiency, and minimize unplanned downtime. Embracing AI-driven analytics empowers organizations to make data-driven decisions, enhance their competitive advantage, and unlock the full potential of their assets.

CHAPTER 64: OPTIMIZING IOT DEVICE PERFORMANCE AND ENERGY EFFICIENCY WITH AI

The proliferation of Internet of Things (IoT) devices has transformed how businesses and individuals interact with the physical world. These devices generate massive amounts of data and require efficient performance and energy management to ensure their optimal operation. By leveraging Artificial Intelligence (AI) technologies, organizations can optimize IoT device performance and enhance energy efficiency. Let us explore how AI can be used to achieve these objectives:

Intelligent Device Configuration:

AI algorithms can analyze data from IoT devices and make intelligent recommendations for optimal configuration settings. By considering factors such as usage patterns, environmental conditions, and device capabilities, AI can suggest configurations that maximize performance while minimizing energy consumption. This intelligent device configuration ensures that each IoT device operates at its peak efficiency.

Predictive Maintenance:

AI-driven predictive maintenance can identify potential issues and proactively address them before they cause device failures or performance degradation. By analyzing historical data and real-time device telemetry, AI algorithms can predict when a device is likely to experience a failure or require maintenance. This enables organizations to schedule maintenance activities, replace components, or address potential issues in a timely manner, reducing downtime and optimizing device performance.

Dynamic Resource Allocation:

AI can optimize the allocation of computing and network resources among IoT devices in real-time. By analyzing data traffic patterns, device loads, and user requirements, AI algorithms can allocate resources efficiently to ensure optimal performance for each device. This dynamic resource allocation enables organizations to balance the workload and prevent overloading or underutilization of resources, resulting in improved device performance and energy efficiency.

Energy Consumption Monitoring and Optimization:

AI algorithms can monitor and analyze energy consumption patterns of IoT devices. By analyzing historical energy usage data and environmental factors, AI can identify energy-saving opportunities and provide recommendations for optimizing device energy efficiency. These recommendations may include adjusting power states, optimizing sleep modes, or implementing energy-saving algorithms. By implementing AI-driven energy optimization strategies, organizations can reduce energy consumption and extend the battery life of IoT devices.

Adaptive Learning and Optimization:

AI algorithms can learn from real-time data collected from IoT devices and continuously optimize device performance and energy efficiency. By analyzing device behavior, usage patterns, and environmental conditions, AI can adapt device configurations and resource allocations to achieve optimal performance. This adaptive learning enables IoT devices to dynamically adjust their operation based on changing conditions, resulting in efficient performance and energy usage.

Context-Aware Decision Making:

AI can make context-aware decisions to optimize device performance and energy efficiency. By analyzing data from various sources, such as IoT sensors, user behavior, and environmental data, AI algorithms can adjust device settings, adjust resource allocation, or trigger specific actions based on the context. For example, an AI-powered smart thermostat can learn user preferences, analyze occupancy patterns, and adjust temperature settings accordingly to optimize energy consumption.

Intelligent Data Filtering and Processing:

AI algorithms can filter and process IoT data at the edge or in the cloud, reducing the amount of data transmitted and processed. By applying AI techniques, such as anomaly detection, data compression, or pattern recognition, IoT devices can filter out irrelevant or redundant data, transmitting only the necessary information. This intelligent data filtering reduces bandwidth requirements, optimizes network utilization, and improves overall system performance and energy efficiency.

Collaborative Edge and Cloud Computing:

AI enables collaborative edge and cloud computing architectures for IoT devices. By leveraging AI algorithms, devices can offload computationally intensive tasks to edge servers or cloud platforms, reducing device workload and energy consumption. Edge and cloud computing allow for distributed processing, enabling real-time analysis, faster response times, and optimized energy utilization.

Predictive Analytics for Energy Demand:

AI-driven predictive analytics can forecast energy demand based on historical data, environmental factors, and usage patterns. By predicting energy demand, organizations can optimize energy allocation and avoid energy wastage. For example, AI algorithms can adjust device schedules, prioritize energy-intensive tasks during off-peak hours, or dynamically allocate energy resources based on predicted demand.

Continuous Improvement through Data Analysis:

AI enables continuous improvement through data analysis of IoT device performance and energy consumption. By analyzing data trends, identifying inefficiencies, and implementing corrective measures, organizations can iteratively optimize device performance and energy efficiency over time. This continuous improvement cycle ensures that IoT devices operate at their best, adapt to changing conditions, and minimize energy consumption.

In conclusion, leveraging AI for optimizing IoT device performance and energy efficiency empowers organizations to maximize the value of their IoT deployments. By utilizing intelligent device configuration, predictive maintenance, dynamic resource allocation, energy consumption monitoring, and adaptive learning, organizations can achieve efficient device operation, extended battery life, and reduced energy consumption. The integration of AI with IoT devices enables intelligent decision-making, context-aware actions, and collaborative computing, leading to enhanced performance and sustainable energy usage. Adopting AI technologies is crucial for organizations looking to unlock the full potential of their IoT investments and drive positive environmental impact.

CHAPTER 65: MANAGING INTELLECTUAL PROPERTY (IP) RIGHTS AND LICENSING IN AN AI-DRIVEN WORLD

The rapid advancement of Artificial Intelligence (AI) technologies is transforming industries and raising new challenges for managing Intellectual Property (IP) rights and licensing. As AI becomes increasingly capable of generating innovative works, organizations must navigate the complex landscape of AI-generated content, ownership, and licensing. Let us explore the key considerations and strategies for managing IP rights and licensing in an AI-driven world:

AI-Generated IP Ownership:

Determining the ownership of AI-generated IP is a complex issue. In many jurisdictions, IP laws attribute ownership to the human creator of the work. However, in the case of AI-generated works, where the contribution of human creators may be minimal or non-existent, determining ownership can be challenging. Organizations should establish clear guidelines and contractual agreements to address the ownership of AI-generated IP, defining the roles and responsibilities of AI systems, human creators, and the organization itself.

Intellectual Property Rights Protection:

Organizations must proactively protect their AI-generated IP through appropriate IP protection mechanisms, such as patents, copyrights, and trademarks. While traditional IP protection methods have generally been applied to human-generated works, emerging legal frameworks are evolving to encompass AI-generated content. It is crucial for organizations to work closely with legal experts to understand the evolving IP landscape and ensure that their AI-generated IP is adequately protected.

Licensing and Commercialization:

Effective licensing strategies are essential for organizations to leverage the value of their AI-generated IP. Organizations can license their AI technologies, algorithms, or datasets to other businesses, researchers, or developers, allowing them to benefit from and build upon their AI innovations. Clear and well-defined licensing agreements should be established, specifying the rights, limitations, and obligations of the parties involved. Licensing models can vary, ranging from royalty-based licensing to open-source licenses, depending on the organization's goals and the nature of the AI-generated IP.

Ethical Considerations and Responsible Use:

When licensing AI-generated IP, organizations must consider the ethical implications and responsible use of their technology. AI systems can inadvertently generate biased or discriminatory content, leading to negative consequences. Organizations should establish guidelines and clauses in licensing agreements to ensure that the AI-generated IP is used responsibly and ethically. This may include provisions for transparency, fairness, and non-discrimination, as well as the monitoring and enforcement of ethical practices by licensees.

Collaboration and Partnerships:

Collaboration and partnerships can play a crucial role in managing IP rights in an AI-driven world. Organizations can engage in cross-industry collaborations, consortia, or research partnerships to collectively address IP challenges and establish industry-wide best practices. Collaborative efforts can help shape legal frameworks, standards, and guidelines related to AI-generated IP, fostering an environment of cooperation and innovation while protecting the interests of all stakeholders.

Monitoring and Enforcement:

Monitoring the use of AI-generated IP and enforcing IP rights is a critical aspect of IP management. Organizations should employ robust monitoring systems to track the use and distribution of their AI-generated content. AI-powered content recognition technologies can help identify instances of unauthorized use or infringement. In cases of infringement, organizations must be prepared to take legal action to protect their IP rights and seek appropriate remedies.

Licensing Agreements for AI Models and Datasets:

In addition to AI-generated content, organizations may also license their AI models and datasets to support AI development in other domains. Licensing agreements for AI models and datasets should outline the terms and conditions for their usage, including limitations, restrictions, and any necessary attribution requirements. Organizations should carefully consider the scope of licenses granted, ensuring they retain appropriate control and safeguard their IP rights.

Continuous Adaptation to Legal Developments:

The legal landscape surrounding AI-generated IP is continuously evolving. Organizations must stay abreast of new legal developments, court rulings, and regulatory frameworks related to AI and IP rights. Engaging legal experts specialized in AI and IP can help organizations navigate the complex legal landscape and ensure compliance with relevant laws and regulations.

International Considerations:

IP rights and licensing in an AI-driven world extend beyond national borders. Organizations operating globally must understand and comply with international IP laws and treaties. They should consider the nuances of IP protection, enforcement, and licensing in different jurisdictions to effectively manage their AI-generated IP on a global scale.

Public Engagement and Education:

Public engagement and education are crucial for fostering a broader understanding of AI-generated IP and its implications. Organizations should engage in public discourse, participate in industry conferences, and collaborate with academia and research institutions to promote awareness and understanding of AI-generated IP, its legal implications, and the need for responsible AI innovation.

In conclusion, managing IP rights and licensing in an AI-driven world requires careful consideration of ownership, protection, licensing strategies, ethical considerations, collaboration, monitoring, and compliance with evolving legal frameworks. By proactively addressing these aspects, organizations can navigate the complexities of AI-generated IP, protect their innovations, and leverage the value of AI while fostering responsible and ethical AI practices.

CHAPTER 66: UTILIZING AI TOOLS FOR PATENT ANALYSIS AND RESEARCH

In today's rapidly evolving technological landscape, organizations rely on patents to protect their innovations and gain a competitive edge. However, with the increasing volume of patent applications and the complexity of patent databases, it can be challenging for organizations to effectively analyze and research existing patents. This is where Artificial Intelligence (AI) tools come into play, offering powerful capabilities to streamline and enhance patent analysis and research processes. Let us explore how AI tools can be utilized for patent analysis and research:

Prior Art Search:

AI tools can significantly expedite the prior art search process, which involves identifying existing patents or other published materials that may be relevant to a patent application. By leveraging Natural Language Processing (NLP) techniques, AI algorithms can analyze patent descriptions, claims, and other textual data to identify relevant prior art. AI tools can sift through vast amounts of patent databases and other sources, significantly reducing the time and effort required for manual searches.

Patent Classification and Categorization:

AI algorithms can automatically classify and categorize patents based on their subject matter, technology domain, or industry. By analyzing patent texts and metadata, AI tools can assign appropriate patent classifications, making it easier to organize and retrieve patents based on specific criteria. This automated classification process enhances efficiency and accuracy, enabling organizations to quickly locate relevant patents within large patent databases.

Patent Portfolio Analysis:

AI tools can assist in analyzing and evaluating patent portfolios. By employing machine learning algorithms, AI tools can extract insights from large patent datasets, identifying patterns, trends, and correlations. This analysis can help organizations identify the strength and value of their patent portfolio, assess the competitive landscape, identify potential licensing opportunities, or make informed decisions regarding patent acquisition or divestment.

Technology Landscaping and Competitive Intelligence:

AI-powered patent analysis tools enable organizations to gain a comprehensive understanding of technology landscapes and monitor their competitors' patent activities. By analyzing patent data, AI algorithms can identify emerging technologies, track patent filing trends, and provide valuable insights into the competitive landscape. This information can help organizations identify white spaces for innovation, evaluate the novelty of their own inventions, and make informed strategic decisions.

Patent Valuation and Market Assessment:

AI tools can assist in assessing the value of patents and evaluating their market potential. By leveraging machine learning algorithms and data analytics, AI tools can analyze various factors such as patent citations, litigation history, market trends, and licensing activities. This analysis helps organizations determine the strength and commercial viability of patents, supporting licensing negotiations, portfolio management, and investment decisions.

Automated Patent Drafting:

AI tools can aid in the process of patent drafting by providing intelligent suggestions and recommendations. By analyzing existing patents, AI algorithms can generate draft patent claims, descriptions, and other sections, helping inventors and patent attorneys create high-quality patent applications. AI-powered drafting tools can improve accuracy, consistency, and efficiency in the patent drafting process, reducing the time and effort required to produce well-crafted patent applications.

Patent Monitoring and Alert Systems:

AI tools can automate the process of monitoring patent publications and notifying organizations about relevant patent updates or potential infringement risks. By analyzing patent databases and utilizing machine learning algorithms, AI-powered systems can deliver timely alerts regarding newly published patents, changes in patent status, or potential conflicts with existing patents. This proactive monitoring allows organizations to stay abreast of developments in their field, protect their IP rights, and make informed decisions.

Language Translation and Cross-lingual Search:

AI-powered tools can overcome language barriers by providing language translation capabilities and enabling cross-lingual patent searches. With multilingual NLP algorithms, AI tools can translate patent texts into different languages, facilitating global patent analysis and research. This enables organizations to access and analyze patent information from different regions, expanding their scope of patent analysis and ensuring comprehensive research.

Patent Data Visualization:

AI tools can transform complex patent data into visual representations, such as interactive graphs, charts, or heatmaps. These visualizations provide intuitive and concise summaries of patent landscapes, enabling researchers and decision-makers to quickly grasp key insights and trends. Visualizations enhance data comprehension, support pattern recognition, and facilitate effective communication of patent analysis results.

Enhanced Patent Examination Processes:

AI tools can assist patent examiners in conducting more efficient and accurate patent examinations. By leveraging AI algorithms, examiners can access relevant prior art, assess the novelty of inventions, and identify potential patent infringements. AI-powered tools can streamline the examination process, reducing the workload of examiners and ensuring consistent and thorough examination of patent applications.

In conclusion, AI tools offer powerful capabilities to streamline and enhance patent analysis and research. By leveraging AI algorithms, organizations can expedite prior art searches, classify patents, analyze patent portfolios, evaluate market potential, automate patent drafting, monitor patent activities, and visualize patent data. The utilization of AI tools empowers organizations to make informed decisions, effectively protect their intellectual property, and leverage patent information for strategic purposes. Embracing AI in patent analysis and research processes enables organizations to stay competitive, foster innovation, and navigate the complex landscape of intellectual property.

CHAPTER 67: DEVELOPING STRATEGIES FOR PROTECTING AI-GENERATED INTELLECTUAL PROPERTY (IP)

As Artificial Intelligence (AI) continues to advance, organizations face the challenge of protecting their AI-generated intellectual property (IP) and ensuring a competitive advantage in the market. AI-generated IP can encompass a wide range of innovations, from machine learning algorithms and predictive models to AI-driven inventions and creative works. Developing effective strategies for protecting AI-generated IP is crucial to safeguarding investments in AI research and development. Let us explore key considerations and strategies for protecting AI-generated IP:

Understanding the Legal Landscape:

To develop effective IP protection strategies, organizations must understand the legal landscape surrounding AI-generated IP. Consultation with IP attorneys and experts specialized in AI-related IP laws is essential. Different jurisdictions may have varying regulations and legal frameworks, so organizations should familiarize themselves with the specific requirements and processes for protecting AI-generated IP in their target markets.

Identifying Patentable Inventions:

Organizations should identify patentable inventions within their AI technology stack. This may include AI algorithms, methods, and applications that are novel, non-obvious, and have industrial applicability. Conducting a comprehensive patent search and analysis, involving AI-generated innovations, can help determine the patentability and potential scope of protection for AI-related inventions.

Patent Protection:

Obtaining patents is one of the primary means of protecting AI-generated IP. Organizations should file patent applications to protect their novel and inventive AI-related technologies. This can cover specific AI algorithms, models, or applications, as well as the underlying hardware or software components. It is crucial to work closely with patent attorneys to draft robust patent applications that effectively describe the AI-generated invention and its technical contributions.

Trade Secret Protection:

In cases where patent protection may not be suitable or desired, organizations can rely on trade secret protection for certain AI-generated IP. By implementing rigorous security measures, access controls, and confidentiality agreements, organizations can maintain the secrecy of proprietary AI algorithms, datasets, or other valuable trade secrets. Adequate safeguards and policies must be in place to ensure the protection and non-disclosure of trade secrets throughout the AI development and deployment process.

Copyright Protection:

Copyright can protect AI-generated creative works, such as artistic creations, literary works, or computer-generated content. Organizations should identify if their AI systems produce copyrightable outputs and consider filing for copyright protection. This includes AI-generated music, artwork, or written content. It is important to review copyright laws and understand the scope of protection for AI-generated works in different jurisdictions.

Collaboration and Non-Disclosure Agreements:

When collaborating with external parties or engaging in AI research partnerships, organizations should establish clear agreements and contracts that address IP ownership, licensing, and confidentiality. Non-disclosure agreements (NDAs) should be implemented to protect sensitive AI-generated IP during collaborations or when sharing AI-related technologies with third parties. These agreements help ensure that valuable AI-generated IP remains protected and confidential.

Monitoring and Enforcement:

Monitoring the market for potential infringements and enforcing IP rights are essential elements of protecting AI-generated IP. Organizations should actively monitor the use of their AI technologies and regularly search for potential infringements. This may involve leveraging AI-driven tools for patent monitoring, using content recognition technologies, or working with IP monitoring services to detect unauthorized use or infringement of AI-generated IP. In case of infringement, prompt action should be taken, including sending cease and desist letters, negotiating licensing agreements, or pursuing legal action when necessary.

International Protection:

Organizations operating globally must consider international IP protection strategies. International treaties, such as the Patent Cooperation Treaty (PCT) or the Madrid Protocol for trademarks, provide mechanisms for seeking IP protection across multiple jurisdictions. It is essential to assess the specific requirements, costs, and timelines for international patent filings and IP protection to ensure comprehensive coverage and effective enforcement of AI-generated IP worldwide.

Defensive Patenting:

Defensive patenting is a strategy used to protect AI-generated IP by building a strong patent portfolio. Organizations may strategically file defensive patents to deter potential competitors, establish prior art, or create a defensive shield against patent litigation. Defensive patenting can provide leverage in negotiations, licensing discussions, or potential cross-licensing arrangements, enhancing the organization's position in the market.

Continuous IP Management:

Developing a comprehensive IP management strategy is crucial for protecting AI-generated IP. This includes regularly reviewing and updating IP portfolios, conducting IP audits, and implementing internal processes and policies for IP protection. Organizations should educate their employees on IP rights, enforce IP policies, and ensure proper documentation of inventions, innovations, and IP-related activities.

In conclusion, developing effective strategies for protecting AI-generated IP is vital to secure investments in AI research and development and maintain a competitive advantage. By understanding the legal landscape, identifying patentable inventions, leveraging patent, trade secret, and copyright protection, implementing collaboration agreements, monitoring the market, and ensuring international coverage, organizations can safeguard their AI-generated IP and maximize its value. Continuous IP management and proactive enforcement are critical to adapt to evolving IP laws and emerging AI technologies, ensuring long-term protection and capitalizing on the benefits of AI innovation.

CHAPTER 68: NAVIGATING THE INTERNATIONAL AI ECOSYSTEM AND REGULATORY ENVIRONMENT

Artificial Intelligence (AI) is a global phenomenon that transcends borders, making it essential for organizations to navigate the international AI ecosystem and regulatory environment. As AI technologies continue to evolve, countries worldwide are implementing regulations and frameworks to address ethical, legal, and societal implications. Understanding the international landscape and complying with relevant regulations is crucial for organizations engaged in AI development and deployment. Let us explore key considerations and strategies for navigating the international AI ecosystem and regulatory environment:

Stay Informed about Global AI Initiatives:

Organizations should stay abreast of global AI initiatives and regulatory developments. International organizations, such as the United Nations, the European Union, and various industry consortia, actively work on AI-related policies, guidelines, and standards. By participating in relevant discussions, conferences, and workshops, organizations can gain insights into emerging trends, best practices, and regulatory expectations on a global scale.

Assess Regional AI Strategies and Policies:

Different countries and regions have varying AI strategies and policies. Organizations should evaluate the AI strategies, national AI plans, and regulatory frameworks in countries where they operate or plan to expand their AI operations. Understanding the specific AI priorities, goals, and guidelines of each region helps organizations align their AI initiatives with local requirements and demonstrate compliance with regional regulations.

Consider Ethical Guidelines and Principles:

Ethical considerations play a significant role in the international AI ecosystem. Organizations should familiarize themselves with ethical guidelines and principles, such as the OECD Principles on AI, the EU's Ethics Guidelines for Trustworthy AI, or industry-specific ethical frameworks. Incorporating ethical principles into AI development and deployment ensures responsible AI innovation and enhances trust among stakeholders in different regions.

Privacy and Data Protection Regulations:

Data protection regulations, such as the EU's General Data Protection Regulation (GDPR), have a significant impact on AI deployment. Organizations must comply with regional data protection laws and ensure that AI systems and processes handle personal data appropriately. This includes implementing privacy-by-design principles, obtaining informed consent, and ensuring the lawful and transparent processing of personal data.

Understand Intellectual Property Laws:

Intellectual Property (IP) laws vary across jurisdictions. Organizations should familiarize themselves with international IP regulations and practices to protect their AI-generated IP. This includes understanding the requirements and processes for patent, copyright, and trade secret protection in different regions. Engaging IP attorneys with international expertise can help navigate the complexities of IP protection in the international AI ecosystem.

Export Controls and Trade Regulations:

Export controls and trade regulations may impact the transfer of AI technologies across borders. Organizations involved in AI research, development, or deployment should assess whether their activities fall under export control regimes. Export controls may apply to AI technologies with military applications or technologies subject to restrictions based on national security concerns. Compliance with export control regulations ensures lawful and responsible AI technology transfer.

International Standards and Certifications:

Standards and certifications play a crucial role in ensuring interoperability, quality, and safety in AI systems. Organizations should evaluate international standards and certifications relevant to their AI applications. Standards bodies, such as ISO and IEEE, develop AI-related standards and certification programs that provide guidance on AI ethics, data governance, algorithmic transparency, and more. Adhering to recognized standards and pursuing certifications demonstrates a commitment to best practices and quality assurance in AI.

Establish International Partnerships:

Building international partnerships is valuable for navigating the international AI ecosystem. Collaborating with international organizations, research institutions, and industry consortia allows for knowledge sharing, collaboration on AI research projects, and access to global expertise. International partnerships facilitate understanding regional nuances, cultural considerations, and regulatory environments, helping organizations effectively navigate the international AI landscape.

Localize AI Solutions:

To succeed in different regions, organizations should consider localizing their AI solutions. This involves adapting AI models, algorithms, and user interfaces to local languages, cultural contexts, and user preferences. Localization ensures that AI systems are aligned with local user needs, regulatory requirements, and societal expectations, enhancing the acceptance and adoption of AI technologies in different regions.

Engage with Regulatory Authorities:

Proactive engagement with regulatory authorities is crucial for organizations operating in the international AI ecosystem. By establishing open lines of communication, organizations can seek guidance, clarify regulatory requirements, and participate in regulatory consultations or public comment processes. Engaging with regulatory authorities fosters constructive dialogue, promotes regulatory compliance, and enables organizations to contribute to shaping AI policies and regulations.

In conclusion, navigating the international AI ecosystem and regulatory environment requires organizations to stay informed about global AI initiatives, assess regional AI strategies and policies, consider ethical guidelines, comply with privacy and data protection regulations, understand intellectual property laws, and adhere to export controls and trade regulations. Engaging with international standards, establishing partnerships, localizing AI solutions, and engaging with regulatory authorities facilitate compliance and foster responsible AI innovation on a global scale. By understanding the diverse regulatory landscapes, organizations can navigate the complexities of the international AI ecosystem and ensure their AI initiatives align with regional requirements and societal expectations.

CHAPTER 69: LEVERAGING AI FOR GLOBAL MARKET EXPANSION AND BUSINESS GROWTH

In today's interconnected world, organizations have immense opportunities for global market expansion and business growth. To seize these opportunities, businesses must leverage advanced technologies, and Artificial Intelligence (AI) stands out as a powerful tool. AI can enable organizations to overcome geographical barriers, understand diverse markets, and drive business growth on a global scale. Let us explore how organizations can leverage AI for global market expansion and business growth:

Market Research and Analysis:

AI can revolutionize market research and analysis by processing vast amounts of data from various sources, including social media, customer feedback, and market trends. AI-powered analytics tools can derive valuable insights about customer preferences, cultural nuances, and market dynamics in different regions. By leveraging AI, organizations can gain a deeper understanding of target markets, identify growth opportunities, and tailor their products or services to specific market needs.

Localization and Personalization:

Localization is essential for successful global expansion. AI can assist in localizing products, services, and marketing strategies by automating language translation, cultural adaptation, and content customization. AI-driven natural language processing (NLP) and machine learning algorithms enable organizations to tailor their offerings to specific regions, ensuring relevance, and resonating with local customers. Personalization powered by AI enables organizations to deliver targeted experiences, recommendations, and offers, enhancing customer engagement and driving business growth in different markets.

Demand Forecasting and Inventory Management:

AI algorithms can analyze historical sales data, market trends, and external factors to forecast demand accurately. This enables organizations to optimize their inventory management, ensure product availability, and minimize the risk of stockouts or excess inventory. AI-powered demand forecasting helps organizations align their supply chain operations with market demand, reducing costs, and improving customer satisfaction in global markets.

Customer Service and Support:

AI-powered chatbots and virtual assistants can enhance customer service and support on a global scale. These intelligent conversational agents can handle customer inquiries, provide real-time assistance, and resolve issues in multiple languages. AI-driven natural language processing enables chatbots to understand and respond to customer queries accurately, improving customer experience, and ensuring consistent support across different regions and time zones.

Sales and Marketing Automation:

AI can automate various sales and marketing processes, enabling organizations to scale their operations and reach a global audience more efficiently. AI-powered lead scoring models can identify high-value prospects, prioritize sales efforts, and increase conversion rates. AI-driven marketing automation tools can optimize digital advertising campaigns, personalize messaging, and target specific customer segments in different markets, maximizing marketing ROI and driving business growth.

Competitive Intelligence and Pricing Optimization:

AI enables organizations to gather competitive intelligence and gain insights into market dynamics. AI algorithms can monitor competitor activities, pricing strategies, and market trends, providing organizations with a competitive edge. AI-powered pricing optimization tools analyze market data, demand patterns, and competitor pricing to determine optimal pricing strategies for different markets, ensuring competitiveness and profitability.

Fraud Detection and Risk Mitigation:

Expanding into global markets comes with the risk of fraud and cybersecurity threats. AI can play a critical role in fraud detection and risk mitigation. AI algorithms can analyze vast amounts of data, identify anomalous patterns, and detect potentially fraudulent activities in real-time. By leveraging AI-powered fraud detection systems, organizations can protect their operations, financial transactions, and customer data, mitigating risks and ensuring trust in global markets.

Language Translation and Communication:

Language barriers can hinder global expansion. AI-powered language translation technologies can bridge this gap by providing real-time translation services for communication, documentation, and customer interactions. AI-driven language translation tools enable organizations to communicate effectively with customers, partners, and employees across different languages, fostering collaboration, and facilitating business growth in international markets.

Supply Chain Optimization:

AI can optimize global supply chains by predicting demand fluctuations, optimizing logistics routes, and improving supply chain efficiency. AI-powered supply chain management systems leverage advanced algorithms and data analytics to optimize inventory levels, reduce lead times, and improve overall supply chain performance. This ensures timely delivery of products and services to global customers, enhancing customer satisfaction and driving business growth.

Market Expansion Strategy and Decision-making:

AI can support organizations in formulating effective market expansion strategies and making data-driven decisions. AI algorithms can analyze market data, customer insights, and competitive intelligence to evaluate potential markets, assess market entry barriers, and identify growth opportunities. AI-powered decision support systems can provide organizations with actionable recommendations, enabling them to make informed decisions on market expansion, investment, and resource allocation.

In conclusion, leveraging AI for global market expansion and business growth offers organizations a competitive advantage in today's interconnected world. By harnessing AI technologies for market research, localization, demand forecasting, customer service, sales and marketing automation, competitive intelligence, fraud detection, language translation, supply chain optimization, and decision-making, organizations can unlock new opportunities, penetrate diverse markets, and drive business growth on a global scale. Strategic adoption of AI empowers organizations to overcome geographical barriers, tailor offerings to local markets, and stay ahead in the global marketplace.

CHAPTER 70: UNDERSTANDING THE IMPACT OF AI ON INTERNATIONAL TRADE AND COMPETITION

Artificial Intelligence (AI) has emerged as a transformative technology with significant implications for international trade and competition. As AI continues to advance, it is reshaping industries, transforming business models, and impacting global economic dynamics. To navigate the evolving landscape, it is crucial to understand the impact of AI on international trade and competition. Let us explore key considerations and insights into this topic:

Increased Efficiency and Productivity:

AI technologies can enhance productivity and efficiency across industries, enabling organizations to streamline operations, automate tasks, and optimize processes. By leveraging AI-powered automation, organizations can improve production processes, reduce costs, and enhance supply chain management. This increased efficiency enhances competitiveness in international trade and allows organizations to deliver products and services more effectively and efficiently.

Disruption of Traditional Industries:

AI's disruptive potential is evident in various industries, transforming business models and value chains. For instance, the rise of AI-powered autonomous vehicles can revolutionize transportation and logistics, impacting global supply chains and trade flows. Similarly, AI-driven innovations in healthcare, finance, manufacturing, and other sectors are reshaping traditional industries, leading to new market dynamics and trade patterns.

Shifts in Comparative Advantage:

AI can influence the comparative advantage of nations in international trade. Countries with advanced AI capabilities and a supportive ecosystem can gain a competitive edge in AI-driven industries. These countries can attract investment, foster innovation, and develop AI talent, leading to the concentration of AI-related activities and the emergence of AI hubs. The distribution of comparative advantage may shift as countries compete in AI-driven sectors, potentially impacting trade balances and global competitiveness.

New Trade Opportunities:

AI opens up new trade opportunities, particularly in the digital economy. AI-driven technologies enable cross-border e-commerce, digital services, and data-driven innovations. Organizations can leverage AI to customize products and services to specific market segments, enhance customer experiences, and tap into global consumer markets. The rise of AI-driven platforms and marketplaces facilitates international trade and provides access to a wider customer base.

Data as a Trade Resource:

AI relies heavily on data, and the availability and quality of data can significantly impact international trade and competition. Countries and organizations with access to large, diverse, and high-quality datasets can develop more robust AI algorithms and models. This can create data-driven competitive advantages and influence global market positions. The ability to collect, analyze, and protect data has become a critical factor in international trade and competitiveness.

Intellectual Property and Technology Transfer:

AI advancements raise important intellectual property (IP) and technology transfer considerations. Protecting AI-related IP rights is crucial for organizations to maintain a competitive edge and secure market positions. At the same time, technology transfer agreements and collaborations can foster AI development, knowledge sharing, and innovation diffusion across borders. Balancing IP protection and technology transfer is essential for promoting global AI development and ensuring fair competition.

Regulatory and Policy Challenges:

The rapid pace of AI development presents challenges for regulatory frameworks and international cooperation. Policymakers face the task of addressing ethical, legal, and societal implications while fostering innovation and ensuring fair competition. Harmonizing AI-related regulations and standards at the international level can promote consistency, facilitate trade, and address concerns such as privacy, cybersecurity, bias, and accountability.

Workforce and Skill Requirements:

AI's impact on international trade extends to workforce dynamics. The adoption of AI technologies can lead to job displacement, particularly in routine or repetitive tasks. However, it also creates opportunities for new types of jobs and demands a workforce with AI-related skills. Countries and organizations must invest in reskilling and upskilling initiatives to equip workers with the necessary AI skills and ensure a smooth transition to the AI-driven economy.

Collaborative Innovation and Partnerships:

International collaboration and partnerships play a crucial role in advancing AI technologies and addressing global challenges. Collaboration between countries, research institutions, and businesses can drive innovation, knowledge exchange, and technology diffusion. Collaborative efforts can foster AI development, promote responsible AI practices, and address global issues like climate change, healthcare, and poverty alleviation.

In conclusion, AI is a transformative force with profound implications for international trade and competition. Organizations and policymakers must understand the impact of AI on productivity, business models, comparative advantage, and trade patterns. Embracing AI-driven opportunities, addressing regulatory challenges, fostering collaborative innovation, and investing in AI skills development will be critical to leveraging the potential of AI for sustainable economic growth and global competitiveness. By embracing AI and its potential, countries and organizations can position themselves for success in the AI-driven global economy.

CHAPTER 71: PREPARING IT SYSTEMS AND NETWORKS FOR AI-DRIVEN DEMANDS

As organizations embrace Artificial Intelligence (AI) technologies, it is essential to ensure that their IT systems and networks are adequately prepared to meet the demands of AI-driven applications. AI introduces unique requirements in terms of computational power, data storage, connectivity, and infrastructure. To leverage the full potential of AI and support its implementation effectively, organizations must proactively prepare their IT systems and networks. Let us explore key considerations and strategies for preparing IT systems and networks for AI-driven demands:

Infrastructure Assessment:

Assessing the existing IT infrastructure is the first step in preparing for AI-driven demands. Evaluate the computational capabilities, storage capacity, and network bandwidth to determine if they can support the increased processing and storage requirements of AI applications. Identify any gaps or limitations that may hinder AI performance or scalability.

High-Performance Computing (HPC):

AI applications often require significant computational power, especially for complex tasks such as deep learning and large-scale data processing. Consider deploying or upgrading to high-performance computing (HPC) systems to handle the computational demands of AI algorithms efficiently.

HPC clusters or cloud-based solutions can provide the necessary processing power to train and deploy AI models effectively.

Scalable Storage Solutions:

AI applications generate and consume vast amounts of data. Ensure that your organization has scalable and high-capacity storage solutions in place to accommodate the data requirements of AI projects. Consider leveraging distributed file systems, object storage, or cloud-based storage solutions that can handle the storage demands of AI-generated data and facilitate seamless data access and retrieval.

Network Bandwidth and Latency:

AI applications often rely on large datasets that need to be processed and analyzed in real-time. To support AI-driven demands, organizations must assess their network bandwidth and latency. High-speed and low-latency networks are crucial for efficient data transfer, model training, and real-time AI inference. Evaluate network infrastructure, consider upgrading network connections, and implement appropriate network architectures to minimize bottlenecks and ensure smooth AI operations.

Data Integration and Data Pipelines:

AI applications require access to diverse and relevant data sources. Establish robust data integration capabilities to collect, aggregate, and preprocess data from various sources. Implement efficient data pipelines that enable data ingestion, transformation, and integration to ensure a continuous and reliable flow of data to AI models. Data pipelines should also incorporate data quality checks, data governance practices, and data security measures.

Cloud Computing:

Leveraging cloud computing can provide several advantages in preparing for AI-driven demands. Cloud platforms offer scalable computing resources, flexible storage options, and AI-specific services. By adopting cloud-based AI infrastructure, organizations can access on-demand computational power, utilize pre-configured AI frameworks, and take advantage of managed AI services. Cloud solutions also facilitate collaboration, scalability, and cost optimization for AI projects.

Edge Computing:

As AI applications increasingly require real-time and low-latency inference, edge computing becomes crucial. Edge computing brings computation closer to the data source, reducing latency and network dependencies. Implementing edge computing infrastructure allows organizations to process AI workloads locally on edge devices or edge servers, improving response times and enabling AI-driven applications in resource-constrained environments or remote locations.

Security and Privacy Considerations:

AI applications handle vast amounts of sensitive data, and organizations must prioritize security and privacy measures. Implement robust cybersecurity measures, including network security, access controls, data encryption, and anomaly detection, to protect AI systems and data. Ensure compliance with privacy regulations, establish data governance frameworks, and implement privacy-enhancing techniques such as differential privacy to protect user data and maintain trust.

Collaboration and Integration with Existing Systems:

AI systems need to seamlessly integrate with existing IT infrastructure and applications. Ensure compatibility and interoperability with existing systems, databases, and software frameworks. Collaborate with IT teams and stakeholders to design integration interfaces, establish data exchange protocols, and ensure smooth interoperability between AI systems and other critical IT components.

Continuous Monitoring and Optimization:

Monitoring and optimizing AI systems and networks is an ongoing process. Implement monitoring tools and processes to track system performance, network utilization, and data flows. Proactively identify bottlenecks, optimize resource allocation, and fine-tune AI models to improve efficiency and performance. Regularly review and upgrade IT systems and networks to keep pace with evolving AI technologies and demands.

In conclusion, preparing IT systems and networks for AI-driven demands is crucial for organizations embarking on AI initiatives. Assessing infrastructure, deploying high-performance computing solutions, ensuring scalable storage and network bandwidth, embracing cloud and edge computing, prioritizing security and privacy, and establishing robust data pipelines are key considerations. Collaboration between IT and other stakeholders, continuous monitoring, and optimization are essential for ensuring that IT systems and networks are capable of meeting the demands of AI-driven applications effectively. By proactively preparing IT systems and networks, organizations can unlock the full potential of AI and drive innovation, productivity, and growth.

CHAPTER 72: EVALUATING EMERGING TECHNOLOGIES FOR POTENTIAL AI INTEGRATION

As technology continues to advance at a rapid pace, organizations are presented with a myriad of emerging technologies that have the potential to integrate with Artificial Intelligence (AI) and drive innovation. Evaluating these emerging technologies is essential for organizations seeking to harness the power of AI and stay at the forefront of technological advancements. Let us explore key considerations and approaches for evaluating emerging technologies for potential AI integration:

Understand the Business Objectives:

Before evaluating emerging technologies, organizations must have a clear understanding of their business objectives and AI strategy. Identify the specific areas where AI integration can create value and support business goals. By aligning technology evaluation with business objectives, organizations can focus on technologies that have the potential to address specific needs and drive desired outcomes.

Stay Informed and Engage in Research:

Keeping up with the latest trends and advancements in technology is crucial for effective evaluation. Stay informed by following industry publications, attending conferences, and participating in technology forums. Engage with research communities and academia to understand the latest breakthroughs in AI and related fields. This ongoing research helps identify emerging technologies that have the potential to enhance AI capabilities and generate new business opportunities.

Assess Technological Maturity:

Evaluate the technological maturity of emerging technologies before considering their integration with AI. Consider factors such as the readiness of the technology for commercial use, the level of industry adoption, and the availability of supporting tools and frameworks. Technologies that are more mature and have proven use cases are generally more suitable for integration with AI applications.

Evaluate Compatibility with Existing Infrastructure:

Assess how well emerging technologies align with the existing IT infrastructure and systems within the organization. Consider factors such as compatibility, scalability, and interoperability. Integration with AI requires seamless data exchange, compatibility with AI frameworks, and the ability to leverage existing resources effectively. Technologies that align well with the organization's existing infrastructure can streamline integration efforts and minimize disruption.

Analyze Data Requirements and Availability:

Evaluate the data requirements and availability for integrating the emerging technology with AI. Consider the type, quality, and volume of data needed to train and operate the technology effectively. Assess if the organization has access to the required data or if there are strategies for acquiring or generating the necessary data. Adequate data availability is critical for AI integration, as it enables organizations to leverage the full potential of emerging technologies.

Consider Ethical and Regulatory Implications:

Examine the ethical and regulatory implications associated with the integration of emerging technologies. Assess if the technology complies with relevant laws, regulations, and ethical guidelines. Consider potential risks, such as privacy concerns, data security, bias, and the impact on human well-being. Evaluating these ethical and regulatory aspects ensures responsible adoption of emerging technologies and mitigates potential risks.

Evaluate Vendor Capabilities and Support:

Assess the capabilities and support provided by technology vendors. Consider factors such as the vendor's track record, expertise, financial stability, and ability to provide ongoing support and maintenance. Evaluate their commitment to research and development, as well as their responsiveness to customer needs. Choosing reliable and capable vendors strengthens the potential for successful integration and long-term support for the technology.

Conduct Proof-of-Concept (PoC) Projects:

Consider conducting proof-of-concept projects to evaluate the integration of emerging technologies with AI in a controlled environment. PoC projects provide hands-on experience and allow organizations to assess the feasibility, performance, and potential benefits of integrating the technology with AI. These projects help identify challenges, uncover limitations, and gather valuable insights for making informed decisions on technology integration.

Collaborate with Industry Peers and Experts:

Engage in collaborations and partnerships with industry peers, experts, and technology ecosystems. Sharing experiences, insights, and best practices can provide valuable perspectives on the integration of emerging technologies with AI. Collaborative initiatives can foster innovation, reduce implementation risks, and accelerate the adoption of emerging technologies.

Assess Return on Investment (ROI) Potential:

Evaluate the potential return on investment of integrating the emerging technology with AI. Consider factors such as cost savings, productivity gains, revenue growth, and competitive advantage. Assess the potential impact on operational efficiency, customer experience, and market differentiation. A comprehensive ROI analysis helps prioritize technologies with the highest potential for delivering significant business value.

In conclusion, evaluating emerging technologies for potential AI integration requires a strategic and comprehensive approach. By aligning evaluation with business objectives, staying informed, assessing technological maturity, considering compatibility, analyzing data requirements, and evaluating ethical and regulatory implications, organizations can make informed decisions. Conducting proof-of-concept projects, collaborating with industry peers, assessing vendor capabilities, and assessing ROI potential further strengthen the evaluation process. By effectively evaluating emerging technologies, organizations can identify the most promising technologies and leverage AI to drive innovation, competitive advantage, and business success.

CHAPTER 73: FUTURE-PROOFING IT INFRASTRUCTURE FOR LONG-TERM AI SUCCESS

As Artificial Intelligence (AI) continues to evolve and play an increasingly prominent role in organizations, it is crucial to future-proof IT infrastructure to ensure long-term success in harnessing the power of AI. Future-proofing involves building a flexible and scalable IT foundation that can adapt to the changing demands of AI technologies and accommodate future advancements. Let us explore key considerations and strategies for future-proofing IT infrastructure for long-term AI success:

Scalability and Elasticity:

Scalability is vital when future-proofing IT infrastructure for AI. As AI workloads and data volumes grow, organizations need the ability to scale their infrastructure to meet increasing demands. Cloud computing offers scalability advantages by providing on-demand access to computing resources. Embracing cloud-based infrastructure allows organizations to easily scale up or down based on AI requirements, enabling cost optimization and agility.

High-Performance Computing (HPC):

AI applications often require significant computational power to process large datasets and train complex models. Investing in High-Performance Computing (HPC) capabilities can future-proof infrastructure for AI. HPC systems, including GPU-accelerated servers and clusters, provide the necessary computational resources to handle the demanding workloads of AI. Evaluating and adopting HPC solutions can ensure the infrastructure can handle future AI advancements.

Edge Computing:

Edge computing has gained prominence with the rise of AI applications that require real-time processing and low-latency inference. Deploying edge computing infrastructure brings computation closer to the data source, reducing latency and network dependencies. By leveraging edge computing, organizations can future-proof their infrastructure for AI-driven applications that require immediate decision-making and localized processing, particularly in IoT environments.

Data Management and Storage:

AI heavily relies on vast amounts of data for training and inference. Future-proofing IT infrastructure requires robust data management and storage solutions. Organizations must ensure they have scalable and secure data storage systems capable of handling the growing volume and variety of data. Distributed file systems, object storage, and data lakes can provide the necessary scalability and flexibility for storing and managing AI data.

Network Infrastructure:

AI applications generate significant network traffic, particularly during training and inference processes. Organizations need to assess their network infrastructure and ensure it can handle the increased bandwidth demands of AI workloads. High-speed and low-latency networks, such as fiber-optic connections and software-defined networks (SDNs), are essential for efficient data transfer between AI components and systems.

AI-Optimized Hardware:

Future-proofing IT infrastructure for AI success involves considering hardware optimizations specifically designed for AI workloads. AI-optimized hardware, such as AI accelerators (e.g., GPUs, TPUs), can significantly improve the performance and efficiency of AI computations.

Evaluating and incorporating AI-optimized hardware into the infrastructure can enhance AI capabilities and ensure compatibility with future AI advancements.

Data Governance and Security:

Data governance and security are critical for long-term AI success. Organizations must establish robust data governance frameworks, ensuring data integrity, privacy, and compliance. Implementing data security measures, such as encryption, access controls, and anomaly detection, protects AI systems and the sensitive data they handle. Future-proofing infrastructure involves continuously enhancing data governance and security measures as AI technologies evolve.

AI-Ready Software Stack:

To future-proof IT infrastructure, organizations must evaluate and adopt an AI-ready software stack. This stack includes AI frameworks, libraries, and development tools that enable efficient development, deployment, and management of AI models. Open-source frameworks like TensorFlow and PyTorch, along with AI-specific platforms and APIs, provide the foundation for building AI capabilities and accommodating future advancements.

Continuous Monitoring and Optimization:

Future-proofing requires continuous monitoring and optimization of the IT infrastructure. Regularly assess system performance, identify bottlenecks, and optimize resource allocation. Monitor AI workloads, network traffic, and data flows to detect anomalies and optimize infrastructure accordingly. Proactive monitoring and optimization ensure that the infrastructure remains resilient, scalable, and capable of accommodating future AI demands.

Collaboration and Knowledge Sharing:

Future-proofing IT infrastructure involves fostering collaboration and knowledge sharing within the organization. Encourage cross-functional collaboration between IT teams, data scientists, and business stakeholders to align infrastructure requirements with AI goals. Collaborate with industry peers, engage in communities, and participate in conferences and events to stay updated on emerging technologies and best practices.

In conclusion, future-proofing IT infrastructure is essential for long-term AI success. By prioritizing scalability, embracing cloud computing and edge computing, investing in high-performance computing and AI-optimized hardware, and implementing robust data management, governance, and security measures, organizations can prepare their infrastructure to accommodate future AI advancements. Continuous monitoring, optimization, collaboration, and knowledge sharing further strengthen the future-proofing process. By future-proofing IT infrastructure, organizations can leverage the full potential of AI and drive innovation, competitiveness, and sustained success.

CHAPTER 74: CULTIVATING A STRATEGIC AI VISION FOR YOUR ORGANIZATION

Artificial Intelligence (AI) has the potential to transform businesses across various industries, enabling organizations to gain valuable insights, automate processes, and make data-driven decisions. However, to fully harness the power of AI, organizations must cultivate a strategic AI vision that aligns with their overall business objectives and drives long-term success. Let us explore key considerations and strategies for cultivating a strategic AI vision for your organization:

Define Business Objectives:

Start by clearly defining your organization's business objectives and identifying areas where AI can create value and drive desired outcomes. Whether it is improving customer experience, enhancing operational efficiency, or driving innovation, understanding your business goals is crucial for aligning your AI vision with strategic priorities.

Conduct a Current State Assessment:

Assess your organization's current state in terms of data maturity, technology infrastructure, skill sets, and AI readiness. Identify existing AI initiatives, ongoing data-related projects, and potential barriers or challenges that may impact AI adoption. This assessment provides a foundation for developing a roadmap to achieve your AI vision.

Educate and Build AI Awareness:

Educate key stakeholders across the organization about AI technologies, benefits, and potential use cases. Foster awareness and understanding of AI's capabilities and its impact on business processes and industry trends. This education creates a shared understanding and lays the groundwork for embracing AI as a strategic tool.

Formulate a Clear AI Strategy:

Develop a comprehensive AI strategy that outlines how AI will be integrated into various aspects of your organization. Define the scope of AI applications, identify key use cases, and prioritize initiatives based on their potential impact and feasibility. Your AI strategy should align with your overall business strategy and address challenges related to data, technology, talent, and ethical considerations.

Establish Cross-Functional Collaboration:

Successful implementation of an AI vision requires collaboration between business units, IT, data scientists, and other stakeholders. Foster cross-functional collaboration to ensure that AI initiatives are aligned with business needs and effectively integrated into existing processes. Encourage open communication, knowledge sharing, and collaboration to drive innovation and maximize the value of AI across the organization.

Build the Right AI Team:

Assemble a multidisciplinary team with the necessary skills and expertise to execute your AI vision. This team may include data scientists, machine learning engineers, domain experts, and business analysts. Ensure a diverse mix of technical and business skills to drive innovation, solve complex problems, and translate AI capabilities into tangible business outcomes.

Invest in Data Infrastructure and Governance:

Data is the foundation of AI, so investing in robust data infrastructure and governance is crucial. Establish data management practices, including data collection, storage, quality assurance, and security measures. Ensure that data is easily accessible, well-organized, and of high quality to support AI initiatives effectively.

Develop AI Ethics Guidelines:

Develop clear guidelines and policies that address ethical considerations in AI. Define principles for responsible AI usage, including fairness, transparency, privacy, and accountability. Ensure that ethical considerations are embedded into the design, development, and deployment of AI solutions, and regularly review and update these guidelines as AI technologies evolve.

Foster a Culture of Experimentation and Learning:

Encourage a culture of experimentation, innovation, and continuous learning. Embrace a growth mindset that encourages employees to explore AI opportunities, take calculated risks, and learn from failures. Provide resources and training programs to upskill employees and enable them to leverage AI technologies effectively.

Monitor and Measure AI Impact:

Establish key performance indicators (KPIs) and metrics to measure the impact of AI initiatives. Regularly monitor and evaluate the progress and effectiveness of AI projects against these KPIs. This feedback loop enables continuous improvement, informed decision-making, and course correction if needed.

Stay Abreast of AI Trends and Developments:

Stay informed about the latest trends, advancements, and best practices in AI. Monitor industry developments, attend conferences, participate in AI communities, and engage with thought leaders. This knowledge helps you stay ahead of the curve, identify emerging opportunities, and adapt your AI vision to evolving technologies and market dynamics.

In conclusion, cultivating a strategic AI vision requires a holistic approach that aligns AI initiatives with business objectives, fosters cross-functional collaboration, builds the right team, invests in data infrastructure and governance, and embraces an ethical and learning-oriented culture. By developing a clear AI strategy, nurturing a collaborative environment, and staying informed about AI trends, your organization can leverage AI as a strategic tool to drive innovation, competitiveness, and long-term success.

CHAPTER 75: DEVELOPING AI LEADERSHIP SKILLS AND COMPETENCIES

In the era of Artificial Intelligence (AI), organizations need leaders who possess the skills and competencies to effectively navigate the complexities of AI-driven environments. Developing AI leadership skills is crucial for driving successful AI adoption, fostering innovation, and leveraging AI technologies to gain a competitive edge. Let us explore key considerations and strategies for developing AI leadership skills and competencies:

Embrace a Growth Mindset:

AI leaders should adopt a growth mindset, which is essential for embracing new technologies and continuously learning. Cultivate a curiosity about AI, its potential applications, and its impact on the business. Be open to exploring new ideas, experimenting with AI technologies, and seeking opportunities to learn and grow in the AI domain.

Understand the Fundamentals of AI:

Develop a foundational understanding of AI concepts, technologies, and applications. AI leaders should be familiar with machine learning, deep learning, natural language processing, computer vision, and other AI techniques. This knowledge enables leaders to effectively communicate with technical teams, make informed decisions, and guide AI initiatives.

Develop Business Acumen:

AI leaders should possess strong business acumen and understand the strategic implications of AI adoption. They should be able to identify AI opportunities that align with business goals, assess the potential impact on revenue, cost optimization, and customer experience. Developing a deep understanding of the organization's industry, competitive landscape, and customer needs helps AI leaders drive meaningful AI-driven business outcomes.

Build a Multidisciplinary Team:

AI leadership involves assembling and managing a multidisciplinary team with diverse skills and expertise. AI leaders should be adept at identifying and recruiting talent across different domains, including data science, machine learning, software engineering, and business analysis. Building a cohesive team and fostering collaboration among team members are crucial for successful AI implementations.

Foster an Ethical and Responsible AI Culture:

AI leaders should prioritize ethics and responsibility in AI adoption. Understanding the ethical implications of AI, such as fairness, bias, and privacy, is crucial for making ethical decisions throughout the AI lifecycle. Encourage an AI culture that values transparency, fairness, and accountability, and ensure that AI initiatives comply with legal and regulatory frameworks.

Promote Data-Driven Decision-Making:

Data is at the core of AI, and AI leaders should promote a data-driven decision-making culture within the organization. Encourage teams to leverage AI-generated insights, analytics, and predictive models to inform decision-making processes. AI leaders should emphasize the importance of data quality, accessibility, and security to enable effective use of AI technologies.

Enhance Communication and Collaboration:

Effective communication is a critical skill for AI leaders. They must be able to explain AI concepts, strategies, and benefits to both technical and non-technical stakeholders. AI leaders should bridge the gap between technical experts and business units, translating technical complexities into actionable insights and strategies. Cultivating a collaborative environment fosters cross-functional alignment and ensures that AI initiatives are effectively integrated into existing processes.

Encourage Innovation and Experimentation:

AI leaders should foster a culture of innovation and experimentation. Encourage teams to explore new AI techniques, experiment with different AI tools and platforms, and take calculated risks. Creating a safe environment for experimentation allows for the exploration of innovative AI-driven solutions and encourages continuous improvement.

Stay Abreast of AI Advances:

AI is a rapidly evolving field, and AI leaders need to stay up to date with the latest advancements and trends. Continuously learn about new AI techniques, frameworks, and emerging technologies. Engage in AI communities, attend conferences, and participate in industry events to stay abreast of the latest developments. Sharing knowledge with peers and encouraging ongoing learning within the organization fosters innovation and positions leaders as thought leaders in the AI space.

Foster Adaptability and Change Management Skills:

AI leadership requires adaptability and effective change management. AI leaders should embrace change, be resilient in the face of challenges, and inspire others to embrace AI-driven transformations. Develop change management skills to effectively communicate the vision, overcome resistance, and navigate organizational changes associated with AI adoption.

In conclusion, developing AI leadership skills and competencies is essential for organizations to leverage AI effectively and drive innovation. By embracing a growth mindset, understanding AI fundamentals, developing business acumen, building a multidisciplinary team, fostering an ethical AI culture, promoting data-driven decision-making, enhancing communication and collaboration, encouraging innovation, staying updated with AI advances, and nurturing adaptability and change management skills, AI leaders can lead their organizations to harness the full potential of AI and create a competitive advantage in the AI-driven landscape.

CHAPTER 76: BUILDING A NETWORK OF AI CHAMPIONS AND ADVOCATES WITHIN YOUR ORGANIZATION

In order to drive successful AI adoption and foster a culture of innovation, organizations need to build a network of AI champions and advocates. These individuals play a crucial role in promoting AI initiatives, driving adoption, and influencing organizational culture. By leveraging the expertise and enthusiasm of these AI champions, organizations can accelerate AI implementation and maximize the benefits of AI technologies. Let us explore key considerations and strategies for building a network of AI champions and advocates within your organization:

Identify Potential AI Champions:

Start by identifying individuals within your organization who possess a strong interest in AI and demonstrate the potential to champion AI initiatives. Look for individuals who are proactive, innovative, and have a good understanding of the organization's goals and challenges. These individuals could come from various departments, including IT, data science, operations, marketing, and customer service.

Provide AI Training and Education:

Offer AI training programs and educational resources to equip potential champions with the knowledge and skills they need to understand AI concepts, technologies, and applications. This training should cover both technical and non-technical aspects of AI, enabling champions to communicate effectively with different stakeholders and promote AI initiatives across the organization.

Foster a Culture of Collaboration and Knowledge Sharing:

Create an environment that encourages collaboration and knowledge sharing among AI champions. Establish forums, such as regular meetings or online platforms, where champions can exchange ideas, share experiences, and discuss AI-related challenges and solutions. This collaborative culture promotes cross-pollination of ideas, accelerates learning, and strengthens the AI community within the organization.

Provide Access to AI Tools and Resources:

Ensure that AI champions have access to the necessary AI tools, platforms, and resources to experiment and explore AI applications within their respective domains. This could include providing access to AI development environments, datasets, and pre-trained models. By providing these resources, champions can gain hands-on experience, develop proofs of concept, and showcase the potential value of AI within their specific areas of expertise.

Encourage Experimentation and Innovation:

Empower AI champions to experiment with AI technologies and explore innovative AI-driven solutions. Create a safe space where champions can take risks, learn from failures, and iterate on their ideas. Encourage them to think outside the box and propose AI applications that could address specific business challenges or create new opportunities. Recognize and celebrate their achievements to inspire others and foster a culture of innovation.

Support Cross-Functional Collaboration:

Promote collaboration between AI champions and other teams or departments within the organization. Encourage champions to share their AI knowledge and insights with colleagues who may benefit from AI-driven solutions. Facilitate cross-functional projects and initiatives that leverage AI technologies to solve complex business problems. This collaboration enhances the impact of AI initiatives, breaks down silos, and fosters a collective approach to AI adoption.

Provide Leadership Opportunities:

Offer leadership opportunities to AI champions to drive AI initiatives and projects. Assign them roles where they can lead cross-functional teams, manage AI-related projects, or act as mentors to other employees interested in AI. These leadership opportunities not only recognize their expertise but also provide a platform for them to influence and drive AI adoption at a broader organizational level.

Communicate Success Stories and Benefits:

Share success stories and communicate the benefits of AI implementations within the organization. Highlight the positive outcomes, such as improved operational efficiency, enhanced customer experiences, or increased revenue, achieved through AI-driven initiatives. These success stories serve as inspiration and demonstrate the tangible value of AI to other employees, creating a ripple effect of enthusiasm and support for AI adoption.

Develop External Networks and Partnerships:

Encourage AI champions to engage with external AI communities, attend conferences, and participate in industry events. These external networks provide opportunities for champions to learn from industry experts, stay updated on the latest AI trends and developments, and bring external perspectives and insights back to the organization. Additionally, seek partnerships with external AI-focused organizations, research institutions, or consultants to augment internal expertise and drive AI initiatives forward.

Recognize and Reward Contributions:

Recognize and reward the contributions of AI champions to reinforce their commitment and dedication. This recognition can take various forms, such as awards, promotions, or opportunities for professional development. Publicly acknowledge their efforts and showcase their achievements to inspire others and reinforce the organization's commitment to AI innovation.

In conclusion, building a network of AI champions and advocates within your organization is crucial for driving successful AI adoption and fostering a culture of innovation. By identifying potential champions, providing AI training and resources, fostering collaboration and knowledge sharing, encouraging experimentation and innovation, supporting cross-functional collaboration, providing leadership opportunities, communicating success stories, developing external networks, and recognizing contributions, organizations can harness the expertise and enthusiasm of their champions to accelerate AI adoption and realize the full potential of AI technologies.

CHAPTER 77: ALIGNING AI STRATEGY WITH CORPORATE SOCIAL RESPONSIBILITY (CSR) AND ETHICAL VALUES

As organizations embrace Artificial Intelligence (AI) technologies, it becomes crucial to align AI strategies with corporate social responsibility (CSR) and ethical values. AI has the potential to significantly impact individuals, communities, and society as a whole, and organizations must proactively consider the social and ethical implications of their AI initiatives. By integrating CSR and ethical considerations into their AI strategies, organizations can ensure that AI deployments are responsible, transparent, and aligned with societal values. Let us explore key considerations and strategies for aligning AI strategy with CSR and ethical values:

Understand the Impact of AI:

Develop a deep understanding of the potential impact of AI on individuals, communities, and society. Consider the ethical challenges associated with AI, such as bias, privacy, transparency, fairness, and accountability. Recognize that AI technologies have the power to shape people's lives, influence decision-making processes, and amplify existing societal biases. Understanding these impacts is the first step in aligning AI strategy with CSR and ethical values.

Define Ethical Principles:

Establish a set of ethical principles that guide AI initiatives within your organization. These principles should reflect your organization's values, respect for individual rights, and commitment to fairness, transparency, and accountability. Ensure that these principles are integrated into every stage of the AI lifecycle, from data collection and model development to deployment and ongoing monitoring.

Foster Cross-Functional Collaboration:

Collaborate with different stakeholders, including ethicists, legal experts, privacy professionals, and community representatives, to inform and shape your AI strategy. Foster cross-functional collaboration to incorporate diverse perspectives and ensure that ethical considerations are adequately addressed. This collaboration helps in identifying potential risks, addressing ethical concerns, and developing comprehensive guidelines and policies for responsible AI deployment.

Embed Privacy and Data Protection:

Privacy and data protection should be a core component of your AI strategy. Ensure that AI initiatives comply with relevant privacy regulations and adhere to established data protection practices. Develop policies and procedures for obtaining informed consent, data anonymization, secure data storage, and secure data sharing. Protecting the privacy of individuals and respecting their data rights is crucial for building trust and maintaining ethical AI practices.

Address Bias and Fairness:

Recognize and mitigate bias in AI algorithms and models. Invest in data quality and diversity to ensure that AI systems are trained on representative datasets. Regularly monitor AI outputs for potential biases and take steps to address them. Implement fairness metrics and testing frameworks to assess the impact of AI systems on different demographic groups. Proactively address bias and fairness concerns to ensure equitable outcomes and avoid perpetuating societal inequalities.

Ensure Transparency and Explainability:

Promote transparency and explainability in AI systems. Ensure that decisions made by AI algorithms can be understood and justified. Provide explanations for AI-generated outputs, especially in high-stakes applications such as healthcare or finance. Strive for transparency in data collection, model training, and decision-making processes. Transparent AI systems foster trust among stakeholders and enable accountability.

Engage in Ethical AI Governance:

Establish robust governance frameworks to oversee AI initiatives. Develop clear roles, responsibilities, and decision-making processes related to AI adoption and use. Consider establishing an AI ethics committee or review board to assess the ethical implications of AI projects. Regularly review and update governance frameworks as AI technologies evolve and ethical standards advance.

Engage with Stakeholders:

Engage with stakeholders, including employees, customers, partners, and the broader community, to understand their concerns and aspirations regarding AI. Conduct regular dialogues, surveys, or focus groups to gather feedback and involve stakeholders in the decision-making process. By incorporating diverse perspectives, organizations can ensure that their AI initiatives align with societal values and serve the interests of all stakeholders.

Support Ethical AI Research and Development:

Invest in research and development efforts focused on advancing ethical AI practices. Support collaborations with academic institutions and research organizations that explore the societal impact of AI and develop ethical guidelines. Encourage your teams to contribute to the AI community through the publication of research papers and participation in conferences and workshops focused on AI ethics.

Embrace Continuous Learning and Improvement:

AI ethics and CSR considerations are evolving fields, and organizations must stay informed and adapt their AI strategies accordingly. Encourage continuous learning among employees, provide training on AI ethics, and allocate resources for staying up to date with emerging ethical frameworks and best practices. Actively seek feedback from stakeholders and be open to revisiting and revising your AI strategy as new ethical challenges arise.

In conclusion, aligning AI strategy with CSR and ethical values is crucial for organizations that seek to leverage AI technologies responsibly and ethically. By understanding the impact of AI, defining ethical principles, fostering cross-functional collaboration, embedding privacy and data protection, addressing bias and fairness, ensuring transparency and explainability, engaging stakeholders, establishing ethical AI governance, supporting ethical AI research, and embracing continuous learning and improvement, organizations can build a foundation of ethical AI practices and contribute to the responsible development and deployment of AI technologies.

CHAPTER 78: IMPLEMENTING ETHICAL AI PRINCIPLES IN YOUR ORGANIZATION'S CULTURE

As organizations adopt Artificial Intelligence (AI) technologies, it becomes essential to embed ethical AI principles into the organization's culture. Ethical AI principles guide the responsible development and use of AI, ensuring that AI systems are fair, transparent, accountable, and aligned with societal values. By integrating ethical AI principles into the organizational culture, organizations can foster trust, mitigate risks, and drive the ethical deployment of AI technologies. Let us explore key considerations and strategies for implementing ethical AI principles in your organization's culture:

Establish a Code of Ethics:

Develop a code of ethics specific to AI that outlines the organization's commitment to responsible AI practices. The code should reflect ethical principles such as fairness, transparency, accountability, privacy, and human rights. Ensure that the code is communicated to all employees and stakeholders, emphasizing the organization's commitment to ethical AI.

Leadership Commitment:

Leadership plays a pivotal role in promoting ethical AI principles. Leaders should demonstrate a strong commitment to ethical AI and lead by example. They should articulate the organization's vision for ethical AI, communicate the importance of ethical considerations, and allocate resources to support ethical AI initiatives. Leadership commitment sets the tone for the organization and reinforces the importance of ethical AI practices.

Develop Ethical AI Guidelines and Policies:

Develop comprehensive guidelines and policies that govern the development, deployment, and use of AI systems within the organization. These guidelines should cover aspects such as data collection and usage, model development, bias detection and mitigation, privacy protection, and algorithmic decision-making. Ensure that the guidelines are accessible, clearly communicated, and aligned with relevant ethical frameworks and regulations.

Integrate Ethical Considerations into AI Development Lifecycle:

Embed ethical considerations into every stage of the AI development lifecycle. From data collection and preprocessing to model training, validation, and deployment, ethical considerations should be systematically addressed. Implement processes for identifying and mitigating biases, ensuring transparency, explainability, and accountability, and regularly auditing AI systems for ethical compliance.

Provide Ethical AI Training and Education:

Equip employees with the knowledge and skills necessary to understand and implement ethical AI principles. Offer training programs and resources that cover topics such as AI ethics, bias detection and mitigation, fairness assessment, privacy protection, and algorithmic transparency. Foster a learning environment where employees can stay up to date with emerging ethical frameworks and best practices in AI.

Foster a Culture of Ethical Decision-Making:

Encourage a culture of ethical decision-making where employees are empowered to raise ethical concerns and make responsible choices when working with AI systems. Create forums for open discussions and ethical dilemmas related to AI. Recognize and reward employees who exhibit ethical leadership and adhere to ethical AI principles.

Promote Transparency and Explainability:

Transparency and explainability are key principles of ethical AI. Encourage teams to adopt transparent practices by documenting the data sources, model architectures, and decision-making processes. Promote the use of interpretable AI models and techniques that provide explanations for algorithmic outputs. This transparency builds trust among stakeholders and ensures accountability for AI systems.

Conduct Ethical Impact Assessments:

Incorporate ethical impact assessments into the development and deployment of AI systems. Assess the potential ethical implications of AI applications on various stakeholders, including customers, employees, and communities. Evaluate the impact on fairness, privacy, bias, and other ethical considerations. These assessments provide insights into the ethical risks and enable organizations to make informed decisions.

Establish Channels for Ethical Concerns:

Implement channels, such as anonymous reporting mechanisms or ethics hotlines, for employees to raise ethical concerns related to AI. Foster a safe and supportive environment where employees feel comfortable reporting ethical violations or seeking guidance on ethical dilemmas. Encourage collaboration between ethics committees, legal teams, and relevant stakeholders to address and resolve ethical concerns promptly.

Regularly Monitor and Review Ethical AI Practices:

Continuously monitor and review the organization's ethical AI practices. Establish processes for regular audits and assessments of AI systems to ensure compliance with ethical guidelines and policies. Stay updated with emerging ethical frameworks, best practices, and regulatory requirements related to AI. Periodically evaluate the effectiveness of ethical AI initiatives and make adjustments, as necessary.

In conclusion, implementing ethical AI principles in your organization's culture is essential for responsible and sustainable AI adoption. By establishing a code of ethics, demonstrating leadership commitment, developing guidelines and policies, integrating ethical considerations into the AI development lifecycle, providing ethical AI training, fostering a culture of ethical decision-making, promoting transparency and explainability, conducting ethical impact assessments, establishing channels for ethical concerns, and regularly monitoring and reviewing ethical AI practices, organizations can embed ethical AI principles into their culture and promote the responsible use of AI technologies.

CHAPTER 79: ENGAGING STAKEHOLDERS IN DISCUSSIONS ABOUT AI ETHICS AND RESPONSIBLE TECHNOLOGY USE

As organizations adopt Artificial Intelligence (AI) technologies, it becomes imperative to engage stakeholders in discussions about AI ethics and responsible technology use. Stakeholder engagement ensures that diverse perspectives are considered, ethical concerns are addressed, and decisions regarding AI deployments are made collaboratively. By involving stakeholders in these discussions, organizations can enhance transparency, build trust, and foster a shared understanding of the ethical implications of AI. Let us explore key considerations and strategies for engaging stakeholders in discussions about AI ethics and responsible technology use:

Identify Stakeholders:

Identify the key stakeholders who are impacted by or have an interest in the organization's AI initiatives. This may include employees, customers, partners, regulators, community representatives, and advocacy groups. Consider both internal and external stakeholders to ensure a comprehensive representation of perspectives.

Foster an Open and Inclusive Environment:

Create an open and inclusive environment where stakeholders feel comfortable sharing their perspectives, concerns, and ideas. Foster a culture of psychological safety, where diverse viewpoints are respected, and individuals are encouraged to voice their opinions without fear of retribution. Establish communication channels, such as forums, workshops, or online platforms, to facilitate dialogue and engagement.

Educate Stakeholders about AI:

Provide educational resources to stakeholders to enhance their understanding of AI concepts, technologies, and their ethical implications. Offer workshops, training sessions, or informational materials that explain the potential benefits and risks associated with AI. This education helps stakeholders participate in discussions more effectively and contribute informed insights.

Promote Transparency and Information Sharing:

Share information about the organization's AI initiatives, including goals, processes, and potential impact, with stakeholders. Provide updates on AI projects, deployments, and any ethical considerations that are being addressed. Transparently communicate the organization's commitment to responsible technology use and ethical AI practices. Timely and transparent information sharing builds trust and ensures stakeholders are well-informed.

Encourage Stakeholder Input:

Actively seek input and feedback from stakeholders on AI ethics and responsible technology use. Establish mechanisms for collecting and considering stakeholder perspectives, such as surveys, focus groups, or public consultations. Create opportunities for stakeholders to share their concerns, suggestions, and expectations regarding the organization's AI initiatives. Demonstrate that their input is valued and considered in decision-making processes.

Collaborate with External Partners:

Engage with external organizations, academic institutions, or industry associations working on AI ethics and responsible technology use. Collaborate on research, share best practices, and participate in industry-wide discussions. These partnerships broaden the scope of stakeholder engagement, provide access to diverse expertise, and contribute to the development of ethical AI frameworks and guidelines.

Establish an Ethics Committee or Advisory Board:

Consider forming an ethics committee or advisory board comprised of internal and external stakeholders with diverse backgrounds and expertise. This committee can provide guidance on AI ethics, review ethical implications of AI projects, and make recommendations for responsible technology use. The committee serves as a platform for ongoing stakeholder engagement and ensures ethical considerations are incorporated into AI decision-making processes.

Communicate the Ethical Implications of AI:

Clearly communicate the ethical implications of AI to stakeholders. Highlight potential risks, such as bias, privacy concerns, and accountability challenges, as well as the measures being taken to address these issues. Provide examples and case studies to illustrate the real-world impact of AI on individuals and communities. This communication fosters a shared understanding of the ethical complexities of AI and encourages stakeholder participation.

Incorporate Stakeholder Feedback into Decision-Making:

Integrate stakeholder feedback and recommendations into the organization's AI decision-making processes. Consider the perspectives shared by stakeholders when defining ethical guidelines, developing AI policies, and implementing AI projects. Incorporating stakeholder input enhances the legitimacy of the organization's AI initiatives and increases the likelihood of responsible technology use.

Provide Feedback and Follow-Up:

Communicate the outcomes of stakeholder engagement initiatives and demonstrate how stakeholder feedback has influenced the organization's AI strategies and practices. Provide opportunities for stakeholders to understand the impact of their input and participate in ongoing discussions. Regularly update stakeholders on the progress of AI projects and any actions taken to address ethical concerns.

In conclusion, engaging stakeholders in discussions about AI ethics and responsible technology use is critical for organizations embracing AI technologies. By identifying stakeholders, fostering an open environment, educating stakeholders, promoting transparency, encouraging input, collaborating with external partners, establishing ethics committees, communicating the ethical implications of AI, incorporating stakeholder feedback, and providing follow-up, organizations can create a collaborative and inclusive approach to AI ethics and ensure responsible technology use. Through meaningful engagement, organizations can build trust, enhance accountability, and promote the ethical deployment of AI technologies.

CHAPTER 80: INTEGRATING AI AS A CRITICAL COMPONENT OF YOUR DIGITAL TRANSFORMATION STRATEGY

Digital transformation has become imperative for organizations seeking to stay competitive in today's rapidly evolving business landscape. As part of this transformation, integrating Artificial Intelligence (AI) has emerged as a critical component for organizations to drive innovation, enhance operational efficiency, and deliver superior customer experiences. By integrating AI into their digital transformation strategy, organizations can unlock new opportunities, gain actionable insights from data, and automate processes to achieve sustainable growth. Let us explore the key considerations and benefits of integrating AI as a critical component of your digital transformation strategy:

Identify Strategic Objectives:

Start by identifying the strategic objectives of your digital transformation strategy. Determine the areas of your business that can benefit from AI, such as customer engagement, operational efficiency, risk management, or product development. Align your AI initiatives with these objectives to ensure they contribute to the overall transformation goals.

Leverage AI for Data-Driven Insights:

AI excels at analyzing vast amounts of data and extracting actionable insights. Integrate AI technologies such as machine learning and data analytics to gain deeper insights into customer behavior, market trends, and operational performance. By leveraging AI-powered data analysis, organizations can make informed decisions and drive data-driven strategies.

Automate and Streamline Processes:

AI can automate repetitive and time-consuming tasks, freeing up employees to focus on higher-value activities. Identify processes that can be streamlined and automated using AI technologies, such as chatbots for customer support, robotic process automation (RPA) for data entry, or predictive analytics for demand forecasting. Automation enhances operational efficiency, reduces costs, and accelerates time-to-market.

Enhance Customer Experiences:

AI-powered technologies, such as natural language processing and sentiment analysis, enable organizations to deliver personalized and seamless customer experiences. Integrating AI into customer engagement channels, such as chatbots, virtual assistants, or recommendation engines, allows organizations to understand customer preferences, deliver targeted content, and provide real-time support. This enhances customer satisfaction and loyalty.

Optimize Decision-Making:

AI empowers organizations to make better and faster decisions by providing real-time insights and predictive analytics. Integrating AI algorithms into decision-making processes can help optimize pricing strategies, inventory management, resource allocation, and risk assessment. AI-driven decision-making enhances agility, competitiveness, and strategic planning.

Drive Innovation and New Revenue Streams:

Integrating AI enables organizations to unlock new avenues for innovation and revenue generation. AI technologies can be leveraged to develop intelligent products, create personalized services, or enhance existing offerings. By harnessing AI's capabilities, organizations can explore new business models, enter new markets, and differentiate themselves from competitors.

Upskill Workforce for AI:

Digital transformation requires organizations to develop AI-related skills within their workforce. Identify the skills and knowledge gaps and invest in training programs to upskill employees on AI concepts, technologies, and applications. Foster a culture of continuous learning and innovation to encourage employees to embrace AI and contribute to its successful integration.

Ensure Ethical and Responsible AI Use:

Ethics and responsible AI use are paramount in the integration of AI into digital transformation strategies. Establish ethical guidelines and governance frameworks that address concerns such as bias, privacy, transparency, and accountability. Regularly assess AI systems for ethical implications and ensure compliance with relevant regulations and standards.

Collaborate with AI Experts and Partners:

Engage with AI experts, consultants, and technology partners to accelerate the integration of AI into your digital transformation strategy. Collaborate with external stakeholders who have expertise in AI to gain insights, access to advanced technologies, and assistance in implementation. These partnerships can provide guidance, reduce implementation risks, and optimize AI adoption.

Continuously Evaluate and Refine:

Digital transformation and AI integration are ongoing processes. Continuously evaluate the outcomes of AI initiatives, measure their impact on business performance, and gather feedback from stakeholders. Use these insights to refine and adjust your AI integration strategy, ensuring it remains aligned with the evolving needs of your organization and market.

In conclusion, integrating AI as a critical component of your digital transformation strategy offers organizations immense opportunities for innovation, operational efficiency, and enhanced customer experiences. By leveraging AI for data-driven insights, automating processes, optimizing decision-making, driving innovation, upskilling the workforce, ensuring ethical AI use, collaborating with experts, and continuously evaluating and refining, organizations can unlock the full potential of AI in their digital transformation journey and gain a competitive edge in the digital era.

CHAPTER 81: LEVERAGING AI TO ENHANCE DIGITAL CUSTOMER EXPERIENCES

In today's digital age, providing exceptional customer experiences is a key differentiator for businesses. To achieve this, organizations are increasingly turning to Artificial Intelligence (AI) technologies. By leveraging AI, organizations can personalize interactions, improve response times, and deliver seamless and tailored experiences across digital channels. Let us explore how organizations can use AI to enhance digital customer experiences:

Personalized Recommendations:

AI algorithms can analyze vast amounts of customer data to understand preferences, behaviors, and patterns. By leveraging this data, organizations can deliver personalized recommendations to customers, whether it is suggesting relevant products or content. Personalization enhances customer engagement, increases satisfaction, and drives conversions.

Chatbots and Virtual Assistants:

Chatbots and virtual assistants powered by AI technologies enable organizations to provide instant and personalized support to customers. These AI-powered assistants can handle common queries, provide information, and guide customers through self-service options. They can be available 24/7, ensuring customers receive timely assistance, leading to improved satisfaction and reduced response times.

Natural Language Processing (NLP):

NLP enables organizations to understand and respond to customer queries in a more human-like manner. AI-powered chatbots equipped with NLP capabilities can interpret natural language, understand customer intent, and provide relevant and accurate responses. This technology allows for more seamless and conversational interactions with customers.

Sentiment Analysis:

AI-driven sentiment analysis helps organizations understand customer sentiment and gauge satisfaction levels. By analyzing customer feedback, social media posts, or online reviews, organizations can gain insights into customer sentiment towards their products, services, or brand. This information can be used to address customer concerns, improve offerings, and enhance overall customer experiences.

Voice Assistants:

Voice assistants, such as Amazon Alexa or Google Assistant, powered by AI technologies, provide customers with hands-free and voice-controlled interactions. Customers can ask questions, make requests, and perform tasks using voice commands. Voice assistants offer convenience, speed, and a natural interface, enhancing the customer experience in various applications, from smart home devices to mobile applications.

Predictive Analytics:

AI-powered predictive analytics can analyze customer data to forecast future behavior, preferences, or needs. By leveraging historical data and AI algorithms, organizations can anticipate customer preferences, recommend relevant products or services, and proactively address customer needs. Predictive analytics enables organizations to deliver targeted offers, personalized content, and proactive support.

Visual Search:

Visual search, powered by AI technologies, allows customers to search for products or information using images instead of text. By analyzing the visual features of an image, AI algorithms can identify relevant products or content. Visual search enhances the customer experience by simplifying product discovery and enabling customers to find what they are looking for more intuitively.

Virtual Try-On:

For industries such as fashion or beauty, AI-powered virtual try-on technologies enable customers to virtually try on products before making a purchase. By leveraging augmented reality (AR) or virtual reality (VR) technologies, customers can see how a product would look on them in real-time. Virtual try-on enhances the customer's experience by reducing uncertainty and increasing confidence in the purchase decision.

Customer Sentiment Monitoring:

AI can monitor customer sentiment in real-time by analyzing customer interactions, social media posts, or feedback. This allows organizations to identify potential issues, track brand perception, and take immediate action to address customer concerns. Real-time sentiment monitoring empowers organizations to proactively manage customer experiences and maintain brand reputation.

Continuous Learning and Improvement:

AI technologies allow organizations to continuously learn from customer interactions and improve the customer experience over time. AI algorithms can analyze customer feedback, behavior, and preferences to identify patterns and trends. This information can be used to refine AI models, update recommendations, and optimize interactions, ensuring ongoing enhancement of the customer experience.

In conclusion, leveraging AI technologies to enhance digital customer experiences offers organizations numerous opportunities to provide personalized, seamless, and engaging interactions. By implementing AI-powered recommendations, chatbots and virtual assistants, NLP, sentiment analysis, voice assistants, predictive analytics, visual search, virtual try-on, customer sentiment monitoring, and continuous learning, organizations can deliver exceptional digital customer experiences, foster customer loyalty, and gain a competitive edge in today's digital landscape.

CHAPTER 82: THE ROLE OF AI IN DRIVING DIGITAL BUSINESS MODEL INNOVATION

In the digital age, organizations are constantly seeking ways to innovate and evolve their business models to stay competitive. One of the most significant drivers of business model innovation is Artificial Intelligence (AI). AI has the potential to revolutionize how organizations operate, create value, and interact with customers. Let us explore the role of AI in driving digital business model innovation:

Data-driven Decision-making:

AI enables organizations to leverage vast amounts of data to make informed decisions. By analyzing data from various sources, AI algorithms can uncover patterns, trends, and insights that humans may miss. This data-driven decision-making enhances the accuracy and effectiveness of strategic choices, enabling organizations to optimize their business models.

Enhanced Customer Understanding:

AI technologies, such as machine learning and natural language processing, enable organizations to gain a deeper understanding of their customers. By analyzing customer data, behaviors, and interactions, AI algorithms can identify preferences, anticipate needs, and personalize experiences. This customer understanding allows organizations to tailor their business models to better meet customer demands.

Personalization and Customization:

AI-powered personalization is transforming business models by enabling organizations to deliver tailored experiences at scale. Through AI algorithms, organizations can analyze customer data to provide personalized recommendations, offers, and services. This level of personalization enhances customer satisfaction, engagement, and loyalty, ultimately driving revenue growth.

Process Automation and Efficiency:

AI technologies, such as robotic process automation (RPA) and cognitive automation, automate repetitive and rule-based tasks. By automating routine processes, organizations can streamline operations, reduce costs, and allocate resources more efficiently. This automation frees up employees to focus on higher-value tasks, fostering innovation and creativity within the organization.

Predictive Analytics and Forecasting:

AI enables organizations to make accurate predictions and forecasts based on historical data and trends. By leveraging machine learning algorithms, organizations can anticipate customer behavior, market trends, demand patterns, and supply chain dynamics. This predictive capability allows organizations to proactively adapt their business models, optimize inventory management, and capitalize on emerging opportunities.

Product and Service Innovation:

AI opens up new avenues for product and service innovation. Organizations can use AI technologies to develop intelligent products, embed AI capabilities into existing offerings, or create entirely new AI-driven solutions. By incorporating AI into their products and services, organizations can deliver enhanced features, functionalities, and user experiences, leading to increased customer satisfaction and market differentiation.

Agile and Adaptive Business Models:

AI enables organizations to create agile and adaptive business models that can quickly respond to changing market dynamics. By continuously monitoring and analyzing data, AI algorithms can identify emerging trends, customer preferences, and competitive threats. Organizations can then adjust their business models, strategies, and offerings in real-time, ensuring relevance and competitiveness.

New Revenue Streams:

AI-driven technologies, such as data monetization, AI-powered marketplaces, or AI-as-a-Service models, enable organizations to explore new revenue streams. By leveraging AI capabilities, organizations can capitalize on their data assets, offer AI-powered solutions to external customers, or monetize AI algorithms. This diversification of revenue sources fuels business model innovation and growth.

Improved Risk Management:

AI technologies enhance risk management by providing organizations with real-time insights and predictive analytics. AI algorithms can analyze vast amounts of data to detect anomalies, identify potential risks, and predict potential disruptions. This information allows organizations to proactively manage risks, mitigate vulnerabilities, and ensure business continuity.

Collaborative Ecosystems:

AI fosters collaboration and ecosystem development by enabling organizations to connect and share data, insights, and resources. Through AI-powered platforms and ecosystems, organizations can form partnerships, exchange information, and co-create value. These collaborative ecosystems facilitate business model innovation by leveraging collective intelligence and expanding market reach.

In conclusion, AI plays a pivotal role in driving digital business model innovation. By enabling data-driven decision-making, enhancing customer understanding, personalization, and customization, automating processes, facilitating predictive analytics, fostering product and service innovation, enabling agile and adaptive business models, creating new revenue streams, improving risk management, and fostering collaborative ecosystems, AI empowers organizations to reimagine their business models and unlock new opportunities for growth and success in the digital era.

CHAPTER 83: UNDERSTANDING THE INTERPLAY BETWEEN AI, BLOCKCHAIN, 5G, AND OTHER EMERGING TECHNOLOGIES

As the world becomes increasingly digital, emerging technologies are playing a crucial role in transforming industries and shaping the future of businesses. Among these technologies, Artificial Intelligence (AI), Blockchain, 5G, and others stand out for their immense potential to revolutionize various sectors. Understanding the interplay between these technologies is vital for organizations looking to leverage their combined power for innovation and competitive advantage. Let us explore how AI, Blockchain, 5G, and other emerging technologies intersect and complement each other:

AI and Blockchain:

AI and Blockchain are two powerful technologies that can work synergistically to enable secure, transparent, and intelligent systems. Blockchain's decentralized and immutable nature enhances the trustworthiness and integrity of AI systems by providing a tamper-proof record of data and algorithms. AI, in turn, can leverage blockchain's distributed ledger technology to verify the authenticity and integrity of data used in training AI models. The combination of AI and Blockchain can create transparent and accountable AI solutions while addressing concerns related to privacy, bias, and trust.

AI and Internet of Things (IoT):

The Internet of Things (IoT) is a network of interconnected devices that collect and exchange data. AI can analyze this massive amount of IoT data to derive meaningful insights, detect patterns, and enable intelligent decision-making. AI algorithms can process real-time data from IoT devices to optimize operations, improve predictive maintenance, and enable autonomous systems. The integration of AI and IoT empowers organizations to create smart, connected ecosystems that drive efficiency, automation, and innovation.

AI and 5G:

The fifth generation of wireless technology, known as 5G, has the potential to revolutionize connectivity with its high speed, low latency, and massive device connectivity. AI and 5G can complement each other to unlock new possibilities. 5G enables the seamless transfer of large volumes of data, facilitating real-time communication between AI systems and devices. AI, on the other hand, can leverage the speed and low latency of 5G to process and analyze data in real-time, enabling enhanced automation, remote operations, and immersive experiences.

AI and Edge Computing:

Edge computing brings computation and data storage closer to the source of data generation, reducing latency and enabling real-time processing. AI algorithms can be deployed at the edge, allowing organizations to harness the power of AI for real-time analytics and decision-making without relying solely on cloud-based processing. Edge computing combined with AI enables faster response times, enhanced privacy and security, and improved performance in applications such as autonomous vehicles, smart cities, and industrial automation.

AI and Robotics:

AI and Robotics are closely intertwined, with AI providing the intelligence and decision-making capabilities to robotic systems. AI enables robots to perceive and interpret the environment, make informed decisions, and perform tasks autonomously. Robotics, in turn, generates valuable data that can be analyzed by AI algorithms to improve performance, optimize operations, and enhance human-robot collaboration. The combination of AI and Robotics opens up new possibilities in fields such as manufacturing, healthcare, logistics, and agriculture.

AI and Augmented Reality/Virtual Reality (AR/VR):

AR/VR technologies create immersive and interactive experiences by blending the digital and physical worlds. AI can enhance AR/VR applications by providing intelligent content generation, object recognition, and personalized experiences. AI algorithms can analyze user behavior, preferences, and environmental data to deliver customized AR/VR content and optimize user experiences. The integration of AI and AR/VR enables realistic simulations, immersive training, and personalized marketing experiences.

AI and Cybersecurity:

AI can strengthen cybersecurity defenses by detecting and mitigating threats in real-time. AI-powered security systems can analyze vast amounts of data, identify patterns, and detect anomalies that indicate potential cyber-attacks. AI can also automate incident response, enabling organizations to respond rapidly to security breaches. Additionally, AI can enhance user authentication and fraud detection systems, providing robust security measures in an increasingly digital world.

AI and Quantum Computing:

Quantum computing has the potential to solve complex problems exponentially faster than traditional computing. AI algorithms can benefit from quantum computing's computational power to accelerate complex computations, optimize AI models, and enable advanced data analysis. Quantum AI holds promise for solving complex optimization problems, improving AI algorithms, and advancing AI research.

In conclusion, understanding the interplay between AI, Blockchain, 5G, and other emerging technologies is crucial for organizations seeking to harness their collective power and drive innovation. The combination of AI, Blockchain, IoT, 5G, edge computing, robotics, AR/VR, cybersecurity, and quantum computing presents unprecedented opportunities to transform industries, create new business models, and deliver enhanced experiences. By strategically integrating and leveraging these technologies, organizations can unlock new possibilities, gain a competitive edge, and navigate the evolving digital landscape successfully.

CHAPTER 84: EVALUATING THE POTENTIAL OF AI-DRIVEN SOLUTIONS IN VARIOUS TECHNOLOGY DOMAINS

Artificial Intelligence (AI) is transforming numerous industries and technology domains, revolutionizing the way organizations operate, make decisions, and deliver value. From healthcare to finance, manufacturing to transportation, AI-driven solutions are being applied across various sectors. Evaluating the potential of AI-driven solutions in different technology domains is crucial for organizations looking to leverage AI to drive innovation and gain a competitive advantage. Let us explore how AI is making an impact in different technology domains:

Healthcare:

AI has significant potential in healthcare, enabling improved diagnostics, personalized treatment plans, and efficient healthcare delivery. AI-driven solutions can analyze medical images, detect anomalies, and assist in early disease diagnosis. AI algorithms can also leverage electronic health records and patient data to provide personalized treatment recommendations based on patient history, genetics, and clinical research. Additionally, AI-powered chatbots and virtual assistants can enhance patient engagement, provide basic healthcare information, and triage patient inquiries.

Finance:

AI is transforming the finance industry, enabling faster, more accurate decision-making, and enhancing risk management. AI-driven algorithms can analyze large volumes of financial data, identify patterns, and predict market trends. This supports portfolio management, algorithmic trading, fraud detection, and credit scoring. AI-powered chatbots can also handle customer inquiries, provide financial advice, and streamline customer service processes. AI-driven solutions in finance improve operational efficiency, mitigate risks, and enable personalized financial services.

Manufacturing:

AI is revolutionizing manufacturing by enabling automation, predictive maintenance, and quality control. AI-driven robots and automation systems can perform complex tasks with precision and efficiency, reducing human errors and increasing productivity. AI algorithms can analyze sensor data to predict machine failures and schedule maintenance proactively. Additionally, AI-driven computer vision systems can inspect product quality, detect defects, and optimize production processes. AI-driven solutions in manufacturing enhance efficiency, reduce costs, and improve product quality.

Transportation and Logistics:

AI is reshaping transportation and logistics by enabling intelligent transportation systems, autonomous vehicles, and optimized logistics operations. AI algorithms can analyze traffic data, weather conditions, and historical patterns to optimize route planning and reduce congestion. AI-powered autonomous vehicles can navigate safely and efficiently, enhancing road safety and reducing accidents. In logistics, AI-driven solutions can optimize supply chain operations, automate inventory management, and enable predictive demand forecasting. AI-driven solutions in transportation and logistics improve efficiency, reduce costs, and enhance customer satisfaction.

Retail and E-commerce:

AI is transforming the retail and e-commerce landscape, enabling personalized customer experiences, targeted marketing, and efficient supply chain management. AI algorithms can analyze customer data to deliver personalized product recommendations, enhance product search capabilities, and enable dynamic pricing strategies. AI-powered chatbots and virtual assistants can provide customer support, answer inquiries, and guide purchasing decisions. AI-driven solutions in retail and e-commerce enhance customer engagement, increase conversion rates, and optimize inventory management.

Energy and Utilities:

AI is playing a crucial role in the energy and utilities sector, enabling energy optimization, predictive maintenance, and demand response. AI algorithms can analyze energy consumption data to optimize energy usage, reduce costs, and improve sustainability. AI-driven predictive maintenance can identify equipment failures before they occur, minimizing downtime and optimizing asset management. AI-powered analytics can also support demand response programs by predicting energy demand patterns and optimizing energy distribution. AI-driven solutions in energy and utilities improve efficiency, enhance sustainability, and optimize resource management.

Agriculture:

AI is revolutionizing agriculture by enabling precision farming, crop monitoring, and yield optimization. AI-powered sensors and drones can collect data on soil moisture, crop health, and weather conditions, enabling farmers to make data-driven decisions. AI algorithms can analyze this data to optimize irrigation, fertilization, and pest control, leading to improved crop yield and reduced environmental impact. AI-driven solutions in agriculture enhance productivity, optimize resource usage, and promote sustainable farming practices.

Education:

AI is transforming education by enabling personalized learning experiences, intelligent tutoring systems, and automated grading. AI algorithms can analyze student data to identify individual learning needs, provide adaptive learning materials, and offer personalized feedback. AI-powered chatbots and virtual assistants can support students in their inquiries, provide educational content, and guide their learning journeys. AI-driven solutions in education enhance learning outcomes, facilitate personalized education, and provide educators with valuable insights.

In conclusion, AI-driven solutions have immense potential across various technology domains. Healthcare, finance, manufacturing, transportation and logistics, retail and e-commerce, energy and utilities, agriculture, and education are just a few examples of sectors where AI is making a significant impact. Evaluating the potential of AI-driven solutions in these domains requires a deep understanding of domain-specific challenges, data availability, regulatory considerations, and business objectives. By leveraging AI strategically, organizations can unlock innovation, drive efficiency, and deliver enhanced value in their respective technology domains.

CHAPTER 85: PREPARING FOR THE CONVERGENCE OF AI AND OTHER DISRUPTIVE TECHNOLOGIES

The convergence of Artificial Intelligence (AI) with other disruptive technologies is shaping the future of industries and societies. As AI continues to advance, its integration with technologies such as Internet of Things (IoT), blockchain, augmented reality (AR), virtual reality (VR), quantum computing, and 5G is creating new opportunities and challenges. Organizations need to be prepared for this convergence to harness its transformative potential effectively. Let us explore how organizations can prepare for the convergence of AI and other disruptive technologies:

Stay Informed and Anticipate Trends:

Organizations must stay abreast of emerging technologies, AI advancements, and industry trends. Engaging with technology experts, attending conferences, and monitoring research and development initiatives can provide valuable insights. By understanding the potential of emerging technologies and the intersection with AI, organizations can proactively identify opportunities for innovation and plan accordingly.

Foster a Culture of Collaboration:

Preparing for the convergence of AI and other disruptive technologies requires collaboration across different teams and departments. Encourage collaboration between data scientists, engineers, domain experts, and business leaders. Facilitate cross-functional teams that can explore the potential synergies between AI and other technologies. By fostering a culture of collaboration, organizations can leverage diverse expertise to drive innovation and uncover new possibilities.

Identify Use Cases and Pilot Projects:

Identify specific use cases where the convergence of AI and other technologies can create value for your organization. Conduct feasibility studies and pilot projects to validate the potential impact and benefits. Start with small-scale initiatives to understand the challenges and opportunities associated with the convergence. Evaluate the feasibility, scalability, and potential risks of implementing AI in conjunction with other technologies.

Build a Flexible and Scalable IT Infrastructure:

Preparing for the convergence of AI and other disruptive technologies requires a flexible and scalable IT infrastructure. Evaluate the current infrastructure and identify any gaps or limitations. Consider cloud-based solutions that provide the flexibility to scale resources based on the demands of AI and other technologies. Embrace scalable data storage, processing power, and networking capabilities to support the increasing volumes of data and computational requirements.

Address Data Integration and Interoperability:

The convergence of AI with other technologies often involves integrating disparate data sources and systems. Organizations must address the challenges of data integration and interoperability to enable seamless communication between different technologies. Establish data governance practices, data standards, and protocols that facilitate data sharing and integration. Consider utilizing APIs, data connectors, and middleware to ensure smooth interoperability.

Invest in Talent Development:

Preparing for the convergence of AI and other technologies requires a skilled workforce capable of understanding and implementing these technologies. Invest in talent development initiatives, including training programs, workshops, and certifications, to upskill employees in AI, IoT, blockchain, and other relevant domains. Encourage cross-training and knowledge sharing between different technology teams to foster a multidisciplinary approach.

Embrace Ethical and Responsible Technology Practices:

As AI converges with other disruptive technologies, ethical considerations become even more critical. Ensure that your organization adheres to ethical and responsible technology practices. Establish guidelines and frameworks for the responsible use of AI and other technologies, addressing issues such as privacy, bias, transparency, and accountability. Engage in ongoing discussions and collaborations with stakeholders to navigate ethical challenges and promote responsible AI adoption.

Foster Partnerships and Collaborations:

Collaborating with external partners, including technology vendors, research institutions, and industry consortiums, can accelerate your organization's preparedness for the convergence of AI and other disruptive technologies. Collaborative partnerships enable access to specialized expertise, shared resources, and insights into emerging technologies. Foster relationships that promote knowledge exchange, co-innovation, and collective problem-solving.

Evaluate Regulatory and Legal Considerations:

The convergence of AI and other technologies may have regulatory and legal implications. Stay updated on relevant regulations and standards applicable to the industry and geography your organization operates in. Assess the compliance requirements related to data privacy, security, intellectual property, and ethical guidelines. Ensure that your organization's AI initiatives align with legal and regulatory frameworks to avoid any legal or reputational risks.

Continuously Monitor and Evolve:

Technology landscapes are ever-evolving, and the convergence of AI and other disruptive technologies is an ongoing process. Continuously monitor emerging trends, technological advancements, and market dynamics. Regularly reassess your organization's strategy, goals, and technology roadmap to adapt to new opportunities and challenges that arise from the convergence.

In conclusion, preparing for the convergence of AI and other disruptive technologies requires a proactive and strategic approach. By staying informed, fostering collaboration, identifying use cases, building a flexible IT infrastructure, investing in talent development, embracing ethical practices, fostering partnerships, evaluating regulatory considerations, and continuously monitoring the landscape, organizations can position themselves for success in the era of AI-driven convergence. Embracing this convergence has the potential to unlock new frontiers of innovation, create competitive advantage, and drive transformational change across industries.

CHAPTER 86: FORMING STRATEGIC ALLIANCES WITH AI TECHNOLOGY PROVIDERS AND PARTNERS

In today's rapidly evolving technological landscape, organizations are recognizing the importance of forming strategic alliances with AI technology providers and partners to drive innovation, gain a competitive edge, and leverage the power of artificial intelligence (AI). By collaborating with AI technology providers and partners, organizations can access cutting-edge AI solutions, tap into specialized expertise, and accelerate their AI adoption journey. Let us explore the benefits and strategies for forming strategic alliances in the realm of AI:

Access to Advanced AI Solutions:

Partnering with AI technology providers gives organizations access to advanced AI solutions that they may not have the in-house capabilities to develop. AI technology providers often specialize in specific AI domains, such as computer vision, natural language processing, or machine learning, and can offer ready-to-use AI tools, platforms, or frameworks. These solutions can enable organizations to leverage AI quickly and effectively, saving time and resources in the development and implementation process.

Specialized Expertise and Knowledge:

AI technology providers and partners bring specialized expertise and knowledge in AI research, development, and implementation. They have a deep understanding of AI algorithms, methodologies, and best practices. By forming strategic alliances, organizations can tap into this expertise and gain valuable insights into how to optimize AI solutions for their specific industry or use cases. Collaborating with AI experts can help organizations avoid common pitfalls, accelerate implementation, and ensure the successful deployment of AI initiatives.

Accelerated Innovation and Time-to-Market:

Partnering with AI technology providers can significantly accelerate innovation and time-to-market for organizations. AI technology providers often have dedicated research and development teams continuously exploring the latest advancements in AI. By leveraging these partnerships, organizations can stay at the forefront of AI innovation and gain a competitive edge. They can access cutting-edge AI algorithms, models, and techniques, enabling them to develop innovative AI-driven products, services, or solutions faster than their competitors.

Cost Optimization and Resource Efficiency:

Building AI capabilities in-house can be resource-intensive and costly. Strategic alliances with AI technology providers and partners offer a cost-effective alternative. Organizations can leverage the expertise and infrastructure of these partners without having to invest heavily in building their own AI teams or infrastructure. This allows organizations to optimize costs, allocate resources more efficiently, and focus on their core competencies while still benefiting from the power of AI.

Scalability and Flexibility:

AI technology providers often offer scalable and flexible solutions that can accommodate the evolving needs of organizations. As AI requirements grow, organizations can easily scale their AI initiatives by leveraging the resources and capabilities of their partners. Additionally, strategic alliances provide flexibility in terms of accessing a wide range of AI capabilities without being limited to a single technology or vendor. This flexibility allows organizations to experiment with different AI approaches and choose the ones that best fit their needs.

Access to Data and Datasets:

Data is a critical component for training AI models and driving AI-driven insights. AI technology providers and partners may have access to large, diverse datasets that organizations can leverage for their AI initiatives. These datasets can help organizations improve the accuracy and performance of their AI models, especially in domains where acquiring data may be challenging or time-consuming. Access to quality data through strategic alliances can give organizations a competitive advantage in AI implementation.

Collaborative Innovation and Co-Creation:

Strategic alliances in the AI space foster collaborative innovation and co-creation between organizations and AI technology providers. Through joint research and development initiatives, organizations can work closely with their partners to explore new AI applications, test novel ideas, and develop customized AI solutions that address specific industry challenges. This collaborative approach encourages knowledge-sharing, fosters innovation, and enhances the potential for breakthrough AI-driven solutions.

Risk Mitigation and Compliance:

AI technology providers can assist organizations in navigating regulatory and compliance challenges associated with AI implementation. They have expertise in addressing privacy, security, and ethical considerations that arise when dealing with AI technologies. Partnering with AI technology providers ensures that organizations adhere to legal and ethical standards, mitigating potential risks and liabilities associated with AI deployments.

When forming strategic alliances with AI technology providers and partners, organizations should consider several key factors:

Alignment of goals, values, and culture between organizations.

Track record and reputation of the AI technology provider.

Compatibility and integration capabilities of the AI solutions with existing systems and infrastructure.

Scalability and future-proofing of the AI solutions to accommodate evolving business needs.

Clear roles, responsibilities, and expectations outlined in partnership agreements.

Proactive communication, collaboration, and knowledge-sharing channels.

In conclusion, forming strategic alliances with AI technology providers and partners offers organizations numerous benefits, including access to advanced AI solutions, specialized expertise, accelerated innovation, cost optimization, scalability, and flexibility. Collaborating with AI technology providers allows organizations to leverage external capabilities, resources, and knowledge, driving AI adoption and gaining a competitive advantage. By choosing the right partners, organizations can navigate the complexities of AI implementation, mitigate risks, and unlock the full potential of AI in their respective industries.

CHAPTER 87: LEVERAGING EXTERNAL AI EXPERTISE AND RESOURCES FOR BUSINESS GROWTH

In today's data-driven world, organizations across industries are recognizing the transformative power of artificial intelligence (AI) in driving business growth and innovation. However, implementing AI successfully requires a deep understanding of AI technologies, methodologies, and best practices. Many organizations may lack the necessary expertise or resources in-house to fully harness the potential of AI. In such cases, leveraging external AI expertise and resources becomes crucial. Let us explore how organizations can leverage external AI expertise and resources to fuel their business growth:

Access to Specialized Knowledge and Skills:

External AI experts bring specialized knowledge and skills that may not be readily available within an organization. They have deep expertise in AI algorithms, data analytics, machine learning, and other AI-related domains. Leveraging external AI expertise allows organizations to tap into this specialized knowledge, gaining insights and guidance on AI implementation strategies, best practices, and emerging trends. External AI experts can provide valuable guidance on how to tailor AI solutions to specific business needs, ensuring optimal results.

Faster Time-to-Market:

Partnering with external AI experts can significantly accelerate the development and deployment of AI initiatives, leading to faster time-to-market. These experts have experience working on similar projects, enabling them to bring proven methodologies and approaches to the table. They can help organizations avoid common pitfalls, reduce trial-and-error cycles, and streamline the AI implementation process. With external AI expertise, organizations can expedite their AI initiatives, gaining a competitive advantage and seizing business opportunities more rapidly.

Cost Optimization:

Building an in-house AI team can be costly, time-consuming, and resource-intensive. Leveraging external AI expertise offers a cost-effective alternative. Rather than investing in hiring, training, and retaining AI professionals, organizations can engage external AI experts on a project-by-project basis or through ongoing collaborations. This allows organizations to allocate their resources more efficiently and focus on their core competencies while still benefiting from the expertise of external AI professionals.

Access to Advanced Tools and Technologies:

External AI experts often have access to advanced AI tools, technologies, and infrastructure that may not be available within an organization. These tools can accelerate AI development, improve accuracy, and enhance performance. By leveraging external AI resources, organizations can tap into cutting-edge AI technologies and platforms, taking advantage of the latest advancements in AI research and development. This access to advanced tools and technologies can give organizations a competitive edge and enable them to deliver AI-powered solutions of higher quality and functionality.

Scalability and Flexibility:

External AI expertise offers scalability and flexibility for organizations. As business needs evolve, organizations can scale their AI initiatives by leveraging external resources. External AI experts can quickly ramp up or down their involvement based on the organization's requirements, ensuring that resources are utilized optimally. This scalability and flexibility allow organizations to respond swiftly to market dynamics, customer demands, and emerging opportunities without being constrained by internal resource limitations.

Risk Mitigation and Compliance:

AI implementations involve inherent risks, including data security, privacy, and regulatory compliance. External AI experts are well-versed in these challenges and can help organizations navigate potential risks and ensure compliance with relevant laws and regulations. They can provide guidance on data governance, ethical considerations, and security protocols, mitigating the risks associated with AI implementations. Collaborating with external AI experts minimizes the chances of costly errors or non-compliance, safeguarding the organization's reputation and bottom line.

Innovation and Outside Perspectives:

External AI expertise brings fresh perspectives and innovative ideas to the table. These experts have worked on diverse projects across various industries, allowing them to identify new opportunities and apply learnings from other domains. They can challenge existing assumptions, uncover hidden patterns, and identify unique applications of AI within the organization's context. This outside perspective can drive innovation, spark creativity, and open up new possibilities for business growth and differentiation.

Collaborative Partnerships and Networking:

Engaging external AI expertise opens doors to collaborative partnerships and networking opportunities. By forming alliances with AI consultants, research institutions, technology vendors, or other organizations in the AI ecosystem, organizations can tap into a broader network of resources, expertise, and potential business opportunities. Collaborative partnerships can lead to knowledge exchange, co-innovation, joint research initiatives, and access to a wider pool of talent, further enhancing business growth potential.

In conclusion, leveraging external AI expertise and resources is a strategic approach for organizations seeking to drive business growth through AI. Access to specialized knowledge and skills, faster time-to-market, cost optimization, access to advanced tools and technologies, scalability, risk mitigation, innovation, and networking opportunities are some of the key benefits organizations can gain from engaging external AI expertise. By leveraging these external resources, organizations can unlock the full potential of AI, make informed decisions, and accelerate their journey towards digital transformation and business success.

CHAPTER 88: COLLABORATING WITH ACADEMIA, RESEARCH INSTITUTIONS, AND INDUSTRY CONSORTIA ON AI INITIATIVES

Collaborating with academia, research institutions, and industry consortia on AI initiatives is a powerful approach for organizations to accelerate innovation, access cutting-edge research, and foster a vibrant ecosystem of knowledge sharing and collaboration. By partnering with these entities, organizations can tap into the expertise of leading researchers, access diverse datasets, leverage advanced technologies, and drive impactful AI initiatives. Let us explore the benefits and strategies of collaborating with academia, research institutions, and industry consortia on AI initiatives:

Access to Research Expertise:

Academic institutions and research organizations are at the forefront of AI research and development. Collaborating with them allows organizations to tap into the expertise of leading researchers and academic professionals. These experts possess deep knowledge in AI algorithms, methodologies, and applications. Their research insights can guide organizations in developing state-of-the-art AI solutions and help address complex technical challenges. Academic collaborations provide access to cutting-edge research papers, conferences, and workshops, enabling organizations to stay updated on the latest AI advancements.

Cutting-Edge Research and Innovation:

Academic institutions and research organizations conduct groundbreaking research that pushes the boundaries of AI. Collaborating with them opens opportunities for joint research initiatives, where organizations can work closely with researchers to explore new AI applications, develop innovative algorithms, and validate new ideas. These collaborations foster a culture of innovation and creativity, enabling organizations to leverage the latest research findings to create novel AI-driven solutions. By partnering with academia, organizations can accelerate their AI innovation journey and gain a competitive edge in their respective industries.

Diverse and Specialized Datasets:

Research institutions often maintain extensive datasets that are crucial for training and validating AI models. Collaborating with these institutions provides access to diverse and specialized datasets, which can significantly enhance the accuracy and performance of AI systems. Organizations can leverage these datasets to build robust AI models, conduct experiments, and validate their AI solutions in real-world scenarios. Access to such high-quality datasets can save organizations time and resources, as acquiring and curating datasets can be a time-consuming and expensive process.

Advanced AI Infrastructure and Tools:

Research institutions and academic organizations often possess advanced AI infrastructure and tools that organizations may not have access to internally. These institutions invest in high-performance computing resources, cloud platforms, AI frameworks, and other cutting-edge technologies. By collaborating with academia, organizations can leverage these resources to develop, test, and optimize their AI models and algorithms. This access to advanced AI infrastructure and tools can accelerate the development and deployment of AI initiatives, enabling organizations to achieve their goals more efficiently.

Interdisciplinary Collaboration:

AI initiatives often require interdisciplinary expertise and perspectives. Collaborating with academia allows organizations to tap into a diverse pool of talent and expertise across various disciplines. By engaging with researchers from different domains such as computer science, mathematics, psychology, and social sciences, organizations can gain a holistic understanding of AI applications and their impact. This interdisciplinary collaboration fosters innovative thinking, encourages cross-pollination of ideas, and leads to the development of AI solutions that address complex challenges from multiple angles.

Networking and Industry Insights:

Industry consortia and collaborative initiatives bring together organizations from various sectors to collectively drive AI innovation. By participating in these consortia, organizations gain access to a network of industry experts, thought leaders, and like-minded peers. This networking opportunity allows organizations to exchange knowledge, share best practices, and learn from the experiences of others in the field. Collaborative initiatives also provide valuable insights into industry trends, regulatory developments, and emerging use cases, helping organizations stay ahead of the curve in the rapidly evolving AI landscape.

Talent Acquisition and Recruitment:

Collaborating with academia and research institutions creates opportunities for talent acquisition and recruitment. Organizations can engage with students, researchers, and faculty members through joint projects, internships, or research collaborations. This engagement enables organizations to identify top talent, assess their skills, and potentially recruit them for AI-related roles within the organization. Collaborating with academia helps bridge the gap between academia and industry, fostering the development of a skilled AI workforce.

When collaborating with academia, research institutions, and industry consortia on AI initiatives, organizations should consider the following strategies:

Clearly define objectives and align expectations with the collaborating entities.

Foster open communication channels and establish a culture of collaboration.

Establish clear roles and responsibilities for each party involved in the collaboration.

Develop mutually beneficial partnerships, ensuring that both sides derive value from the collaboration.

Leverage the strengths of each partner and encourage knowledge sharing and co-creation.

Establish mechanisms for intellectual property protection and fair sharing of research outcomes.

Provide adequate resources, funding, and support to enable successful collaborations.

In conclusion, collaborating with academia, research institutions, and industry consortia on AI initiatives offers organizations numerous benefits, including access to research expertise, cutting-edge research, diverse datasets, advanced infrastructure and tools, interdisciplinary collaboration, networking opportunities, and talent acquisition. These collaborations foster innovation, drive impactful AI solutions, and create a thriving ecosystem of knowledge sharing and collaboration. By embracing these partnerships, organizations can accelerate their AI initiatives, gain a competitive advantage, and contribute to the advancement of AI technology on a broader scale.

CHAPTER 89: PREPARING FOR THE IMPACT OF AI ON WORKFORCE COMPOSITION AND SKILL REQUIREMENTS

Artificial intelligence (AI) is revolutionizing the way organizations operate, leading to significant changes in workforce composition and skill requirements. As AI technologies continue to advance, organizations must proactively prepare for the impact AI will have on their workforce. This includes understanding the implications of AI on job roles, reskilling and upskilling employees, and creating a workforce strategy that embraces the collaboration between humans and AI. Let us explore how organizations can prepare for the impact of AI on workforce composition and skill requirements:

Understand the Impact of AI on Job Roles:

Organizations need to assess how AI will impact different job roles within their workforce. While AI can automate repetitive tasks, it can also augment human capabilities and create new opportunities. It is essential to identify which job roles are at risk of automation and which roles will require new skills to effectively collaborate with AI systems. By understanding the impact of AI on job roles, organizations can better plan for reskilling initiatives and ensure a smooth transition for employees.

Reskilling and Upskilling Employees:

To navigate the changing landscape, organizations should invest in reskilling and upskilling initiatives to empower employees with the skills needed to work alongside AI technologies. This involves identifying skill gaps and designing training programs that equip employees with AI-related skills, such as data analytics, machine learning, and algorithm design. Upskilling employees enables them to take on more complex and strategic tasks that leverage the capabilities of AI, fostering a more efficient and productive workforce.

Foster a Culture of Lifelong Learning:

As AI continues to evolve, organizations must foster a culture of lifelong learning to keep up with the rapid pace of technological advancements. Encouraging employees to engage in continuous learning and development helps them stay relevant and adaptable in the face of AI-driven changes. Providing learning opportunities, such as online courses, workshops, and mentorship programs, enables employees to acquire new skills and knowledge that align with the evolving demands of the AI-powered workforce.

Promote Human-Machine Collaboration:

Rather than viewing AI as a replacement for human workers, organizations should emphasize the importance of human-machine collaboration. AI excels at tasks involving data analysis, pattern recognition, and automation, while human workers bring unique qualities such as creativity, critical thinking, empathy, and complex problem-solving skills. Promoting a collaborative mindset and facilitating effective collaboration between humans and AI systems can lead to greater productivity, innovation, and job satisfaction.

Redefine Job Roles and Responsibilities:

With the integration of AI, job roles and responsibilities may evolve. Some tasks may be automated, while new roles that require managing AI systems, interpreting AI-generated insights, or ensuring ethical use of AI may emerge. Organizations should redefine job roles and responsibilities to reflect the changing landscape and equip employees with the necessary skills and knowledge to thrive in their updated roles. This can include creating hybrid roles that combine AI expertise with domain-specific knowledge.

Develop Soft Skills:

While technical skills are crucial in the AI era, the demand for soft skills, such as creativity, critical thinking, emotional intelligence, and adaptability, will continue to grow. These skills complement the capabilities of AI systems and are essential for tasks that require human judgment, ethical decision-making, and effective communication. Organizations should prioritize the development of these soft skills to enhance the overall capabilities of their workforce and ensure successful collaboration with AI technologies.

Embrace a Growth Mindset:

Preparing for the impact of AI on workforce composition requires embracing a growth mindset at all levels of the organization. Leaders must foster an environment that encourages experimentation, risk-taking, and learning from failures. Employees should feel empowered to explore new technologies, propose innovative solutions, and adapt to changing circumstances. Embracing a growth mindset promotes agility, resilience, and the ability to seize new opportunities in the AI-driven landscape.

Foster Collaboration and Change Management:

Preparing for the impact of AI on workforce composition requires effective collaboration and change management. Organizations should involve employees in the decision-making process, communicate transparently about AI initiatives, and provide the necessary support during the transition. Employees should be encouraged to share their insights, concerns, and suggestions. This collaborative approach creates a sense of ownership and fosters a smooth adoption of AI technologies within the organization.

In conclusion, preparing for the impact of AI on workforce composition and skill requirements is essential for organizations to thrive in the AI-driven era. By understanding the impact of AI on job roles, investing in reskilling and upskilling programs, fostering a culture of lifelong learning, promoting human-machine collaboration, redefining job roles, developing soft skills, embracing a growth mindset, and fostering collaboration and change management, organizations can successfully navigate the changing workforce dynamics and unlock the full potential of AI while empowering their employees for future success.

CHAPTER 90: LEVERAGING AI TO ENHANCE WORKFORCE PLANNING AND TALENT MANAGEMENT

Workforce planning and talent management are critical aspects of organizational success. With the advent of artificial intelligence (AI), organizations have an opportunity to leverage AI-powered tools and technologies to optimize their workforce planning and talent management processes. AI can enable organizations to make data-driven decisions, improve recruitment and retention strategies, enhance employee development and engagement, and optimize workforce productivity. Let us explore how organizations can leverage AI to enhance workforce planning and talent management:

Data-driven Decision Making:

AI can process vast amounts of workforce data, including employee demographics, performance metrics, skills, and experience. By analyzing this data, AI-powered workforce planning tools can provide valuable insights and predictions about future talent needs, workforce gaps, and potential areas for improvement. This data-driven approach helps organizations make informed decisions when it comes to workforce planning, such as identifying critical skill gaps, predicting attrition rates, and developing strategies to address talent shortages.

Efficient Recruitment and Selection:

AI can streamline and improve the recruitment and selection process by automating repetitive tasks, such as resume screening, candidate matching, and initial assessments. AI-powered tools can quickly analyze resumes, identify relevant skills and experience, and match candidates to job requirements. This saves time for HR professionals and allows them to focus on more strategic aspects of the recruitment process, such as conducting interviews and assessing cultural fit. AI can also help reduce bias in the recruitment process by focusing on objective criteria and minimizing human bias.

Enhanced Employee Development and Learning:

AI can play a significant role in identifying skill gaps and providing personalized learning and development opportunities for employees. AI-powered learning platforms can analyze employee performance data, career aspirations, and learning preferences to recommend relevant training programs, courses, or learning resources. This personalized approach to employee development enhances skills, increases engagement, and fosters a culture of continuous learning. AI can also provide real-time feedback and performance insights to help employees track their progress and make informed decisions about their career paths.

Predictive Analytics for Workforce Optimization:

AI can leverage predictive analytics to optimize workforce planning and scheduling. By analyzing historical data, AI algorithms can predict future workforce demand, identify patterns of absenteeism or turnover, and optimize work schedules accordingly. This ensures that organizations have the right people with the right skills in the right place at the right time, minimizing staffing gaps and maximizing productivity. Predictive analytics can also help identify high-potential employees, allowing organizations to proactively develop and retain top talent.

Employee Engagement and Retention:

AI can contribute to employee engagement and retention by identifying factors that contribute to job satisfaction and employee turnover. By analyzing employee sentiment data from surveys, performance reviews, and social media platforms, AI-powered tools can identify trends, patterns, and areas of concern. Organizations can then take proactive steps to address these issues, such as improving leadership practices, enhancing work-life balance, or providing targeted rewards and recognition programs. AI can also assist in identifying flight risks, allowing organizations to implement intervention strategies to retain valuable talent.

Intelligent Succession Planning:

Succession planning is crucial for organizations to ensure a smooth transition of leadership and critical roles. AI can help identify high-potential employees, assess their readiness for promotion, and recommend suitable candidates for succession planning. By analyzing employee performance data, skills, and career aspirations, AI can provide insights into potential successors, enabling organizations to develop and groom talent effectively.

Automation of Administrative Tasks:

AI can automate administrative tasks, freeing up HR professionals to focus on more strategic initiatives. For example, AI-powered chatbots can handle routine employee inquiries, provide information about policies and benefits, and facilitate self-service options. This not only saves time but also improves the employee experience by providing quick and accurate responses to their queries.

Ethical Considerations:

While leveraging AI in workforce planning and talent management, organizations should consider ethical considerations. AI algorithms should be designed to be fair, transparent, and unbiased. There should be clear guidelines and safeguards in place to ensure that AI is used responsibly and that decisions made based on AI recommendations are reviewed and validated by human experts.

In conclusion, leveraging AI to enhance workforce planning and talent management can provide organizations with valuable insights, optimize decision-making processes, improve recruitment and selection, enhance employee development and engagement, optimize workforce scheduling, and support succession planning. By harnessing the power of AI, organizations can make data-driven decisions, improve productivity, and create a more efficient and engaged workforce, ultimately driving business success. However, it is important for organizations to strike a balance between leveraging AI and maintaining ethical considerations to ensure the responsible use of AI in talent management processes.

CHAPTER 91: ENCOURAGING A CULTURE OF LIFELONG LEARNING AND ADAPTABILITY IN THE AGE OF AI

In the age of artificial intelligence (AI), where technological advancements are rapidly transforming industries, organizations must foster a culture of lifelong learning and adaptability. The ability to continuously acquire new knowledge, develop new skills, and adapt to changing circumstances is essential for individuals and organizations to thrive in the AI-driven era. Let us explore why encouraging a culture of lifelong learning and adaptability is crucial and how organizations can promote it:

Embracing Continuous Learning:

Lifelong learning involves the commitment to continuous personal and professional development. In the context of AI, this means staying updated on the latest trends, technologies, and best practices in AI. Organizations should encourage employees to pursue learning opportunities, such as online courses, workshops, webinars, and conferences, to deepen their understanding of AI and its implications for their roles and industries. By embracing continuous learning, employees can enhance their skills and knowledge, and organizations can benefit from a more knowledgeable and adaptable workforce.

Nurturing a Growth Mindset:

A growth mindset is the belief that abilities and intelligence can be developed through effort, practice, and learning. Organizations should foster a culture that promotes a growth mindset, where employees are encouraged to embrace challenges, learn from failures, and persist in their pursuit of mastery. This mindset creates an environment that values learning and growth, where individuals are motivated to continually acquire new skills and adapt to new technologies, including AI.

Providing Learning Opportunities:

Organizations can provide various learning opportunities to facilitate lifelong learning and adaptability. This includes offering formal training programs, mentorship initiatives, and access to online learning platforms. In-house training sessions, workshops, and knowledge-sharing sessions can also be organized to encourage employees to share their expertise and learn from one another. Additionally, organizations can allocate dedicated time and resources for employees to engage in learning activities, signaling their commitment to continuous development.

Encouraging Experimentation and Innovation:

To foster a culture of lifelong learning and adaptability, organizations should create an environment that encourages experimentation and innovation. Employees should be empowered to explore new ideas, experiment with AI technologies, and take calculated risks. This freedom to innovate encourages employees to step out of their comfort zones, learn from their experiences, and adapt to new ways of working. Celebrating and recognizing innovative initiatives can further reinforce the importance of learning and adaptability.

Building Collaborative Learning Communities:

Organizations can create collaborative learning communities where employees can connect, share knowledge, and learn from one another. This can be achieved through internal social platforms, online discussion forums, or communities of practice. By fostering a sense of community, individuals can tap into collective intelligence, seek advice, and collaborate on solving problems related to AI. Peer learning can be a powerful mechanism for acquiring new skills and perspectives.

Providing Supportive Leadership:

Leaders play a crucial role in promoting a culture of lifelong learning and adaptability. They should lead by example, actively engage in learning activities, and communicate the value of continuous development to their teams. Leaders should support employees' learning journeys by providing resources, mentoring, and creating opportunities for skill-building. Additionally, leaders should provide feedback and recognition that acknowledges and reinforces the importance of learning and adaptability.

Emphasizing Agility and Flexibility:

In the AI-driven era, organizations must emphasize agility and flexibility. This includes promoting cross-functional collaboration, agile work practices, and the ability to quickly adapt to changing circumstances. By embracing flexibility, organizations can respond effectively to technological disruptions, leverage emerging opportunities, and proactively address challenges. Agility and flexibility require a mindset of continuous learning and adaptation, which should be embedded in the organizational culture.

Recognizing and Rewarding Learning:

Organizations should recognize and reward employees' learning efforts and achievements. This can be done through performance evaluations, promotions, career advancement opportunities, and incentives for acquiring new skills or completing relevant certifications. Recognizing and rewarding learning reinforces the importance of continuous development and motivates employees to continue their learning journeys.

In conclusion, in the age of AI, organizations must encourage a culture of lifelong learning and adaptability to thrive in a rapidly changing landscape. By embracing continuous learning, nurturing a growth mindset, providing learning opportunities, encouraging experimentation and innovation, building collaborative learning communities, providing supportive leadership, emphasizing agility and flexibility, and recognizing and rewarding learning, organizations can create an environment where employees are empowered to acquire new skills, adapt to technological changes, and drive innovation. This culture of lifelong learning and adaptability positions organizations and individuals for long-term success in the AI-driven era.

CHAPTER 92: INTEGRATING AI INTO BOARD-LEVEL DISCUSSIONS AND DECISION-MAKING

As artificial intelligence (AI) continues to reshape industries and drive digital transformation, it is crucial for organizations to integrate AI into board-level discussions and decision-making processes. Boards of directors play a vital role in setting the strategic direction of organizations and ensuring long-term success. By embracing AI at the board level, organizations can harness its transformative potential, make informed decisions, and gain a competitive edge. Let us explore why integrating AI into board-level discussions is important and how organizations can effectively do so:

Understanding the Strategic Implications of AI:

Board members must have a comprehensive understanding of the strategic implications of AI for their organization. This includes awareness of AI trends, emerging technologies, and their potential impact on the industry. By staying informed, board members can identify opportunities for leveraging AI to drive growth, enhance operational efficiency, and improve customer experiences. Understanding the strategic implications of AI enables boards to make informed decisions that align with the organization's goals and vision.

Appointing AI-Competent Board Members:

To effectively integrate AI into board-level discussions, organizations should consider appointing board members with expertise in AI or technology. These individuals bring valuable insights and a deep understanding of AI's capabilities, risks, and opportunities. AI-competent board members can provide guidance on AI-related strategies, investments, and governance, ensuring that board discussions are well-informed and aligned with the organization's AI initiatives.

Educating Board Members on AI:

Board members may not have a technical background or comprehensive knowledge of AI. Therefore, organizations should prioritize educating board members on the fundamentals of AI, its potential applications, and its impact on the industry. This can be done through board education programs, workshops, guest speakers, and presentations by AI experts. By providing educational resources, organizations can equip board members with the necessary knowledge to effectively contribute to AI-related discussions and decision-making.

Incorporating AI in Strategic Planning:

Organizations should integrate AI considerations into their strategic planning processes. This involves assessing the organization's current AI capabilities, identifying areas where AI can drive value, and setting strategic goals and initiatives related to AI adoption. By explicitly including AI in strategic planning, boards can ensure that AI-related decisions are aligned with the organization's overall direction and objectives. This also helps boards allocate appropriate resources and prioritize AI investments.

Risk Assessment and Management:

Boards should actively assess and manage the risks associated with AI adoption. AI introduces unique risks, such as data privacy, algorithmic bias, and cybersecurity vulnerabilities. Boards must ensure that adequate safeguards and governance frameworks are in place to address these risks effectively. Regular risk assessments and ongoing monitoring of AI initiatives allow boards to proactively identify potential issues and take appropriate actions to mitigate risks.

Engaging with AI Experts:

Boards should engage with AI experts, both internal and external, to gain insights and guidance on AI-related matters. This can include inviting AI experts to board meetings, establishing advisory boards or committees with AI expertise, or seeking external consultations. Engaging with AI experts enables boards to tap into specialized knowledge, understand emerging trends, and make well-informed decisions regarding AI strategies, investments, and ethical considerations.

Ethical Considerations and Responsible AI:

As AI technologies continue to advance, ethical considerations become increasingly important. Boards should actively participate in discussions around the ethical implications of AI and ensure that AI initiatives align with the organization's values and societal expectations. This includes addressing issues related to algorithmic bias, transparency, privacy, and responsible AI use. Boards should advocate for responsible AI practices and establish governance frameworks that promote ethical decision-making.

Monitoring and Evaluation:

Boards play a crucial role in monitoring the progress and outcomes of AI initiatives. They should establish key performance indicators (KPIs) and metrics to assess the effectiveness and impact of AI adoption. Regular monitoring and evaluation enable boards to identify areas of success, address any challenges, and make informed adjustments to AI strategies and investments.

In conclusion, integrating AI into board-level discussions and decision-making is essential for organizations seeking to capitalize on the potential of AI. By ensuring board members have a solid understanding of AI's strategic implications, appointing AI-competent board members, educating board members on AI, incorporating AI in strategic planning, assessing and managing AI-related risks, engaging with AI experts, addressing ethical considerations, and monitoring and evaluating AI initiatives, organizations can leverage AI effectively and make informed decisions that drive sustainable growth and success. Integrating AI at the board level positions organizations at the forefront of innovation and empowers them to navigate the complexities of the AI-driven landscape.

CHAPTER 93: ENSURING ACCOUNTABILITY AND TRANSPARENCY IN AI ADOPTION AND USE

As artificial intelligence (AI) becomes more prevalent across industries, ensuring accountability and transparency in AI adoption and use is of utmost importance. AI technologies have the potential to impact various aspects of society, including decision-making processes, customer experiences, and privacy. To build trust and mitigate risks, organizations must prioritize accountability and transparency in their AI initiatives. Let us explore why accountability and transparency are crucial in AI adoption and how organizations can ensure them:

Responsibility and Ethical Considerations:

Accountability and transparency are essential to ensure responsible and ethical AI use. Organizations should establish clear guidelines and principles for AI adoption, taking into account ethical considerations such as fairness, bias, privacy, and human values. By holding themselves accountable for the ethical implications of AI, organizations demonstrate their commitment to responsible AI practices and build trust among stakeholders.

Governance Frameworks and Policies:

Organizations should develop governance frameworks and policies that provide guidance on AI adoption and use. These frameworks should include guidelines for data handling, algorithmic decision-making, and risk assessment. They should also address issues like algorithmic bias, explainability, and accountability for AI-generated outcomes. Transparent governance frameworks promote responsible AI practices and enable organizations to align AI initiatives with their values and objectives.

Data Quality and Bias Mitigation:

Accountability and transparency require organizations to ensure the quality and integrity of the data used to train AI models. Organizations should implement robust data governance practices, including data collection, storage, processing, and protection. It is crucial to identify and mitigate biases in training data to prevent AI algorithms from perpetuating or amplifying existing biases. Transparent data practices and bias mitigation techniques contribute to fair and accountable AI systems.

Explainability and Interpretability:

AI systems should be designed to be explainable and interpretable to ensure transparency. Organizations should strive to understand how AI models make decisions and provide explanations to stakeholders, especially when the decisions have significant consequences. Explainable AI helps build trust, facilitates auditing, and allows users to understand and challenge AI-generated outcomes. Organizations should prioritize the development and adoption of explainable AI techniques and provide clear explanations to stakeholders when AI is involved in decision-making.

External Audits and Certification:

External audits and certifications can enhance accountability and transparency in AI adoption. Independent audits can assess the compliance of AI systems with ethical guidelines, regulatory requirements, and organizational policies. Organizations can seek certifications from recognized bodies that validate their AI practices and demonstrate their commitment to responsible and transparent AI use. External audits and certifications provide third-party validation, build trust among stakeholders, and demonstrate accountability in AI adoption and use.

Open Collaboration and Peer Review:

Organizations should encourage open collaboration and peer review to foster transparency in AI adoption. Sharing research findings, methodologies, and best practices allows for external scrutiny and promotes knowledge exchange. Organizations can participate in collaborative research initiatives, publish research papers, and engage with the academic and AI community. Open collaboration and peer review contribute to the identification and mitigation of potential biases, errors, and limitations in AI systems, improving their transparency and accountability.

Stakeholder Engagement and Communication:

Accountability and transparency require effective stakeholder engagement and communication. Organizations should proactively engage with stakeholders, including customers, employees, regulators, and the public, to communicate their AI practices, the benefits they provide, and the safeguards in place. Transparent communication about AI adoption and use builds trust, manages expectations, and addresses concerns. Organizations should actively seek feedback from stakeholders and demonstrate responsiveness in addressing their queries and concerns related to AI.

Continuous Monitoring and Evaluation:

To ensure accountability and transparency, organizations should implement robust monitoring and evaluation mechanisms for AI systems. This involves continuously assessing the performance, fairness, and impact of AI models and algorithms. Regular audits and evaluations help identify potential biases, errors, or unintended consequences and allow organizations to take corrective measures. Monitoring and evaluation contribute to ongoing improvement, accountability, and transparency in AI adoption.

In conclusion, accountability and transparency are critical in AI adoption and use. Organizations should prioritize responsibility and ethical considerations, establish governance frameworks and policies, ensure data quality and bias mitigation, promote explainability and interpretability, conduct external audits and seek certifications, encourage open collaboration and peer review, engage stakeholders through effective communication, and implement continuous monitoring and evaluation. By fostering accountability and transparency, organizations can build trust, mitigate risks, and realize the full potential of AI while ensuring its responsible and beneficial use for society.

CHAPTER 94: MANAGING THE IMPACT OF AI ON CORPORATE GOVERNANCE AND RISK MANAGEMENT

As artificial intelligence (AI) becomes increasingly integrated into business operations, organizations must proactively manage the impact of AI on corporate governance and risk management. AI technologies have the potential to transform decision-making processes, enhance operational efficiency, and create new opportunities. However, they also introduce unique challenges and risks that organizations need to address. Let us explore why managing the impact of AI on corporate governance and risk management is crucial and how organizations can effectively do so:

Enhancing Board Oversight:

AI technologies require robust oversight from boards of directors to ensure ethical and responsible use. Boards should actively engage in discussions related to AI adoption, monitor its impact on organizational strategies, and review policies and frameworks governing AI use. By enhancing board oversight, organizations can align AI initiatives with their overall strategic direction and ensure adherence to ethical guidelines.

Establishing AI Governance Frameworks:

Organizations should develop AI governance frameworks that provide clear guidelines and principles for AI adoption and use. These frameworks should outline roles and responsibilities, define decision-making processes, and establish accountability mechanisms. AI governance frameworks ensure that AI technologies are aligned with organizational goals, ethical considerations, and regulatory requirements.

Risk Assessment and Mitigation:

Organizations must conduct thorough risk assessments to identify and mitigate potential risks associated with AI adoption. This includes assessing data privacy and security risks, algorithmic biases, legal and regulatory compliance, and reputational risks. Risk mitigation strategies should be implemented to minimize potential adverse effects of AI technologies. Regular risk assessments and ongoing monitoring are essential to address emerging risks in a dynamic AI landscape.

Ethical Considerations:

AI technologies raise ethical considerations that organizations need to address. This includes ensuring fairness, transparency, and accountability in AI algorithms, mitigating biases, and respecting privacy rights. Organizations should establish ethical guidelines and review AI systems to prevent unintended consequences and potential harm. By integrating ethical considerations into corporate governance frameworks, organizations can build trust and uphold ethical standards.

Data Governance and Quality:

AI relies on data, making effective data governance critical for ensuring accurate and reliable AI outcomes. Organizations should implement robust data governance practices, including data collection, storage, processing, and quality assurance. Data quality and integrity are vital for generating trustworthy insights and avoiding biased or unreliable outcomes. Proper data governance ensures that AI models are built on reliable and representative data.

Compliance with Regulatory Requirements:

Organizations must ensure compliance with relevant legal and regulatory requirements related to AI adoption. This includes data protection and privacy regulations, intellectual property rights, anti-discrimination laws, and industry-specific regulations. Compliance with these requirements helps mitigate legal and reputational risks and demonstrates the organization's commitment to responsible AI use.

Talent and Expertise:

Organizations need to invest in talent and expertise to effectively manage AI-related risks. This includes having individuals with AI expertise on the board and within the organization's risk management and compliance functions. Having a multidisciplinary team with diverse skill sets can help organizations navigate the complexities of AI and address associated risks.

Continuous Monitoring and Evaluation:

Organizations should implement ongoing monitoring and evaluation processes to assess the effectiveness of AI systems and risk management strategies. Regular audits, testing, and performance evaluations are crucial to identify potential issues, biases, or limitations in AI systems. Continuous monitoring and evaluation help organizations make informed decisions and take necessary actions to address emerging risks or optimize AI performance.

Stakeholder Engagement:

Effective stakeholder engagement is essential in managing the impact of AI on corporate governance and risk management. Organizations should engage with regulators, customers, employees, and other relevant stakeholders to communicate their AI practices, address concerns, and gather feedback. Engaging stakeholders helps organizations gain insights, build trust, and ensure that AI initiatives align with societal expectations.

Training and Awareness:

Organizations should invest in training programs and awareness initiatives to educate employees about AI technologies, their impact, and associated risks. This helps foster a culture of AI literacy and responsible AI use throughout the organization. Training programs should cover topics such as ethical considerations, bias mitigation, data governance, and compliance.

In conclusion, managing the impact of AI on corporate governance and risk management is crucial for organizations embracing AI technologies. By enhancing board oversight, establishing AI governance frameworks, conducting risk assessments, addressing ethical considerations, implementing robust data governance, ensuring compliance with regulatory requirements, investing in talent and expertise, continuous monitoring and evaluation, engaging stakeholders, and providing training and awareness programs, organizations can navigate the complexities of AI while managing associated risks effectively. Proactive management of the impact of AI on corporate governance and risk management positions organizations for success in the AI-driven era.

CHAPTER 95: REFLECTING ON THE KEY INSIGHTS AND TAKEAWAYS FROM THE GUIDE

As we come to the end of this guide, it is important to reflect on the key insights and takeaways we have explored throughout the chapters. The journey through various aspects of artificial intelligence (AI) has provided valuable knowledge and practical guidance for organizations seeking to leverage AI for their business success. Let us summarize some of the key insights and takeaways from the guide:

AI's Impact on Businesses:

AI has the potential to revolutionize businesses by driving digital transformation, enhancing decision-making processes, improving customer experiences, and enabling operational efficiency. Organizations that embrace AI can gain a competitive edge and position themselves for long-term success in the rapidly evolving digital landscape.

Types of AI:

Machine learning, deep learning, natural language processing, and computer vision are the core types of AI. Understanding these technologies helps organizations identify the most suitable AI applications for their specific needs and industry.

AI in Digital Transformation:

AI plays a crucial role in digital transformation efforts by enabling organizations to automate processes, enhance customer experiences, optimize operations, and drive innovation. Integrating AI as a critical component of digital transformation strategies can lead to sustainable growth and increased competitiveness.

Aligning AI Strategies with Business Goals:

To maximize the benefits of AI, organizations must align their AI strategies with their overall business goals. This alignment ensures that AI initiatives are purposeful, relevant, and contribute to the organization's strategic objectives and vision.

Building the Right Team:

Building a diverse and skilled team comprising data scientists, engineers, and analysts is essential for successful AI adoption. These professionals bring the necessary expertise to develop and implement AI solutions, extract insights from data, and drive business value.

Collaboration between IT and Business Units:

Collaboration between IT and business units is crucial for effective AI adoption. IT teams provide technical expertise, infrastructure, and support, while business units offer domain knowledge and insights. By working together, organizations can align AI initiatives with business needs and drive successful outcomes.

Identifying Use Cases and Prioritizing Projects:

Identifying use cases and prioritizing AI projects based on their potential impact and feasibility is key to achieving successful outcomes. Organizations should focus on projects that align with their strategic objectives, address pain points, and have a high likelihood of delivering tangible benefits.

Assessing AI Maturity:

Assessing an organization's AI maturity helps identify strengths, weaknesses, and areas for improvement. Understanding the current level of AI adoption and capabilities enables organizations to develop realistic goals and create a roadmap for AI implementation.

Creating an AI Roadmap:

Developing an AI roadmap provides a strategic plan for AI adoption and guides organizations in deploying AI solutions effectively. The roadmap outlines key milestones, timelines, resource requirements, and metrics for measuring progress.

Data Quality and Governance:

Data quality and governance are crucial for successful AI implementation. Organizations must prioritize data quality, ensure proper data governance practices, and establish mechanisms to address biases, privacy concerns, and ethical considerations.

Cloud-based vs. On-premises AI Solutions:

Organizations need to consider the advantages and trade-offs of cloud-based and on-premises AI solutions based on factors such as scalability, security, data privacy, and cost. The choice depends on specific requirements and organizational capabilities.

Evaluating AI Tools and Platforms:

Thorough evaluation of AI tools and platforms helps organizations select the most suitable solutions for their needs. Considerations include functionality, ease of use, scalability, vendor reputation, support, and integration capabilities.

Ethical Considerations in AI:

Ethical considerations, including fairness, transparency, privacy, and accountability, must be integrated into AI practices. Organizations should develop frameworks and policies that promote responsible and ethical AI use.

Continuous Learning and Development:

Continuous learning and development are crucial for organizations to keep pace with the evolving AI landscape. Investing in upskilling and reskilling employees and fostering a culture of innovation and learning are essential for long-term success.

Monitoring and Evaluation:

Continuous monitoring and evaluation of AI projects and initiatives help organizations measure success, identify areas for improvement, and ensure ongoing value creation. Key performance indicators and evaluation methods should be established to assess the impact of AI adoption.

Collaboration and Stakeholder Engagement:

Collaboration with external partners, academia, and industry consortia fosters knowledge sharing, innovation, and the exchange of best practices. Engaging stakeholders, including customers, employees, and regulators, promotes transparency, trust, and responsible AI use.

Managing Risk and Compliance:

Organizations must actively manage the risks associated with AI adoption, including data security, bias, regulatory compliance, and reputation. Implementing robust risk management strategies and adhering to relevant regulations are critical for mitigating risks.

Future Readiness:

Preparing for the future requires organizations to stay informed about emerging AI technologies, adapt to regulatory changes, and continuously refine their AI strategies. Being agile, flexible, and proactive positions organizations to leverage AI effectively in an ever-evolving business landscape.

These key insights and takeaways provide organizations with a solid foundation for embarking on their AI journey and realizing the benefits of AI adoption. By leveraging AI technologies responsibly, organizations can drive innovation, enhance operational efficiency, improve decision-making processes, and deliver exceptional customer experiences in the digital age. Embracing AI for long-term success requires a strategic approach, a commitment to continuous learning, and a focus on ethics, transparency, and accountability. With the right strategy, team, and mindset, organizations can navigate the complexities of AI and position themselves as leaders in their respective industries.

CHAPTER 96: ASSESSING YOUR ORGANIZATION'S PROGRESS ON THE AI JOURNEY

Embarking on the AI journey is an ongoing process that requires continuous assessment to evaluate your organization's progress, identify areas of improvement, and ensure the successful integration and adoption of artificial intelligence (AI) technologies. Assessing your organization's progress on the AI journey is crucial for understanding the impact of AI initiatives, aligning them with strategic objectives, and maximizing the value derived from AI investments. Let us explore some key considerations for assessing your organization's progress on the AI journey:

Clearly Defined Objectives:

Start by revisiting your organization's AI objectives and goals. Assess whether these objectives are well-defined, measurable, and aligned with your overall business strategy. Evaluate how effectively your AI initiatives contribute to achieving these objectives and whether they are generating the expected outcomes.

AI Adoption and Maturity:

Evaluate the level of AI adoption and maturity within your organization. Assess the extent to which AI technologies have been integrated into your business processes, systems, and decision-making. Consider the capabilities, expertise, and resources available within your organization to support AI initiatives. This assessment helps determine your organization's readiness and potential for further AI integration.

Impact on Key Performance Indicators (KPIs):

Measure the impact of AI initiatives on your organization's key performance indicators (KPIs). Assess whether AI technologies have improved efficiency, productivity, customer satisfaction, revenue generation, or any other metrics relevant to your business. Compare current performance with historical data to gauge the effectiveness of AI adoption in driving positive outcomes.

User Adoption and Satisfaction:

Evaluate user adoption and satisfaction with AI technologies within your organization. Assess how well employees have embraced and incorporated AI tools into their daily workflows. Conduct surveys or interviews to gather feedback on user experiences, challenges, and suggestions for improvement. This assessment helps identify potential barriers to adoption and opportunities for enhancing user engagement.

Data Quality and Availability:

Assess the quality and availability of data for AI applications. Evaluate the data management practices, data governance frameworks, and data infrastructure in place to support AI initiatives. Consider the accuracy, completeness, relevance, and timeliness of data used for training AI models. Identify any gaps or limitations in data accessibility and quality that may impact AI effectiveness.

Integration and Scalability:

Evaluate the integration of AI technologies with existing systems and processes. Assess whether AI solutions have been seamlessly integrated into your organization's infrastructure and workflows or if there are any compatibility issues. Consider the scalability of AI implementations and whether they can accommodate future growth and evolving business needs.

Ethical and Regulatory Compliance:

Assess the adherence to ethical guidelines and regulatory compliance in your AI initiatives. Evaluate whether your organization is actively addressing issues such as fairness, transparency, privacy, and bias mitigation. Consider the steps taken to ensure compliance with data protection, security, and industry-specific regulations.

Continuous Learning and Improvement:

Assess the organization's commitment to continuous learning and improvement in the AI domain. Evaluate the initiatives in place to upskill employees, foster a culture of innovation, and stay updated on the latest AI trends and technologies. Assess whether feedback loops and mechanisms for continuous improvement exist to optimize AI models and algorithms.

Stakeholder Perception and Trust:

Gauge the perception of AI initiatives among stakeholders, including customers, employees, and partners. Assess whether stakeholders perceive AI as valuable, trustworthy, and aligned with their expectations. Consider conducting surveys, focus groups, or feedback sessions to gather insights and address any concerns or misconceptions.

Return on Investment (ROI):

Evaluate the return on investment (ROI) of your AI initiatives. Assess whether the expected benefits and outcomes of AI adoption have been realized. Consider the financial impact, cost savings, revenue growth, or other measurable returns achieved through AI implementations. This assessment helps justify future AI investments and align them with business priorities.

Regularly assessing your organization's progress on the AI journey provides valuable insights to refine your AI strategy, prioritize investments, and make informed decisions. It helps identify areas for improvement, address challenges, and capitalize on opportunities for innovation and growth. By continuously evaluating your organization's progress, you can ensure that your AI initiatives remain on track, deliver value, and drive long-term success in the era of artificial intelligence.

CHAPTER 97: ENVISIONING THE FUTURE OF YOUR ORGANIZATION IN AN AI-DRIVEN WORLD

In today's rapidly evolving business landscape, artificial intelligence (AI) is transforming industries and reshaping the way organizations operate. To thrive in an AI-driven world, it is crucial for organizations to envision their future and harness the power of AI to drive innovation, create value, and stay ahead of the competition. Envisioning the future of your organization in an AI-driven world involves strategic thinking, proactive planning, and a focus on long-term sustainability. Let us explore some key considerations for envisioning the future of your organization in an AI-driven world:

Embrace a Data-Driven Culture:

To leverage AI effectively, organizations must foster a data-driven culture. This involves valuing data as a strategic asset, collecting and analyzing data to gain insights, and making data-backed decisions. Establish processes for data collection, storage, and analysis, and ensure that employees have the necessary skills and tools to work with data. A data-driven culture creates a foundation for AI-driven innovation and empowers organizations to capitalize on the full potential of AI technologies.

Identify AI Opportunities:

Identify areas within your organization where AI can have the most significant impact. Explore processes, workflows, and tasks that can be optimized, automated, or enhanced through AI technologies. Engage with stakeholders across different functions to understand their pain points, challenges, and opportunities for improvement. Conduct thorough assessments to identify specific AI use cases that align with your strategic objectives and have the potential to deliver tangible benefits.

Develop a Strategic AI Roadmap:

Develop a strategic roadmap that outlines how AI will be integrated into your organization's operations and processes. Define short-term and long-term goals, milestones, and key performance indicators (KPIs) to measure progress. Consider the necessary resources, infrastructure, and partnerships required to implement the roadmap effectively. The roadmap should be agile and adaptable to accommodate emerging AI technologies and changing business needs.

Foster Collaboration and Partnerships:

Collaboration and partnerships are vital for success in an AI-driven world. Engage with external stakeholders such as technology providers, research institutions, startups, and industry networks to exchange knowledge, share best practices, and stay updated on the latest AI trends and developments. Seek opportunities for collaboration to drive innovation, co-create AI solutions, and explore new business models. By leveraging the collective expertise and resources of external partners, you can accelerate your organization's AI initiatives and unlock new opportunities.

Invest in AI Talent:

Developing and nurturing AI talent is essential to achieve your organization's AI-driven vision. Invest in recruiting, training, and retaining AI professionals, including data scientists, AI engineers, and AI strategists. Create a supportive environment that encourages continuous learning, experimentation, and knowledge sharing. By building a strong AI talent pool, you can drive innovation, stay at the forefront of AI advancements, and build a competitive advantage.

Continuously Monitor and Adapt:

In an AI-driven world, change is constant. Continuously monitor AI trends, emerging technologies, and market dynamics to stay ahead of the curve. Regularly evaluate the effectiveness of your AI initiatives, measure their impact, and make necessary adjustments. Be proactive in adopting new AI technologies and adapting your strategies to leverage the latest advancements. Agility and adaptability are key to maintaining a competitive edge and capitalizing on evolving opportunities.

Ethical and Responsible AI Use:

Integrate ethical considerations and responsible AI practices into your organization's AI strategy. Ensure that AI systems are designed to be fair, transparent, and unbiased. Establish governance frameworks and guidelines to address ethical concerns, privacy issues, and regulatory compliance. Engage in ongoing dialogue with stakeholders, including customers, employees, and regulators, to build trust and ensure that your AI initiatives align with societal expectations.

Foster a Culture of Innovation:

Create a culture that encourages experimentation, risk-taking, and innovation. Empower employees to explore new ideas, challenge the status quo, and propose AI-driven solutions. Implement mechanisms such as innovation labs, hackathons, and idea-sharing platforms to foster creativity and collaboration. Recognize and reward innovative initiatives to reinforce the importance of innovation within your organization.

Embrace Lifelong Learning:

Encourage a mindset of lifelong learning and adaptability. Promote continuous learning opportunities for employees to develop AI-related skills and stay updated on industry trends. Encourage cross-functional collaboration and knowledge sharing to foster a holistic understanding of AI's potential across different departments and functions.

Emphasize Customer-Centricity:

In an AI-driven world, customer-centricity becomes even more critical. Leverage AI technologies to gain a deep understanding of customer preferences, behaviors, and needs. Personalize customer experiences, deliver hyper-personalized recommendations, and provide proactive customer support through AI-driven insights. Use AI-powered analytics to anticipate customer demands and deliver exceptional experiences.

Envisioning the future of your organization in an AI-driven world requires a strategic mindset, a focus on innovation, and a commitment to embracing the transformative power of AI. By harnessing the potential of AI technologies, fostering a data-driven culture, collaborating with stakeholders, and embracing continuous learning, your organization can position itself for success and drive sustainable growth in the dynamic landscape of AI.

CHAPTER 98: THE ROLE OF AI IN REVOLUTIONIZING HEALTHCARE DELIVERY

AI (Artificial Intelligence) has emerged as a powerful tool in revolutionizing healthcare delivery. With its ability to analyze vast amounts of data and identify patterns, AI has the potential to enhance medical diagnosis, treatment, and overall patient care. In this article, we will explore the role of AI in healthcare, focusing on its applications in medical diagnosis and treatment, AI-enabled precision medicine, personalized healthcare, and the ethical considerations that accompany AI adoption in healthcare.

AI Applications in Medical Diagnosis and Treatment:

One of the significant contributions of AI in healthcare is its potential to improve medical diagnosis and treatment. By analyzing medical images, such as X-rays, CT scans, and MRIs, AI algorithms can assist radiologists in identifying abnormalities and providing accurate diagnoses. AI can quickly process and analyze vast amounts of imaging data, potentially reducing diagnostic errors and improving patient outcomes.

AI algorithms can also be utilized in the interpretation of pathology slides, allowing for faster and more accurate detection of cancerous cells. By leveraging AI in pathology, clinicians can benefit from improved accuracy, reduced workload, and increased efficiency.

Furthermore, AI can assist in the interpretation of clinical data, including patient histories, lab results, and genetic information. By analyzing these data points, AI algorithms can help healthcare providers make more informed decisions regarding diagnosis and treatment plans.

AI-Enabled Precision Medicine and Personalized Healthcare:

Another critical role of AI in healthcare is in the field of precision medicine and personalized healthcare. AI algorithms can analyze large-scale genomic data to identify genetic variations associated with specific diseases. This information can aid in predicting disease risks, selecting appropriate treatments, and developing personalized healthcare plans.

Additionally, AI can integrate data from various sources, including electronic health records, wearable devices, and patient-reported data, to provide comprehensive insights into an individual's health status. This holistic view allows healthcare providers to tailor treatment plans and interventions to each patient's specific needs.

Ethical Considerations in AI Adoption in Healthcare:

As with any technological advancement, the adoption of AI in healthcare comes with ethical considerations. It is crucial to address these ethical considerations to ensure responsible and ethical AI implementation. Some of the key ethical considerations in AI adoption in healthcare include:

Data Privacy and Security: AI algorithms require access to sensitive patient data for analysis. Protecting patient privacy and ensuring the security of personal health information is paramount. Healthcare organizations must establish robust data protection measures and adhere to regulatory guidelines to safeguard patient privacy.

Algorithm Bias and Fairness: AI algorithms can be influenced by biases present in the training data, potentially leading to biased decisions and unequal access to healthcare services. It is essential to develop algorithms that are fair, transparent, and unbiased, and to regularly evaluate and mitigate any potential biases.

Explainability and Transparency: AI algorithms can be complex and difficult to interpret. In healthcare, it is crucial to ensure that AI systems provide explanations and justifications for their decisions, enabling healthcare professionals to understand and trust the algorithms' outputs. Transparent AI systems enhance accountability and facilitate better patient care.

Patient Autonomy and Informed Consent: AI systems may influence clinical decisions, including treatment plans. It is essential to ensure that patients are adequately informed about the role of AI in their care and have the autonomy to participate in decision-making. Patients should have the opportunity to understand how AI algorithms contribute to their diagnosis and treatment and provide informed consent.

Liability and Accountability: As AI becomes more integrated into healthcare, questions arise regarding liability and accountability for errors or adverse outcomes. Clear guidelines and regulations must be established to address the legal and ethical responsibilities of healthcare providers and technology developers when using AI in patient care.

In conclusion, AI has the potential to revolutionize healthcare delivery by improving medical diagnosis and treatment, enabling precision medicine, and providing personalized healthcare. However, it is essential to address the ethical considerations that accompany AI adoption in healthcare, including data privacy, algorithm bias, explainability, patient autonomy, and liability. By addressing these considerations, we can harness the full potential of AI while ensuring responsible and ethical use in healthcare, ultimately leading to improved patient outcomes and a more efficient healthcare system.

CHAPTER 99: ENHANCING EDUCATION WITH AI-POWERED TOOLS

AI (Artificial Intelligence) has the potential to revolutionize education by providing innovative solutions to enhance learning experiences. With its ability to analyze vast amounts of data and adapt to individual needs, AI can personalize education, provide adaptive assessments, and assist in educational administration and management. However, it is essential to address ethical concerns and privacy issues to ensure responsible and effective AI-enabled education. In this article, we will explore the role of AI in enhancing learning experiences, focusing on personalized learning, adaptive assessment, AI applications in educational administration, and addressing ethical concerns in AI-enabled education.

Personalized Learning:

One of the significant contributions of AI in education is its ability to personalize learning experiences. AI-powered educational tools can analyze student data, such as performance, learning styles, and preferences, to provide customized content and recommendations. By adapting to each student's needs, AI can create personalized learning pathways, offering tailored content, activities, and assessments. This approach promotes student engagement, motivation, and individualized support, leading to improved learning outcomes.

Adaptive Assessment:

AI can also enhance assessment practices by providing adaptive assessments. Traditional assessments often follow a one-size-fits-all approach, which may not effectively capture the diverse abilities and needs of students. AI-powered assessment tools can dynamically adjust the difficulty and format of questions based on individual student performance. This adaptive approach ensures that students are challenged appropriately, receiving questions that match their skill level and provide meaningful feedback. Adaptive assessments enable educators to gain deeper insights into student progress, identify areas for improvement, and offer targeted interventions.

AI Applications in Educational Administration and Management:

AI has the potential to streamline educational administration and management processes. AI-powered systems can automate administrative tasks such as scheduling, grading, and record-keeping, freeing up valuable time for educators to focus on teaching and student support. Additionally, AI can analyze large datasets to identify patterns and trends in student performance, attendance, and behavior. This information can assist educational institutions in making data-informed decisions, such as identifying at-risk students, optimizing resource allocation, and developing personalized interventions.

Addressing Ethical Concerns and Privacy Issues in AI-Enabled Education:

While AI presents significant opportunities in education, it is crucial to address ethical concerns and privacy issues to ensure responsible and effective implementation. Some key considerations include:

Data Privacy and Security: AI-enabled educational tools require access to sensitive student data. Protecting student privacy and ensuring data security are paramount. Educational institutions must establish robust data protection measures and adhere to regulatory guidelines to safeguard student information.

Algorithm Bias and Fairness: AI algorithms can be influenced by biases present in the training data, potentially leading to biased decisions and unequal treatment. It is crucial to develop and evaluate algorithms that are fair, transparent, and unbiased. Regular monitoring and audits can help identify and address any biases that may emerge.

Informed Consent and Student Agency: Students and parents should have a clear understanding of how AI is used in their education and have the autonomy to participate in decision-making. Transparent communication and consent processes can empower students to make informed choices about their engagement with AI-enabled educational tools.

Teacher-Student Relationship: AI should complement the teacher-student relationship, not replace it. While AI can provide valuable support and feedback, it should not undermine the critical role of human teachers. Ensuring a balance between AI-powered tools and human interaction is essential to maintain the quality of education.

Continuous Monitoring and Evaluation: Regular monitoring and evaluation are crucial to assess the effectiveness and impact of AI-enabled educational tools. This evaluation should include feedback from teachers, students, and other stakeholders to identify strengths, weaknesses, and areas for improvement.

In conclusion, AI-powered educational tools have the potential to enhance learning experiences by personalizing education, providing adaptive assessments, and streamlining administrative processes. However, it is essential to address ethical concerns and privacy issues to ensure responsible and effective AI-enabled education. By prioritizing data privacy, fairness, informed consent, and continuous evaluation, we can harness the full potential of AI to create a more inclusive, engaging, and effective learning environment for all students.

CHAPTER 100: OPTIMIZING TRANSPORTATION SYSTEMS WITH AI-DRIVEN SOLUTIONS

The transportation industry plays a vital role in our modern society, enabling the movement of goods and people efficiently and safely. With the advent of artificial intelligence (AI), there is significant potential to optimize transportation systems and revolutionize the way we travel, transport goods, and manage logistics. In this article, we will explore the role of AI in optimizing transportation systems, focusing on AI applications in autonomous vehicles and drones, AI-powered logistics and supply chain management, as well as the safety, security, and ethical implications of AI in transportation.

AI Applications in Autonomous Vehicles and Drones:

One of the most prominent areas where AI is transforming transportation is in autonomous vehicles and drones. AI algorithms can analyze vast amounts of data from sensors, cameras, and other sources to make real-time decisions for safe and efficient navigation. Autonomous vehicles powered by AI can enhance road safety, reduce congestion, and provide more accessible transportation options.

AI enables autonomous vehicles to perceive and interpret their environment, make decisions, and navigate complex traffic situations.

Machine learning algorithms allow these vehicles to learn from data and improve their driving capabilities over time. AI also facilitates advanced features such as lane-keeping assistance, adaptive cruise control, and automatic emergency braking, which enhance driver safety and convenience.

Similarly, AI-powered drones have the potential to revolutionize industries like package delivery, surveillance, and emergency response. Drones equipped with AI algorithms can navigate dynamically, avoid obstacles, and adapt to changing environments. They can optimize flight paths for efficiency and deliver goods or provide services with speed and accuracy.

AI-Powered Logistics and Supply Chain Management:

AI is also transforming logistics and supply chain management, improving efficiency, and reducing costs. AI algorithms can analyze large amounts of data, including historical shipping patterns, demand forecasts, and real-time data, to optimize routes, schedules, and inventory management. AI enables intelligent decision-making in areas such as demand forecasting, warehouse management, and transportation optimization.

Predictive analytics powered by AI can forecast demand patterns, allowing companies to adjust inventory levels and allocate resources efficiently. AI can optimize route planning, considering factors such as traffic conditions, weather, and fuel consumption, leading to more efficient transportation and reduced emissions. AI algorithms can also monitor the condition of goods during transportation, identifying potential risks and optimizing storage and handling practices.

Safety, Security, and Ethical Implications of AI in Transportation:

While AI offers numerous benefits in transportation, it also raises important considerations regarding safety, security, and ethics. Some key aspects to address include:

Safety: Safety is paramount in transportation, and AI-powered systems must prioritize it. Ensuring the reliability and robustness of AI algorithms is crucial to prevent accidents and protect human lives. Thorough testing, validation, and regulation are necessary to ensure the safety of autonomous vehicles and drones.

Security: With increased connectivity and data exchange in transportation systems, cybersecurity becomes a critical concern. Protecting AI-driven transportation systems from cyber threats, such as hacking or tampering, is essential. Implementing robust security measures, encryption protocols, and regular system updates are crucial to safeguarding the integrity and privacy of data.

Ethical Implications: AI algorithms in transportation raise ethical considerations, particularly regarding decision-making in critical situations. For example, autonomous vehicles may face moral dilemmas when faced with potential accidents. Developing ethical frameworks and guidelines that prioritize human safety, transparency, and accountability is crucial in addressing these ethical challenges.

Equity and Accessibility: AI-driven transportation solutions should address equity and accessibility concerns, ensuring that advancements benefit all individuals and communities. It is essential to avoid exacerbating existing inequalities in transportation access and to ensure that autonomous vehicles and other AI-driven systems are accessible to everyone, including individuals with disabilities or in underserved areas.

Data Privacy: AI relies on vast amounts of data, including personal information. Protecting individuals' privacy and ensuring compliance with data protection regulations are essential. Transportation systems must establish robust data privacy policies, secure data storage, and transparent data usage practices.

In conclusion, AI has the potential to optimize transportation systems, enhance safety, and transform logistics and supply chain management. However, it is crucial to address the safety, security, and ethical implications that accompany AI adoption in transportation. By prioritizing safety, implementing robust security measures, addressing ethical concerns, and ensuring equitable access, we can harness the full potential of AI to create efficient, sustainable, and people-centered transportation systems for the future.

CHAPTER 101: TRANSFORMING THE ENERGY SECTOR WITH AI-DRIVEN INNOVATIONS

The energy sector is undergoing a significant transformation, driven by the need for clean, sustainable, and efficient energy sources. In this era of transition, artificial intelligence (AI) has emerged as a powerful tool for optimizing energy systems, improving renewable energy management, enabling predictive maintenance, and addressing environmental and sustainability concerns. In this article, we will explore the role of AI in transforming the energy sector, focusing on AI applications in renewable energy optimization and management, AI-powered predictive maintenance in utility infrastructure, and the environmental impact and sustainability considerations in AI adoption.

AI Applications in Renewable Energy Optimization and Management:

Renewable energy sources, such as solar and wind, are crucial in the transition to a sustainable energy future. AI plays a significant role in optimizing the generation, distribution, and consumption of renewable energy. AI algorithms can analyze vast amounts of data, including weather patterns, energy demand, and grid conditions, to optimize energy production and grid integration.

For example, AI can predict solar and wind energy production based on weather forecasts, enabling utilities to optimize their operations and balance supply and demand. AI algorithms can also optimize the placement and configuration of renewable energy systems, maximizing their efficiency and output. By leveraging AI in renewable energy optimization and management, the energy sector can enhance grid stability, increase renewable energy penetration, and reduce carbon emissions.

AI-Powered Predictive Maintenance in Utility Infrastructure:

Maintaining the reliability and efficiency of utility infrastructure is crucial for the energy sector. AI-powered predictive maintenance offers a proactive approach to infrastructure management, helping to identify potential failures and optimize maintenance schedules. By analyzing data from sensors, IoT devices, and historical maintenance records, AI algorithms can detect patterns and anomalies, enabling utilities to take timely actions and prevent unplanned downtime.

AI algorithms can predict equipment failure, identify maintenance needs, and optimize maintenance schedules to minimize costs and maximize the lifespan of assets. This approach improves the efficiency of maintenance operations, reduces operational risks, and enhances the overall reliability of energy systems.

Environmental Impact and Sustainability Considerations in AI Adoption:

While AI presents significant opportunities for the energy sector, it is crucial to consider its environmental impact and sustainability implications. Here are some key considerations:

Energy Efficiency: AI systems themselves consume energy, so it is important to ensure that the energy consumed by AI infrastructure and operations is justified by the benefits achieved. Developing energy-efficient AI algorithms, optimizing computing resources, and using renewable energy sources for AI infrastructure are important steps in minimizing the carbon footprint of AI technologies.

Data Center Footprint: AI requires large-scale computing infrastructure, which often involves data centers that consume significant amounts of energy. Optimizing data center operations, adopting energy-efficient technologies, and leveraging renewable energy sources for data centers are essential for reducing their environmental impact.

Responsible Data Usage: AI relies on vast amounts of data for training and analysis. Ensuring the responsible and ethical collection, storage, and usage of data is crucial to mitigate privacy risks and potential negative environmental consequences associated with data storage and processing.

Life Cycle Assessment: Assessing the environmental impact of AI technologies throughout their life cycle is important. This includes considering the environmental footprint of hardware manufacturing, energy consumption during operation, and proper disposal or recycling of AI systems at the end of their life.

Collaboration and Standards: Collaboration between industry stakeholders, policymakers, and researchers is vital to establish standards and guidelines for environmentally sustainable AI adoption. This includes promoting energy-efficient AI solutions, encouraging transparency in AI algorithms, and supporting research on the environmental impact of AI technologies.

In conclusion, AI-driven innovations have the potential to transform the energy sector by optimizing renewable energy management, enabling predictive maintenance, and addressing sustainability concerns. However, it is crucial to consider the environmental impact and sustainability implications of AI adoption. By promoting energy efficiency, responsible data usage, and collaboration, the energy sector can leverage AI to accelerate the transition to a sustainable, clean energy future.

CHAPTER 102: IMPROVING THE AGRICULTURE INDUSTRY CROP YIELD AND RESOURCE EFFICIENCY WITH AI TECHNOLOGIES

The agriculture industry faces numerous challenges, including the need to increase crop yields, optimize resource efficiency, ensure food safety, and meet the demands of a growing global population. In recent years, artificial intelligence (AI) technologies have emerged as valuable tools to address these challenges. AI applications in precision agriculture and smart farming enable farmers to make data-driven decisions, optimize resource allocation, and enhance overall productivity. Additionally, AI-enabled technologies play a crucial role in ensuring food safety and quality assurance. However, it is essential to consider the ethical and social implications of AI in agriculture. In this article, we will explore the role of AI technologies in improving crop yield and resource efficiency, AI applications in precision agriculture and smart farming, AI-enabled food safety and quality assurance, as well as the ethical and social considerations surrounding AI adoption in agriculture.

AI Applications in Precision Agriculture and Smart Farming:

Precision agriculture utilizes AI technologies to analyze data and provide actionable insights for optimizing farming practices. Through the integration of sensors, satellite imagery, and other data sources, AI algorithms can monitor and analyze various parameters, including soil moisture, nutrient levels, weather conditions, and crop health. This real-time data enables farmers to make informed decisions regarding irrigation, fertilization, pest management, and other critical factors that influence crop yield and resource efficiency.

AI-powered systems can also automate and enhance farm operations. For example, autonomous drones equipped with AI algorithms can survey fields, identify crop stress, and facilitate targeted interventions. Additionally, AI-enabled robotics systems can automate tasks such as planting, harvesting, and weeding, improving efficiency and reducing labor costs.

AI-Enabled Food Safety and Quality Assurance:

Ensuring food safety and quality is of utmost importance in agriculture. AI technologies play a crucial role in enhancing food safety and quality assurance processes. AI algorithms can analyze vast amounts of data, including historical quality control data, sensor readings, and consumer feedback, to detect anomalies, identify potential risks, and optimize quality control measures.

For example, AI-powered systems can identify pathogens in food products, detect contaminants, and predict shelf-life. AI algorithms can also assist in optimizing supply chain management, facilitating traceability, and enhancing product labeling to ensure transparency and compliance with food safety regulations.

Ethical and Social Implications of AI in Agriculture:

The adoption of AI technologies in agriculture raises ethical and social considerations that need to be addressed. Some key aspects to consider include:

Data Ownership and Privacy: AI technologies rely on large volumes of data, including sensitive information about crops, farms, and farmers. Ensuring data ownership, privacy, and security is crucial to protect farmers' interests and prevent misuse of data. Clear policies and regulations must be in place to govern data collection, storage, and sharing.

Access and Equity: AI technologies have the potential to increase productivity and efficiency in agriculture. However, it is essential to ensure that small-scale farmers and disadvantaged communities have access to these technologies. Bridging the digital divide and providing equal opportunities for all farmers is crucial to prevent inequalities in agricultural productivity.

Dependence on Technology: The increasing reliance on AI technologies in agriculture raises concerns about the potential loss of traditional farming knowledge and skills. Balancing the integration of AI technologies with traditional farming practices and knowledge is essential to preserve cultural heritage and maintain social sustainability in rural communities.

Displacement of Farm Labor: The automation of certain farm tasks through AI-powered robotics and machinery may result in the displacement of farm labor. It is important to consider the social implications of this transition, ensuring that affected workers have access to retraining programs and alternative employment opportunities.

Environmental Sustainability: While AI technologies can enhance resource efficiency, it is crucial to consider their overall environmental impact. For example, the energy consumption of AI infrastructure and the ecological consequences of large-scale data collection should be evaluated. Striking a balance between resource optimization and environmental sustainability is key.

In conclusion, AI technologies offer significant opportunities to improve crop yield, resource efficiency, food safety, and quality assurance in agriculture. Precision agriculture and smart farming, coupled with AI-enabled technologies, enable farmers to make data-driven decisions and optimize their operations. However, it is important to address the ethical and social implications of AI adoption in agriculture, including data ownership, access and equity, the preservation of traditional knowledge, labor concerns, and environmental sustainability. By adopting a responsible and inclusive approach, AI technologies can contribute to a more sustainable and productive agriculture sector.

CHAPTER 103: CREATING INTELLIGENT CITIES AND SUSTAINABLE URBAN ENVIRONMENTS WITH AI

As the world becomes more urbanized, the need to create intelligent and sustainable cities is of paramount importance. Artificial intelligence (AI) has emerged as a powerful tool to address the complex challenges of urbanization. By leveraging AI technologies, cities can enhance urban planning, optimize infrastructure management, improve public safety and security, and foster more inclusive and sustainable communities. However, the adoption of AI in urban environments also presents challenges related to privacy, inclusivity, and governance. In this article, we will explore the role of AI in creating intelligent and sustainable urban environments, AI applications in urban planning and infrastructure management, AI-driven public safety and security systems, and the challenges surrounding privacy, inclusivity, and governance in smart cities.

AI Applications in Urban Planning and Infrastructure Management:

AI plays a crucial role in urban planning and infrastructure management, enabling cities to make data-driven decisions and optimize resource allocation. AI algorithms can analyze large volumes of data from various sources, including sensors, social media, and public records, to gain insights into population dynamics, traffic patterns, and environmental factors. This information allows urban planners to design efficient transportation systems, allocate resources effectively, and develop sustainable infrastructure.

For instance, AI-powered systems can analyze real-time traffic data to optimize traffic signal timings, reduce congestion, and improve transportation efficiency. AI algorithms can also predict energy demand patterns to optimize energy distribution and facilitate the integration of renewable energy sources into the grid. By leveraging AI in urban planning and infrastructure management, cities can enhance resource efficiency, reduce environmental impact, and improve the overall quality of life for residents.

AI-Driven Public Safety and Security Systems:

Public safety and security are critical aspects of urban environments. AI technologies offer significant opportunities to improve safety, prevent crime, and respond to emergencies more effectively. AI algorithms can analyze large amounts of data from surveillance cameras, social media, and other sources to identify potential threats, detect anomalies, and facilitate proactive interventions.

For example, AI-powered video analytics systems can monitor public spaces and identify suspicious activities or objects in real-time. AI algorithms can also analyze social media data to identify potential public safety concerns, such as posts indicating criminal activities or emergency situations. By harnessing the power of AI, cities can enhance situational awareness, improve emergency response times, and create safer environments for their residents.

Privacy, Inclusivity, and Governance Challenges in Smart Cities:

While AI technologies offer immense potential for intelligent and sustainable urban environments, they also raise challenges related to privacy, inclusivity, and governance. Some key considerations include:

Privacy: The use of AI technologies in smart cities involves the collection and analysis of vast amounts of data, raising concerns about individual privacy. It is essential to establish robust privacy frameworks, ensure data anonymization, and obtain informed consent when collecting personal information. Clear guidelines and regulations must govern data storage, usage, and sharing to protect the privacy of residents.

Inclusivity: AI-driven technologies should be designed with inclusivity in mind, ensuring that all residents can benefit from smart city initiatives. It is crucial to bridge the digital divide and provide equal access to AI-enabled services for marginalized communities. Efforts should be made to address socioeconomic disparities and ensure that AI technologies do not exacerbate existing inequalities in urban environments.

Governance and Transparency: The governance of AI technologies in smart cities is a complex issue. Clear guidelines, regulations, and standards must be established to ensure transparency, accountability, and responsible use of AI. Additionally, stakeholders, including residents, should be involved in the decision-making processes surrounding AI adoption in urban environments to foster trust and inclusivity.

Bias and Fairness: AI algorithms can inherit biases from the data they are trained on, potentially leading to discriminatory outcomes. It is crucial to address bias in AI systems and ensure fairness in the decision-making processes. Regular audits and evaluations of AI systems should be conducted to detect and mitigate biases, promoting equitable outcomes for all residents.

In conclusion, AI technologies offer significant potential for creating intelligent and sustainable urban environments. AI applications in urban planning, infrastructure management, public safety, and security can lead to more efficient resource allocation, enhanced safety, and improved quality of life for residents. However, it is essential to address the challenges related to privacy, inclusivity, and governance. By establishing robust privacy frameworks, fostering inclusivity, and ensuring transparent and accountable governance, cities can harness the full potential of AI to create intelligent and sustainable urban environments for the benefit of all residents.

CHAPTER 104: REVOLUTIONIZING BANKING AND FINANCE WITH AI TECHNOLOGIES

The banking and finance industry is experiencing a significant transformation driven by the adoption of artificial intelligence (AI) technologies. AI has revolutionized various aspects of banking and finance, including fraud detection and risk management, customer service, and regulatory compliance. In this article, we will explore the role of AI technologies in revolutionizing banking and finance, AI applications in fraud detection and risk management, AI-powered chatbots and virtual assistants in customer service, as well as the importance of regulatory compliance and transparency in AI adoption in the finance sector.

AI Applications in Fraud Detection and Risk Management:

Fraud detection and risk management are critical areas in the banking and finance industry. AI technologies play a crucial role in identifying and mitigating fraudulent activities, as well as managing risks effectively. AI algorithms can analyze vast amounts of data, including transaction records, customer behavior patterns, and external factors, to detect anomalies and suspicious activities.

For example, AI-powered systems can flag potential fraudulent transactions by detecting unusual spending patterns, geographic inconsistencies, or deviations from normal customer behavior. AI algorithms can also identify emerging risks by analyzing market trends, news, and social media data. By leveraging AI in fraud detection and risk management, banks and financial institutions can improve their ability to detect and prevent fraudulent activities, as well as make more informed decisions regarding risk mitigation.

AI-Powered Chatbots and Virtual Assistants in Customer Service:

Customer service is another area in which AI technologies have made significant advancements in the banking and finance industry. AI-powered chatbots and virtual assistants provide efficient and personalized customer support, enhancing the overall customer experience. These AI systems can understand natural language, interpret customer inquiries, and provide prompt and accurate responses.

Chatbots and virtual assistants can handle routine customer queries, such as balance inquiries, transaction history, and account management, freeing up human agents to focus on more complex customer needs. AI-powered systems can also analyze customer data to offer personalized product recommendations and financial advice. By leveraging AI in customer service, banks and financial institutions can provide round-the-clock support, improve response times, and enhance customer satisfaction.

Regulatory Compliance and Transparency in AI Adoption in Finance:

As AI technologies are integrated into the banking and finance industry, it is essential to prioritize regulatory compliance and transparency. Financial institutions must ensure that AI systems adhere to relevant regulations, such as anti-money laundering (AML) and know-your-customer (KYC) requirements. AI algorithms should be designed to minimize the risk of biased decision-making and discrimination, ensuring fair outcomes for all customers.

Transparency is also crucial in AI adoption in finance. Banks and financial institutions should be able to explain how AI algorithms make decisions, especially when those decisions have significant impacts on customers' financial lives. Explainable AI (XAI) techniques can be employed to provide transparency and ensure that AI-powered systems are accountable and trustworthy.

Moreover, ethical considerations play a crucial role in the adoption of AI in finance. Ensuring data privacy and security is essential to protect customer information from unauthorized access or misuse. Financial institutions should implement robust data governance frameworks and adhere to strict data protection regulations.

Additionally, as AI systems become more sophisticated, continuous monitoring and audits are necessary to detect and rectify any biases or errors that may arise. Regular assessments and evaluations of AI models and algorithms should be conducted to ensure their accuracy, fairness, and compliance with regulations.

In conclusion, AI technologies have revolutionized the banking and finance industry, transforming fraud detection and risk management, improving customer service through AI-powered chatbots and virtual assistants, and emphasizing regulatory compliance and transparency. By effectively integrating AI into banking and finance operations while prioritizing ethical considerations and regulatory compliance, financial institutions can enhance efficiency, reduce risks, and provide better customer experiences. However, ongoing vigilance and accountability are crucial to ensure the responsible and ethical use of AI in the finance sector.

CHAPTER 105: ENHANCING USER EXPERIENCES WITH AI IN ENTERTAINMENT CONTENT

The entertainment industry has witnessed a significant transformation with the integration of artificial intelligence (AI) technologies. AI has revolutionized various aspects of entertainment, including content creation, recommendation systems, data analytics, and audience insights. These advancements have resulted in enhanced user experiences, personalized content recommendations, and improved understanding of audience preferences. However, it is crucial to address ethical concerns and biases that may arise with AI-generated content. In this article, we will explore the role of AI in enhancing user experiences in entertainment, AI applications in content creation and recommendation systems, AI-driven data analytics and audience insights in media, and the importance of addressing ethical concerns and biases in AI-generated content.

AI Applications in Content Creation and Recommendation Systems:

AI technologies have transformed the content creation process in the entertainment industry. AI algorithms can analyze vast amounts of data, including scripts, images, and music, to generate or assist in the creation of engaging and captivating content. For example, AI-powered systems can analyze patterns in successful films or TV shows to generate storylines, dialogue, or even entire scripts. Additionally, AI algorithms can assist in video editing, special effects, and sound design, optimizing the post-production process.

AI-powered recommendation systems have also become integral to the entertainment industry. These systems analyze user data, including viewing habits, preferences, and demographics, to provide personalized content recommendations. By leveraging AI, streaming platforms can deliver tailored suggestions that match users' interests, increasing engagement and satisfaction. Recommendation algorithms continuously learn and adapt based on user feedback, leading to increasingly accurate and relevant content suggestions over time.

AI-Driven Data Analytics and Audience Insights in Media:

Data analytics and audience insights play a crucial role in understanding user preferences and improving content delivery in the entertainment industry. AI technologies enable the analysis of vast amounts of data, including user interactions, social media trends, and demographic information, to gain actionable insights.

For example, AI-driven data analytics can identify trends in user behavior, content consumption patterns, and engagement metrics. This information allows entertainment companies to make data-driven decisions regarding content acquisition, production investments, and marketing strategies. AI algorithms can also help predict audience preferences, allowing for targeted content creation and strategic content distribution.

Addressing Ethical Concerns and Biases in AI-Generated Content:

While AI technologies offer significant benefits in entertainment, it is essential to address ethical concerns and biases that may arise with AI-generated content. Some key considerations include:

Representation and Bias: AI algorithms can inadvertently perpetuate biases present in the training data, leading to underrepresentation or misrepresentation of certain groups. It is crucial to address bias in AI systems and ensure diverse representation in content creation, recommendation systems, and casting decisions. Regular audits and evaluations of AI models can help detect and mitigate biases, promoting fairness and inclusivity.

Intellectual Property and Copyright: The use of AI in content creation raises questions about ownership and copyright. While AI algorithms can generate content based on existing works, it is important to ensure compliance with intellectual property laws and respect the rights of original creators. Clear guidelines and regulations must be in place to govern the use of AI-generated content and protect the rights of content creators.

Privacy and Data Security: AI technologies rely on vast amounts of user data for content recommendations and audience insights. It is crucial to handle user data with utmost privacy and security, adhering to applicable data protection regulations. Transparency about data collection, storage, and usage is essential to gain user trust and maintain data privacy.

Accountability and Transparency: The use of AI in entertainment raises questions about accountability and transparency. Users should be made aware when interacting with AI-generated content or recommendations. Additionally, explainable AI (XAI) techniques can be employed to provide transparency and ensure that AI systems are accountable and understandable to users.

In conclusion, AI technologies have significantly enhanced user experiences in entertainment through content creation, recommendation systems, and data analytics. However, it is crucial to address ethical concerns and biases that may arise with AI-generated content. By promoting diversity, addressing bias, ensuring data privacy, and fostering transparency and accountability, the entertainment industry can harness the full potential of AI to create engaging, inclusive, and ethical entertainment experiences for users.

CHAPTER 106: ADVANCEMENTS IN AI FOR GAME DEVELOPMENT AND GAMEPLAY

The field of game development has been significantly transformed by advancements in artificial intelligence (AI) technologies. AI has revolutionized various aspects of game development and gameplay, including game design, procedural content generation, player behavior analysis, and adaptive game experiences. These advancements have resulted in more immersive and engaging gaming experiences for players. However, it is crucial to consider the aspects of fairness, inclusivity, and ethics when implementing AI-enhanced gaming. In this article, we will explore the advancements in AI for game development and gameplay, AI-powered game design and procedural content generation, AI-driven player behavior analysis and adaptive game experiences, and the importance of fairness, inclusivity, and ethics in AI-enhanced gaming.

AI-Powered Game Design and Procedural Content Generation:

AI technologies have revolutionized game design and procedural content generation, allowing for more dynamic and immersive gameplay experiences. AI algorithms can generate game levels, landscapes, characters, and even narratives based on predefined rules and constraints. This enables game developers to create vast and varied game worlds that adapt to the player's actions and preferences.

For example, AI algorithms can generate procedurally generated maps, ensuring that each playthrough of a game is unique. AI-powered game design can also analyze player preferences and behaviors to dynamically adjust the difficulty level, pacing, and challenges within a game. By leveraging AI in game design, developers can create more engaging, challenging, and personalized experiences for players.

AI-Driven Player Behavior Analysis and Adaptive Game Experiences:

AI technologies can analyze player behavior and adapt game experiences in real-time, enhancing player engagement and enjoyment. AI algorithms can track player actions, decision-making patterns, and interactions to understand player preferences and skill levels. This information can then be used to tailor the game experience to individual players.

For instance, AI algorithms can dynamically adjust the difficulty level of a game based on the player's performance, ensuring that the game remains challenging yet enjoyable. AI can also analyze player behavior to provide personalized recommendations, such as suggesting alternative paths or game strategies based on the player's preferences and playstyle.

Fairness, Inclusivity, and Ethics in AI-Enhanced Gaming:

As AI technologies become more prevalent in gaming, it is crucial to ensure fairness, inclusivity, and ethical considerations. Some key considerations include:

Fairness: AI algorithms should be designed to avoid unfair advantages or biases that may arise based on player characteristics such as gender, race, or socioeconomic status. Developers must carefully monitor and test AI systems to identify and address any biases that may impact gameplay or player experiences.

Inclusivity: AI-enhanced games should be designed with inclusivity in mind, ensuring that all players can enjoy the game regardless of their abilities or disabilities. Game interfaces should be accessible, and AI algorithms should accommodate different play styles and preferences to provide an inclusive gaming experience for all players.

Transparency and Explainability: AI algorithms used in gaming should be transparent and explainable to players. Players should have visibility into how AI is used in the game, including how AI influences gameplay, decision-making, and adaptive experiences. This transparency builds player trust and understanding.

Data Privacy and Security: As AI systems collect and analyze player data, it is essential to prioritize data privacy and security. Developers must handle player data with care, ensuring compliance with relevant data protection regulations. Clear guidelines and policies should be in place to address data privacy concerns and protect player information.

Additionally, ongoing monitoring, evaluation, and auditing of AI systems in gaming are essential to ensure that they remain fair, inclusive, and aligned with ethical considerations.

In conclusion, advancements in AI for game development and gameplay have transformed the gaming industry, offering more immersive experiences through AI-powered game design, procedural content generation, player behavior analysis, and adaptive game experiences. As AI becomes increasingly prevalent in gaming, it is crucial to prioritize fairness, inclusivity, and ethical considerations. By promoting fairness, inclusivity, transparency, and data privacy, game developers can harness the full potential of AI to create engaging and ethical gaming experiences for players.

CHAPTER 107: LEVERAGING AI FOR SOCIAL GOOD AND HUMANITARIAN INITIATIVES

Artificial intelligence (AI) technologies have the potential to bring about significant positive impact in various domains, including social good and humanitarian initiatives. AI can be utilized to address critical challenges and drive positive change in areas such as disaster response and relief efforts, healthcare access and support in underserved communities, and other social impact projects. However, it is essential to consider ethical considerations and promote responsible AI practices to ensure the equitable and responsible use of AI in these initiatives. In this article, we will explore the potential of leveraging AI for social good and humanitarian initiatives, AI applications in disaster response and relief efforts, AI-powered healthcare access and support in underserved communities, as well as ethical considerations and responsible AI practices in social impact projects.

AI Applications in Disaster Response and Relief Efforts:

Disaster response and relief efforts can greatly benefit from the integration of AI technologies. AI algorithms can analyze real-time data, such as satellite imagery, social media feeds, and sensor data, to provide valuable insights for decision-making and resource allocation during emergencies. For example, AI can help in rapid damage assessment, identifying critical infrastructure damage, and predicting areas that require immediate attention.

AI-powered predictive analytics can aid in early warning systems for natural disasters, enabling authorities to take proactive measures and save lives. Moreover, AI algorithms can optimize logistics and supply chain management in disaster scenarios, ensuring the efficient distribution of relief supplies and resources. By leveraging AI in disaster response and relief efforts, humanitarian organizations and emergency responders can enhance their capabilities, improve response times, and save more lives.

AI-Powered Healthcare Access and Support in Underserved Communities:

AI technologies can play a crucial role in improving healthcare access and support, particularly in underserved communities. AI-powered systems can assist in diagnosis, disease prevention, and personalized healthcare delivery, even in areas with limited medical resources. For instance, AI algorithms can analyze medical imaging data, such as X-rays and MRI scans, to assist doctors in detecting diseases and making accurate diagnoses.

In underserved communities, where healthcare professionals may be scarce, AI-powered chatbots and virtual assistants can provide basic medical information, answer health-related queries, and offer guidance on self-care and prevention measures. This technology can help bridge the healthcare gap and provide support to individuals who may not have easy access to healthcare facilities.

Ethical Considerations and Responsible AI Practices in Social Impact Projects:

While AI has immense potential for social good, it is crucial to consider ethical considerations and promote responsible AI practices in social impact projects. Some key considerations include:

Bias and Fairness: AI algorithms should be trained on diverse and representative datasets to avoid perpetuating biases or discrimination. It is important to continuously monitor and evaluate AI systems for fairness and ensure that they do not disproportionately impact certain individuals or communities.

Data Privacy and Security: Social impact projects involving AI must prioritize data privacy and security. Sensitive information should be handled with care, and proper measures should be in place to protect individuals' data from unauthorized access or misuse. Transparent data governance frameworks and privacy policies are essential to gain the trust of the communities involved.

Human-Centered Design: It is crucial to ensure that AI systems designed for social impact projects are human-centered and consider the needs, values, and cultural contexts of the communities they aim to serve. Engaging and involving the affected communities in the design and development process helps to address their specific requirements and concerns.

Accountability and Transparency: Responsible AI practices require accountability and transparency. Organizations involved in social impact projects should clearly communicate how AI is being used, its limitations, and potential risks to the communities and stakeholders involved. Transparency builds trust and allows for meaningful engagement and collaboration.

Additionally, ongoing evaluation and assessment of AI systems, as well as collaboration with domain experts, community leaders, and relevant stakeholders, are essential to ensure that AI is deployed responsibly and effectively.

In conclusion, leveraging AI for social good and humanitarian initiatives has the potential to address critical challenges and drive positive change in society. By applying AI in disaster response and relief efforts, healthcare access in underserved communities, and other social impact projects, we can make significant strides in improving lives. However, it is crucial to approach these initiatives with ethical considerations and responsible AI practices to ensure equitable, fair, and inclusive outcomes for all.

CHAPTER 108: A COMPREHENSIVE OVERVIEW OF AI IN PRACTICE

"AI in Practice: A Comprehensive Guide to Leveraging Artificial Intelligence in Business" has offered a rich and comprehensive exploration of the practical applications, strategies, and considerations involved in harnessing the power of artificial intelligence (AI) in various business domains. Throughout the book, readers were taken on a journey that covers the fundamentals of AI, aligning AI strategies with business goals, building the right team, developing an AI roadmap, data management, AI technologies, implementation methodologies, ethical considerations, measuring success, workforce development, emerging trends, and much more. This book provides a holistic and practical understanding of AI in practice, empowering organizations to embark on their AI journey with confidence and clarity.

The book began by laying the foundation with an overview of AI and its impact on businesses. Readers gained a solid understanding of the different types of AI, including machine learning, deep learning, natural language processing, and computer vision, and how they can be applied in various industries. It highlighted the role of AI in digital transformation, emphasizing its potential to revolutionize businesses and drive innovation in customer experiences, operations, and overall organizational strategies.

Aligning AI strategies with business goals is a key focus throughout the book. Readers were guided on the importance of understanding organizational objectives and developing AI initiatives that align with and enhance those goals. The book emphasized the need for collaboration between IT and business units, emphasizing the value of cross-functional teams in driving successful AI adoption and implementation.

Creating an AI roadmap is another critical aspect covered in the book. Readers gained insights into identifying use cases, prioritizing projects, and assessing the AI maturity of their organization. With this knowledge, they can develop a clear roadmap that outlines the steps, timelines, and resources needed to achieve their AI objectives.

Data management and infrastructure were explored in depth, stressing the significance of data quality, governance, and storage in AI projects. The book discussed the considerations of cloud-based versus on-premises AI solutions, enabling readers to make informed decisions based on their specific needs and requirements.

Selecting the right AI tools and platforms is a vital aspect covered in the book. Readers were provided with a framework for evaluating AI vendors and partners, considering criteria such as functionality, scalability, and compatibility with existing systems. The book also explored the pros and cons of open-source versus proprietary AI solutions, empowering readers to make well-informed choices.

The book highlighted the importance of agile methodologies for AI projects, promoting iterative development and continuous improvement. It emphasized the need to integrate AI solutions with existing systems and processes, ensuring seamless integration and minimal disruption.

Ethical considerations in AI adoption are given significant attention. The book explores topics such as bias and fairness in AI algorithms, transparency and explainability, privacy, and data protection. By addressing these ethical considerations, organizations can ensure responsible and accountable AI adoption.

Measuring AI success and assessing ROI were explored, with a focus on defining appropriate key performance indicators (KPIs) and evaluating the value created by AI projects. The book emphasized the use of both quantitative and qualitative evaluation methods to capture the impact and effectiveness of AI initiatives.

Upskilling and reskilling the workforce was discussed, highlighting the importance of continuous learning and development in the AI-driven landscape. The book guided readers through identifying skill gaps and training needs within their organization, emphasizing the creation of a culture of innovation and learning.

The book also offered insights into emerging AI trends and technologies, providing readers with a glimpse into the future of AI and its potential impact on businesses. It emphasized the importance of staying informed, adapting to regulatory changes, and continuously refining and evolving AI strategies to stay ahead in the competitive landscape.

Throughout the book, real-world case studies, examples, and best practices were provided to illustrate how organizations from various industries have successfully implemented AI solutions to achieve their business objectives. These practical examples bring the concepts and strategies to life, providing readers with tangible insights and inspiration.

In conclusion, "AI in Practice: A Comprehensive Guide to Leveraging Artificial Intelligence in Business" is a valuable resource for organizations seeking to embrace the potential of AI. By providing a holistic overview of AI in practice, the book equips readers with the knowledge, strategies, and considerations necessary to navigate the AI landscape, implement AI solutions effectively, and drive innovation and success in the digital age.

Whether starting the AI journey or looking to refine existing AI initiatives, this book serves as a trusted guide to unlocking the transformative power of AI in businesses.

CHAPTER 109: D&C

Disclaimer & Copyright

 First Printing, 2023

www.ingramcontent.com/pod-product-compliance
Lightning Source LLC
LaVergne TN
LVHW080011210926
848481LV00011B/2986
* 9 7 9 8 2 2 3 4 1 0 9 8 0 *